A-Z

of

CROSSWORDS

JONATHAN CROWTHER

Collins

HarperCollins Publishers
Westerhill Road
Bishopbriggs
Glasgow
G64 2QT
Great Britain

First Edition 2006

© Jonathan Crowther 2006

ISBN-13 978-0-00-722923-9
ISBN-10 0-00-722923-2

Collins® is a registered trademark of HarperCollins Publishers Limited

www.collins.co.uk

A catalogue record for this book is available from the British Library

Typesetting by Davidson Pre-Press, Glasgow

Printed in Germany by Bercker

A-Z owl created by Reg Boulton

Contents

Acknowledgements

This book is dedicated to my dear, long-suffering wife Alison
('O, this rare clown!').

I am most grateful to all my fellow crossword setters featured
in its pages for their generous help and cooperation in providing
me with material relating to our abstruse occupation. I must also
thank Ross Beresford for his meticulous checking of the
crosswords included in the book.

Introduction

This is a book for people who do crosswords. I use 'do' here to mean (principally) 'solve' but also 'set'. It is not primarily a book on how to solve crossword puzzles. There are plenty of those already, and in my experience the ability to solve crosswords comes from practice rather than from diligent application to 'how-to' books, though these clearly have their place.

A preliminary word or two on terminology is called for. In the absence of standard descriptive terms, I prefer the simple 'set' and 'setter' to refer to the process of producing crosswords and those engaged in it, though readers will encounter in the following pages such terms as 'compile' and 'construct' in this context. The puzzle format itself may be the 'grid' or the 'diagram' or even the 'square' (which it isn't always). There is also a basic distinction between 'blocked' and 'barred' puzzles: blocked puzzles – the commonest type – use blacked-in squares to indicate where words end, and barred puzzles use thick black bars to perform the same function. In a barred grid every square in the completed puzzle will therefore contain a letter. The answers to be entered in a puzzle of either type are sometimes referred to as 'lights', like church windows (presumably to get over the fact that they may consist of more than one word or not be real words at all), and further to confuse matters 'lights' may also be used to refer to the clues themselves. I personally prefer to stick to 'clues' for clues and 'answers' for answers, whatever form they take.

Many people solve crosswords. All daily and weekly newspapers, and most weekly and other periodicals, contain at least one crossword, and it goes without saying that they wouldn't do this if they weren't convinced that such diversions are popular with a sizable section of the readership. (Other types of puzzle are also popular, of course, but I don't intend to be drawn into the relative merits of crosswords and, say, Sudoku and comparable oriental puzzles.) The history of the crossword puzzle is relatively short (little over a century), but it has firmly established itself as an intrinsic part of our culture. This development has been described elsewhere, but what has received less attention is the people behind it, the often anonymous or pseudonymous setters who strive to satisfy the apparently insatiable public demand for this particular type of mental stimulus. This book attempts for the first time to reveal something of the personalities behind these challenges to our intelligence, with some examples of their work to illustrate contrasting styles. Readers who are familiar with setters working for a particular paper but unaware of their identity may discover this through the index of sources which lists setters according to the outlets where their work appears.

What emerges about these shadowy figures? It is hard to make any generalizations about the sort of person who becomes a crossword setter. As one might expect perhaps, the roll-call includes a fair number of teachers (many with classics or mathematics degrees) and computer scientists, but the list also includes a wood scientist, a former racing driver, and a would-be opera singer, so there appears to be no common denominator. All setters began as solvers, self-taught or with encouragement from parents or others, who at some stage were persuaded or inspired to have a go at leaping the barrier between solving and setting, and to submit their efforts to this or that newspaper. Their ideas on setting, in particular on the writing of clues, are expounded in the following pages and, unsurprisingly, differences of opinion emerge. I have my own firmly held views on the art of clue writing, which I shall develop further on in this introduction, but I accept that they are not universally shared and readily acknowledge that the solver is the judge.

I have picked the setters in this book on the basis of three broad criteria: they are all alive and, with a few exceptions, still setting crosswords; they all set for British papers and periodicals;

and they all set crosswords on a regular basis, rather than as an occasional pastime. Each of these criteria needs further comment. A number of distinguished setters are no longer with us. Readers will come across reference to them in one or more of the entries, and two are mentioned more than the rest as having been an inspiration to setters at work today: Derrick Macnutt (Ximenes) and Alec Robins (Custos, Zander). Both wrote seminal works on crosswords (respectively *Ximenes on the Art of the Crossword* and *Teach Yourself Crosswords*, later reissued as *The ABC of Crosswords*), both were teachers of classics, and both as it happens set puzzles for *The Observer*, where my own crosswords appear. Ximenes himself had taken over from the legendary Torquemada (Edward Powys Mathers), who is remembered now by a dwindling band of older solvers. Torquemada's puzzles appeared in *The Observer* between 1926 and 1939 and attracted a large and devoted following, though by today's standards his cluing style would be regarded as eccentric and often unfair. In addition to creating many fine crosswords, Macnutt (1902–71) and Robins (who died in 1998) are remembered chiefly because they set down, possibly better than and certainly before anyone else, the principles of crossword making in all its aspects, and therefore remain essential reading for aspiring setters. Other important figures in the history of the crossword include Afrit (Alistair Ferguson Ritchie), Hubert Philips, Alan Cash, and more recently Richard Whitelegg (a contemporary of mine at Cambridge and yet another classicist) and Michael Rich (a pupil of Derrick Macnutt's at Christ's Hospital School in Horsham and – you've guessed it – a classics graduate), who gave much help and encouragement to younger setters. I must also mention Eric Chalkley (Apex), who died shortly before this book went to press. His puzzles appeared in *The Guardian, The Independent*, and (as Hysterix) in the *Sunday Times*, among other publications, but he will perhaps be best remembered for the competition puzzles he circulated privately for many years around Christmastime to a small group of friends. This tradition has been continued in his memory by Paul Henderson (Phi).

I have limited myself to British setters (or rather setters for the British market) mainly because I feel unqualified to cover the wider picture. Leaving aside crosswords in other languages, English-speaking countries around the world have developed their own crossword traditions, but it is fair to say that Britain is the home of the cryptic clue and it is therefore reasonable to focus attention principally on those at work in this country. (An interesting treatise remains to be written on the separate development of crosswords in Britain and the US.) I have also chosen regular 'professional' setters and not included the much larger group of those who set only occasionally as a pastime, though I am conscious that in so doing I have had to exclude many brilliantly inventive people, and hope that they will understand the reasons for my decision. The public appetite for crosswords is such that there are now more full-time setters than there have ever been, and some of them have achieved a quite staggering output, producing puzzles for a wide range of papers and with multiple pseudonyms. Finally, it must be said that my choice has been determined to some extent by the response I received from crossword editors around the country to whom I initially wrote for details of the regular setters on their books. If I have, inadvertently or through ignorance, omitted any setters who feel that they qualify for inclusion, I apologize unreservedly and appeal to them to contact me in case further editions of this book allow me to repair the omissions.

Most crossword setters are not acknowledged by name alongside their work, unlike other contributors to the journal that employs them. If there is an acknowledgement of authorship it is usually in the form of a pseudonym. Why is this? Are crossword setters so innately modest or self-effacing that they prefer to avoid explicit recognition of their work? I suspect not. The enthusiasm with which almost all the setters featured in this book responded to my request for information about themselves convinces me that they are not the shrinking violets one might have supposed. On the contrary, they appear anxious to receive the credit they have perhaps been too long denied, so I am happy to set the record straight. The use of pseudonyms is long established, though it is still not the norm in most daily newspapers. The majority of entries in the main section of this book are headed by pseudonyms, and readers will find explanations of most of these. Some setters do not have one and appear under their own names, or have chosen to appear under their real names despite having one or more pseudonyms. For those with two or more pseudonyms, there are cross-references from each to the main entries. In a few cases (e.g. Beelzebub, Mephisto, Polymath, Simplex) the pseudonym 'belongs' to a particular puzzle shared by a number of setters or passed on by each incumbent to the next. Just when and why the habit of using this form of disguise originated I have not been able to discover. I suspect it simply goes with the territory, a *jeu d'esprit* that appeals to those whose daily business is wordplay. Some are fairly obvious, others much less so. I didn't realize, for example, (until he told me) that Cinephile, the occasional pseudonym also used by the distinguished setter Araucaria when setting puzzles for the *Financial Times*, is an anagram of Chile pine. Very pleasing.

Setting crosswords is clearly a skill, but is it a form of art, as is implied by the title of Ximenes's book mentioned above? Most solvers will approach a puzzle as a form of mental diversion, to be set aside and most likely forgotten when it is completed or other matters claim their attention, but for some, and for all setters I guess, there is an aesthetic pleasure to be had from a puzzle that is cleverly (dare I say beautifully?) constructed and clued. Almost all the setters featured in these pages claim that they set out to entertain and amuse (the importance of humour is stressed repeatedly), but not everyone is amused by the same things. Solvers will tend to remain loyal to one or more regular setters whose style they like, and it is hoped that learning more about their favourites will help them to account for these loyalties. But, as with any art, there are many different styles. Crossword setting, as has often been remarked, is not an exact science, and this book contains a variety of views expressed, at times forcefully, on what constitutes a good clue. These views can, however, be divided into two broad schools of thought, representing what might be termed the 'Ximenean' (i.e. rule-based) and the 'libertarian' (i.e. anything goes) approaches. I make no secret of the fact that I belong to the former camp, and later in this introduction I shall set out the basic principles I regard as essential, and to which I adhere when setting my puzzles. At the same time I recognize that ours is a broad church, and that in the last analysis it is the solvers who decide what they like best. It should also be said that most setters agree on many, if not most, aspects of clue writing and that to represent the two groups as warring factions is misleading and unhelpful.

One of the main reasons for my belief in firm cluing principles (I dislike calling them 'rules') has to do with the special nature of the Azed series in *The Observer*. Following a tradition established by my predecessor Ximenes, I produce a competition puzzle once a month which requires competitors to submit with their solutions a clue of their own to a given word. I then award prizes to the clues I judge the best. This process inevitably involves detailed analysis of clue construction, and without a clear set of principles to base this on, adjudication would be impossible, or at best highly subjective. Given the generally very high standard of clues submitted, I need to have good reasons for my choice and to be able to justify these if challenged. This I regularly do in the 'slip', a monthly newsletter or comment sheet on each competition, available on subscription and posted on the Guardian Unlimited website. Each slip lists the three prize-winners for the month and the twenty or so judged to be VHC (very highly commended) together with their clues, and the HCs (highly commended, a longer list). Each year an honours list is presented, showing how the top solvers have performed and who will receive the coveted Azed silver salver by beating the rest. Competitors – the keener ones anyway – therefore have a good idea of what is expected of them. And if all this sounds a bit like school exams, I will readily concede that there is a strong competitive element among regular entrants, but over the years many exceptionally brilliant clues have emerged, a number of which are quoted as favourites in these ensuing pages.

The puzzle section of this book (pages 195–333) contains crosswords, all of which have already appeared in print, by about half of the setters listed, chosen by them as representative of their own style and illustrating a wide variety of types and levels of difficulty. I have not attempted to 'grade' these, preferring to let readers explore them at will, but they range from relatively straightforward 'plain' puzzles typical of daily newspapers to fiendishly complex thematic crosswords (and even one in Latin). Solvers who are initially put off by the idea of really tough puzzles, which can include obscure vocabulary and may require considerably more than the odd half-hour to complete, may find that with a bit of application they can lift their game and so move to a new level of enjoyment. There is, in any case, something here for everybody, and, perhaps more importantly, a rare opportunity to compare directly the contrasting styles of the top setters in the country. Occasional reference is made to 'Playfair', a code which has found its way into advanced crosswords more frequently than the many other codes at the disposal of cryptographers. Afrit (A. F. Ritchie) was probably the first to exploit it in this way. This is not the place to explain in detail how the Playfair code works, except to say that it was originally devised in the 1850s by Charles Wheatstone (he of the Bridge) and subsequently promoted in a military context by his friend Baron Playfair. In crosswords it usually depends on a codeword (to be deduced) in which no letter recurs, so setters enjoy hunting for words that are suitable, especially long ones, like UNCOPYRIGHTABLE and DERMATOGLYPHIC.

In the biographical section (pages 23–194) the setters reveal their various different methods of working. In my own case the setting process, for plain puzzles (the bulk of my output), consists of three distinct stages. Starting with a totally blank grid I first design the grid's symmetrical pattern (of bars in my case) so that it will contain a reasonable spread of word lengths and a fair number of 'unchecked' squares, also known as 'unches', i.e. ones occupied by letters belonging to only one answer which cannot therefore be verified by another answer crossing them. Many newspapers and other periodicals use a fixed number of different patterns to which their setters are restricted, as a means of minimizing errors in the preparation of grids for printing. I would myself find such a restriction irksome and am glad to have a completely free hand in preparing my own patterns. After a bit of practice it becomes quite easy to do and doesn't take long. The next stage, filling the patterned grid with words, takes somewhat longer (and a lot longer when certain pre-selected words have to be included, as happens in some thematic puzzles). There now exist a number of software packages with huge lexical databases, designed to fill grids in an instant, and these can be a godsend to the hard-pressed setter with no time to spare, though he or she will have little control over the words the computer comes up with. Despite the extra time it takes I still prefer to fill my grids by hand in a squared ('quadrille') exercise book, using words of my own choice. This stage of the process takes on average about two hours, assuming the mental wheels are running smoothly, but it is still a somewhat technical skill that can be acquired by practice and is not creatively demanding. The creativity all comes in the final, most protracted, stage: the writing of the clues. Few solvers will pause to admire an elegant grid, if they notice it at all, but their attention will be caught, even if only briefly, by a good clue, or their sense of fair play offended by a bad one. This is therefore an appropriate point to explain what I mean by good clue writing.

It is worth remembering that cryptic cluing devices, like jokes or the basic plots of novels, can be reduced to quite a short list. With minor variations these are exhaustively analyzed in all the books on how to solve crosswords, most notably in Don Manley's excellent *Chambers Crossword Manual* (4th edition, 2006), for those who are keen to become solvers. Regular solvers, to whom this volume is primarily addressed, will already be familiar with these devices, even if they have not consciously categorized them like this. Briefly, they can be summarized as follows (with examples from Azed puzzles):

I TWO OR MORE DEFINITIONS

Though there are few exact synonyms in English, many words have several different senses, whether or not they are separate homographs (words with the same form but distinct meanings, often because of different etymologies). A simple form of cryptic clue exploits this diversity by juxtaposing two or more definitions of the same word, leaving the solver to identify the word that fits both or all. Example: 'Low standard' (BASE).

II SEQUENTIAL PARTS

Words can often be split into their component parts, each of which is a real word in its own right. Thus REINVENT can be split into REIN and VENT. In clues of this type these parts are isolated and clued separately (usually by definition), the correct order of the parts being maintained. (Note that such a device, sometimes also called 'charades', is best used when the separate parts of the full word are both unconnected to it etymologically or morphologically. Cluing GRANDSTAND by splitting it into GRAND and STAND would be decidedly feeble.) Example: 'Refer to part of newspaper for leak?' (SEEPAGE).

III CONTAINER AND CONTENTS

A word can often be seen as formed from two separate words, one inserted at some point inside the other (or, less commonly, like a Russian doll, from one word inside another inside another), e.g. LOCK in BED = BLOCKED. The clue writer may then clue the full word as such, using any of a wide range of words or phrases to indicate the insertion. Example: 'Flexible growth? I invested' (PLIANT).

IV REVERSALS

Words can often be formed by reversing other words. The solver may spot clues exploiting this by looking out for words like 'reversed', 'back', 'turning', and 'round' (which could also indicate a clue of type III above, of course). Note, however, that 'back' and 'round' are best not used to indicate reversal in clues to down words, where 'up', 'rising', etc. would be more appropriate. Example: 'I hadn't turned round carvings' (TONDI).

V HIDDEN

Words can be secreted in one or more other words without disturbing the order of the letters. Thus DROP can be seen as a 'piece' of ol*d rop*e. Clues that use this device should be used sparingly since they can be rather easy to solve (not in itself necessarily a bad thing – solvers welcome a sprinkling of easier clues to get them started), but if subtly worded they can be quite testing. Example: 'Rarely goes in for medley as part of swimming lessons' (IMMINGLES).

VI HOMOPHONES

Our language is full of words that sound, when spoken, the same or virtually the same as other words, despite their different spelling (e.g. bow/bough; threw/through). Such puns may be exploited by the clue writer, and solvers should be on the look-out for tell-tale phrases like 'we hear' and 'by the sound of it', in addition to other possibly less obvious indicators. (A word of caution, however. Pronunciation varies regionally, despite what dictionaries record as standard. In Scotland, for example, the letter 'r' is usually pronounced wherever in a word it occurs, but in most regional accents in England, and in Received Pronunciation, 'r' is omitted at the end of a word that is not followed by a vowel sound. The careful clue writer should take this on board.) Example: 'Old-fashioned club, exclusive group by the sound of it' (CLEEK).

VII ANAGRAMS

The anagram (formed by jumbling the letters of one or more other words) is perhaps the device most familiar to word puzzlers, and less experienced solvers tend to look for one in every clue they read. The ways in which the clue writer can indicate an anagram are many and varied – anything that suggests disturbance or an abnormal state may serve – but whichever is chosen the anagram indicator must be there, and be fair and grammatically sound. Furthermore the component letters of the anagram, or an unequivocal indication of them, must be given explicitly in the anagram-based clue. A clue such as 'Stupid translation of Greek letter' for MORONIC (an anagram of OMICRON) involves what is generally called an *indirect anagram*, which won't do. Even though there are only three seven-letter characters in the Greek alphabet (well, four if you include DIGAMMA), which narrows the field somewhat, it is unfair to expect the solver to know this and to have to deduce the word from which the anagram is to be formed.

A more complex development of the anagram is what I have called the *composite anagram* (abbreviated to 'comp. anag.' in solution notes). In it the clue writer implies that x (the answer to the clue) is that which + y (another word or words) + an anagram indicator could produce z, or alternatively that x (again the answer to the clue) is that which z − y + an anagram indicator could produce. Examples of simple and composite anagrams: 'Herb Iron Age cultivated' (ORIGANE); 'Valve of a kind, such as gets radio set working' (TRIODE). In the second of these examples, x (the answer to the clue) is 'valve of a kind', y is 'as', z is 'radio set', and the anagram indicator is 'working'. So 'triode as' can be arranged to form 'radio set'.

VIII ADDITION AND SUBTRACTION

In clues of this type the setter views a word as another word plus or minus a letter at either end or both ends (or even somewhere within it). So PATE may be treated as SPATE minus S, PATELLA minus LLA, PAT plus E, ATE plus P, PLATE minus L, or PASTE minus S, and so on, according to choice. How the bits added or subtracted are dealt with is up to the setter, provided that he or she gives a clear and fair indication of what is going on. I myself use 'a bit of', 'the head of', 'the end of', 'the last of', etc., referring always to a single initial or final letter (more than one seems too vague), whereas 'the middle of', 'the heart of', etc. may consist of one or more letters, provided that they are centrally positioned in their 'parent' word. Example: 'Calls HE ignored from 'her at No. 10', singular' (CRIES), a clue that may become dated before too long!

IX '& LIT.'

This is a rather special clue type, with a rather obscure label. I am uncertain who invented the name (Ximenes possibly) but it has stuck, despite occasional attempts to rechristen it. As I shall be emphasizing in the next section, I firmly believe that every cryptic clue should consist of a definition of the answer, plus a cryptic treatment of that answer, using one or more of the devices just listed. Sometimes, however, it is possible to construct a clue, of whichever type, in such a way that the definition and the cryptic treatment are *one and the same*. In other words the clue as a whole can be read in two different ways, once as a literal definition of the answer and once as a cryptic indication of it. Many setters would agree with me that such clues are especially satisfying to setter and solver alike. Example: 'Room temperature's favoured for this' (CHAMBERTIN).

Setters may of course pick and mix from the list above, so innumerable permutations are possible. Armed with this toolbox the clue writer should be able to deal effectively with any word or phrase in the lexicon. He or she should also, however – and here we come to what I might call my crossword philosophy – keep a number of precepts (well, ten to be precise) firmly in mind at all times.

Azed's maxims

SAY WHAT YOU MEAN

...even if you may not mean what you say or appear to be saying. In my professional life as a lexicographer writing dictionaries for foreign learners of English, I learnt the importance of *disambiguation* – explaining the meanings and usage of words in language that was unambiguously clear and simple. As a crossword setter you are not bound by the same restrictions and are free to exploit the many ambiguities offered by the language (words which have multiple meanings, which can be two or more different parts of speech, etc.) in order to hoodwink the solver into thinking you mean one thing when you actually mean another. *But*, when the penny drops, the clue must be seen to work and lead unmistakably to the answer, even if not via the route originally explored by the solver. So 'The sort of leaves that hold up trains?' may initially conjure up images of the rail companies and their tired excuses for delays, but with a bit of lateral thinking it can only lead in the end to PAGES.

MAKE SENSE

Clues are small pieces of English prose, and as such they should convey something with a reasonable degree of 'surface meaning', an image (even if a misleading one) which solvers can relate to as part of their real-world knowledge. I really do not like clues which concentrate so much on the cryptic treatment of their answers that they lose touch with reality and end up as gobbledegook. The more normal a clue sounds when read out, the better it will be in my view. (At one time 'narrative' crosswords were quite common, in which the setter contrived to link the clues in order in one continuous piece of prose, thus imposing on himself an even more demanding need for textual cohesion. They are no longer fashionable, probably because they were so hard to construct.)

REMEMBER YOUR GRAMMAR

As a piece of prose, each clue should also observe the normal rules of grammar and syntax. These are, of course, many and varied, but here are a few key points, often overlooked by even experienced setters.

First, the part of speech of the solution should be clearly indicated in the clue. So, for example, a clue which can only lead to an adjective will not do if the word sought is unmistakably a noun. (I make an exception in the case of verb phrases as clues to nouns that could stand as their subjects: 'wags its tail and is man's best friend' is therefore acceptable in defining DOG, whereas 'furry and four-legged' on its own is not.) The fact that many words in English can have more than one part of speech helps the setter, who can, as I have said, exploit this ambiguity.

Second, the fact that "s" can stand for 'is' or 'has', as well as indicating a possessive, is useful to the clue writer, when the literal reading of a clue requires it to mean one thing and the cryptic reading requires one of the other meanings. This is an entirely legitimate deception.

Third, a clue such as 'I am hugged by crazy girl' for MAID won't do. It makes sense in the literal reading, but in the cryptic reading what is meant is 'I is hugged ...', which is bad English. 'We are tucking into jellied pudding' for SWEET is equally flawed. Help is at hand in the shape of verb forms like 'will' and 'must', which can be equally first and third person forms, so 'I'll be hugged by crazy girl' and 'We must tuck into jellied pudding' are fine and circumvent the problem.

Finally, few issues divide crossword setters so fundamentally as the noun anagram indicator, a manifestation of what linguists mean (among other things) by the Sanskrit word *tatpurusha*, a common feature of English and some other languages defined by *The Chambers Dictionary* (2003) as 'a class of compound words in which the first element modifies the second by standing next to it in various types of relationship, e.g. possession, as in *goatskin*, location, as in *fieldmouse*, as the object of an action, as in *guitar-player*, and as agent, as in *man-made*'. Juxtaposing two nouns to indicate that one must modify the other to form an anagram of it is highly questionable in my view, unless that is what is actually implied *in the real world*. I concede (just) that for cluing purposes 'prawn cocktail' means 'a mixture of prawns' and could therefore indicate an anagram of the letters in 'prawn' (while pointing out that there are other ingredients involved and it is in fact a melange of 'prawns' not 'prawn' – you see how picky we have to be), but 'dolly mixture' is certainly not a mixture of dollies (or even of a single dolly), so it simply cannot imply an anagram of 'dolly'. When it comes down to it, it's a case, as always, of saying what you mean. I make it a personal rule to avoid noun anagram indicators at all times.

RESPECT PUNCTUATION

Punctuation performs a useful function in the written form of the language, and even though it is widely misunderstood or misapplied, the huge success of Lynne Truss's little book *Eats Shoots and Leaves* (the title almost reads like a crossword clue) is an indication of how much people care about it. There is no justification for the clue writer ignoring punctuation marks (or, worse, telling the solver to ignore them). I am thinking particularly of the comma and the hyphen. If there is a comma in a clue, but the cryptic reading of the clue only works without it being there, the setter is taking unwarrantable liberties and not playing fair by solvers. Similarly, a hyphen between parts of a word binds the two parts into a single compound unit. Expecting solvers then to treat this unit as two separate words in order for the clue to work is also unfair.

ORTHOGRAPHY MATTERS

This goes hand in hand with grammar and punctuation, and emphasizes again the fact that the medium in which clues are written should be real English, not a special variant of the language that ignores or subverts standard usage. So I do not accept (as some do) that Gateshead is the same as 'gate's head' (i.e. G) or that 'indeed' can be treated as if it were 'in deed', still less that 'cocktail' could be used to indicate K. I equally reject the notion that the capital initial of a proper name can be downcased in a clue because it suits the setter to do this. (The converse of this – upgrading a lower-case initial to a capital one – I regard as acceptable, just.)

DON'T WAFFLE

Every clue should contain a definition or equivalent of the answer plus a cryptic treatment of its component parts, *and nothing else*. Every word in the clue must have a function as part of the whole, and there should be no superfluous verbiage. Such padding can be grossly misleading to solvers, especially in 'hidden' clues (see III in the clue taxonomy above), who may reasonably feel that it has been included merely to put them off the scent, as it were. And while we're on the subject, I disapprove of clues which omit any definition of the answer, relying on the 'Ho-ho' factor to gloss over this omission: the much-quoted 'Gegs' (or possibly 'Gges', 'Sgeg', 'Gseg', etc.) for SCRAMBLED EGGS is a prime offender in this, and I've never really understood why it is so often held up as a model clue. (Why not equally 'Lligr', 'Rlilg', etc?) The setter is only doing half the job by omitting any indication of the meaning of the answer to be entered. Clues which consist solely of a punning definition (such as 'A stiff examination' *tout simple* for POST MORTEM) are equally culpable in this regard, however witty they may be.

THE SPICE OF LIFE

The crossword setter must aim for variety in each set of clues. The predominance of one or two different types of clue in any one crossword is surprisingly noticeable to the solver, who may feel short-changed as a result. It is worth thinking about this before a single clue has been written, i.e. during the grid-filling process, since different words undoubtedly lend themselves more to one type of cluing approach than to others. (I have mentioned the attraction for setters of the '& lit.' type of clue, IX above, but use too many of this type in a single puzzle and you will definitely be over-egging the pudding.)

BEWARE OF SPECIALIZED KNOWLEDGE

Do you ever get irritated by Jeremy Paxman on *University Challenge* when he gives vent to his exasperation with students who are ignorant of something he regards as common knowledge (something dear old Bamber would *never* have done)? It is dangerous for setters to assume that solvers will be as well up in certain specialized areas of knowledge as they are. I know I am occasionally guilty of this myself, and I usually regret it, regarding it – if I'm honest – as a form of showing off. I am talking here of encyclopaedic knowledge generally. We all have a fair amount of this, some more than others, but no two people have the same 'mix', and this should be respected. An exception can be made in the case of thematic puzzles which are based on a particular area of specialized vocabulary; here solvers know from the start, or discover as solving progresses, which field they are in, and can direct their search for the necessary information accordingly.

BE A GOOD LOSER

While many occasional solvers may not mind if they fail to finish a puzzle, most who are keen derive satisfaction when the last answer goes in and they can admire their handiwork in having completed the grid. This is the ideal end result of the tussle of wits between setter and solver, and the setter does well to remember it. In other words, if a puzzle is so fiendishly complex that few can solve it, it represents so much wasted effort all round. The setter may feel he or she has created a masterpiece but it will remain largely unappreciated. As one whose puzzles are at the tougher end of the scale in terms of the challenge they offer, I am especially mindful of the need to avoid unnecessary complexity.

DON'T BE TOO SELF-EFFACING

This is a difficult one to pin down, but it is important just the same. Setters, like writers generally, should develop a style that is unmistakably their own, so that their personalities can be seen to shine through their clues. In other words they should not be afraid to reveal their interests, preferences, even prejudices in the clues they write. Most of the setters featured in this book declare that they see the need to amuse and entertain as their primary objectives. I agree wholeheartedly, and further assert that the application of the principles I have enumerated does not (or need not) lead to boring clues, as some have claimed.

If I had to boil down my ideas on good clue writing to the basic minimum requirements, they would be these: setters should strive at all times for the three key ingredients of accuracy, economy, and wit, with if possible that elusive marriage of a brilliant idea with elegant wording that lifts a clue into the alpha-plus class. *And always, always think of the solver.*

Not all of the setters featured in this book share the views I have set out above. Some disagree strongly with this or that maxim, and here we must agree to differ. I invited those who submitted puzzles to choose one that typified their style, not necessarily the one they are proudest of because of its special subtlety or cleverness. Many are 'plain' puzzles with no particular theme, the type with which many readers will be most familiar. Quite a few *are* thematic, since such puzzles are without doubt becoming increasingly common and no longer the special preserve of a few periodicals. Pre-eminent among the latter has for many years been *The Listener* puzzle in *The Times* on Saturday. The late lamented *Listener*, apart from being a wonderfully readable periodical that reproduced material from radio and (later) television, each week included a thematic crossword. In its early days (the 1930s), these crosswords were the work of a small group of gifted amateur setters and often very difficult, solved by very few (cryptic crosswords as a genre being then still in their infancy), with comments published each week to accompany the solution, such as 'This was easier than usual, and twenty-nine competitors sent in correct solutions.' In later years *The Listener* crossword became a forum for many aspiring setters, with such a dedicated following that when *The Listener* itself ceased publication, a group of concerned crossworders persuaded *The Times* to adopt the puzzle, where it continues today as an outlet for creative setters and a must for enthusiastic solvers of difficult puzzles. A number of other such outlets deserve mention, especially for the opportunities they offer to newer setters. The Enigmatic Variations series in the *Sunday Telegraph*, created some years ago and still edited by James Leonard (Mr Lemon), features thematic crosswords by a range of setters. 1 *Across*, a monthly crossword magazine edited by Tom Johnson (Doc) *puzzler@btinternet.com* and available on subscription, features regular puzzles by Araucaria and others; Brian Head founded the Crossword Club *www.thecrosswordclub.co.uk*, whose monthly magazine *Crossword* he edits; and *The Magpie* (a monthly edited by Mark Goodliffe and Simon Anthony and also available on subscription, *gooders@emperors.freeserve.co.uk*) took over from *Tough Puzzles*, founded by Michael Rich, after the latter's death. None of these series and periodicals is tailored to the needs of the occasional solver unfamiliar with thematic puzzles or disinclined to tackle anything out of the ordinary, but they all offer a fascinating variety of puzzles at the more difficult (and indeed most difficult) end of the spectrum.

I am conscious of the fact that, in this introduction, I have touched on many aspects of crossword setting and solving which, thoroughly treated, would cover many pages. One day, perhaps, I shall get down to a full study of the crossword in all its aspects. And then again I may not. Though I hold increasingly firm views on the principles that should guide setters in their construction of puzzles, I doubt whether it is possible to establish permanent 'rules' for every single type of clue, and am comforted by this realization. There should always remain an area of creativity which defies categorization, to which we setters all aspire, and on the whole I prefer to let my puzzles speak for themselves.

Jonathan Crowther
Oxford
May 2006

Biographies

'Dummy' entries indicate
setters with more than
one pseudonym, and refer
readers to the main entries
for such setters. SMALL
CAPITALS within entries
indicate the first mention
within an entry of a setter
with his or her own entry.

Adam

Adam Sobey was born in Sutton Coldfield in 1925, and at the age of five found himself in rural Dorset, where he began a lifelong love affair with nature. A daily cycle ride of fifteen miles to and from the local grammar school in Sherborne, combined with a keen interest in healthy games at school, has enabled him to acquire the kind of body that has endured into old age with his enthusiasm for life undimmed. His education continued at Christ's College, Cambridge (mathematics) and Imperial College, London (aeronautical structures), which prepared him for a career at the Royal Aircraft Establishment, Farnborough, where he carried out research on structural problems of aircraft, particularly the vibration problems of helicopters. On being timed out at sixty, he joined a company building computer models of complex mechanical systems, where he worked for eleven years. Since giving up paid employment, he has pursued his academic interests in elasticity as a visiting fellow of City University, London, as well as local charitable work.

Adam's interest in crosswords began at an early age with attempts to fill the blocked grids of highly interlocking words (the old *Evening News* standard puzzle). At about thirteen he began solving cryptics, starting with the Saturday prize puzzle in the now defunct *Daily Sketch*; by the age of fourteen he was into the *Daily Telegraph* cryptic and by fifteen happily through and out of it. Crosswords then took a back seat until his first university long vacation, when he came across *The Listener* puzzle (around No. 750), a life-changing experience. He fondly recalls a Pangloss puzzle of narrative type that began 'The obit of the temulent greengrocer was an orra one ...'. In those days only the original *Chambers's Twentieth Century Dictionary* was available to solvers, there being no short-cuts to inspiration such as *Chambers Words*, and of course no electronic aids. Solving almost every *Listener* crossword over the following sixty years has enabled him to make comparisons between the puzzles and setters of several decades. With his particular interest in the entertainment value of puzzles, for him those by Proton stand out for their brilliance. He reckons that Proton's Jabberwocky of physicists ('Twas Soddy and the Gay-Lussacs …') has not been surpassed. Today's fare is different: the socio-demographic changes that have taken place, and modern work practices with their paucity of leisure time, make comparisons impossible.

Adam's first published puzzle ('Exit Lines' in 1955) has been followed by a long string in *The Listener* and *Times Listener* series, his latest being his fiftieth. His puzzles have also appeared in *Crossword* and *The Magpie*. His pet dislikes are crosswords that require most of the clues to be solved before the pencil can get busy or depend on the services of Google, and preambles that lack generosity to the solver in their wording. He looks forward to an early demise of extraneous letters and misprints.

Adamant
See **GOLDMAN, HAZEL**

Aelfre
See **SALAMANCA**

Aelred
See **CORYLUS**

Alaun

Nuala Considine (whose pseudonym is a reversal of her forename) was born in London and brought up in a diplomatic environment. Her father was Irish ambassador to various countries, so her schooling was largely abroad. After leaving school she studied piano at the Accademia di Santa Cecilia in Rome and operatic singing with Maestro Mario Ranucci, one of whose claims to fame was that he could sing in a perfect (non-falsetto) soprano voice as well as in a rich baritone one. In fact, he could sing any opera duet for the two voices single-handed, outdoing both his female and his male pupils simultaneously.

At the age of eighteen Nuala met the love of her life and gave up any idea of becoming a concert pianist or an operatic star in favour of marriage. It was, incidentally, her husband Brian who introduced her to cryptic crosswords. After marriage she also did some photographic modelling.

Nuala and Brian together, for fun, compiled a crossword which they submitted to the *Irish Times*. It was accepted, and became the first of many on which they collaborated for that paper. Nuala then worked for the newspaper features agency Morley Adams, writing everything from theatre and film reviews and horoscopes to advice to couples on how to lead a happy married life. Morley Adams also produced crosswords, and it was here that Nuala found her true milieu, finally doing little else but compiling puzzles. She has provided crosswords for, among many others, the *Daily Telegraph*, *Daily Express* (for some years setting all their daily cryptics single-handed), *Evening Standard*, *Daily Mail*, *Financial Times*, *Washington Post*, *New Scientist*, *Daily Sketch*, *Sunday Correspondent* (of which she was crossword editor as well as a contributor until its demise) and numerous magazines.

Nuala also compiled a crossword called 'The Stinker' for the *Weekend Mail*, which had a large and devoted following.

One group, who worked together and regularly attempted to solve it jointly, became so frustrated that they wrote to the paper asking for a photograph of the setter so that they could throw darts at it, a request that was politely refused on the grounds that the setter was a lady.

Nuala now limits herself to setting for the *Sunday Telegraph*, Friday's *Evening Standard*, and the Saturday *Daily Mail*. She likes pithy clues and dislikes 'tortured' ones in which the word is dismembered letter by letter. She hates gobbledegook clues that make no normal readable sense. She greatly enjoys humour in other setters and tries to inject some into her own creations whenever possible.

See the puzzle section for an example of this setter's work.

Anobium
See JAGO

Antares
See BROWNE, RICHARD

Antico
See COLUMBA

Aquila
See MUTCH, JEREMY

Aragon

Richard Rogan's pseudonym is derived not from his own name, but from that of the French poet Louis Aragon. Richard was born in 1961 in Ballymoney, Northern Ireland, and educated at Coleraine Academical Institution and the universities of Reading, Nantes, and Lancaster. After seventeen years, first as a linguist and then as an IT specialist at GCHQ, Cheltenham, he now works for an IT consultancy based in Oxford.

Richard's introduction to crosswords was through his father, a Church of Ireland clergyman who battled regularly with the *Daily Telegraph* puzzle; it was a memorable day when Richard completed his first Saturday prize puzzle without parental guidance. Sunday papers were something only read about until his father's retirement, upon which Richard was introduced to *The Observer*, and in particular the AZED puzzle, which fascinated him with its unfamiliar barred grid and strange vocabulary. He also bought early anthologies of *Listener* puzzles in a spirit of youthful optimism. He persevered, nevertheless, and began compiling puzzles, painstakingly building two 100-puzzle collections in hardback notebooks, the grids carefully ruled in pencil, the blocks inked in with black biro. These puzzles never saw the light of publication and to this day probably reside in an outhouse at his sister's house in County Antrim, waiting to be discovered and snapped up by some connoisseur!

Richard's secret ambition had been to compile for *The Times*, whose puzzle he started solving in the Seventies, but he realized that if this ever came to pass it would disqualify him from entering *The Times* crossword championship. Four years after finishing fifth in the national final, he had his first puzzle published in *The Times*, and he now contributes two puzzles a month, with a jumbo puzzle every two months. He has to date had seven puzzles published in the *Times Listener* series, but finds the challenge of coming up with fresh themes difficult alongside the satisfying process of devising acceptable clues for plain puzzles, while at the same time doing a full-time job. He envies those who can manage this, in particular SABRE, whose combination of intriguing themes and artful and subtle clues he much admires.

As he sits at his computer today, interactively filling the latest *Times* grid with the aid of bespoke software, Richard wonders how he ever managed to cope with ruler and pencil. But clues are still dreamt up far from the PC, when he is surrounded by a heap of dictionaries and armed with only paper and pencil. He finds that the 'clever' clue, which causes a smile of satisfaction, is often the one most likely to fall foul of further inspection. If he has learned anything, it is that one should never try to be too clever or too obscure. He always tries to put himself in the position of the commuter on the underground.

Outside crosswords, Richard has competed for many years in cross-country and road running events for his club, whose (largely crossword-free) newsletter he edits. His wife, a Polish-Chechen Ukrainian citizen with Russian step-parents, is just about reconciled to the amount of time he devotes to crosswords. He remembers with some misgivings the occasion on which he tried to explain *The Listener* crossword to an attendant in a Kiev internet café, realizing as he did so how ridiculous he was sounding.

Araucaria

John Graham was born in 1924 and has been setting puzzles in *The Guardian* as Araucaria (also known as the monkey puzzle or the Chile pine) since 1958, though as a young man he read the old left-leaning *News Chronicle*. He grew up in Oxford, where his father was dean of Oriel College, and read classics at King's College, Cambridge, until the war intervened. He joined the RAF and flew in about thirty operations as an observer, after failing to become a pilot. Forced to bale out over Italy and go into hiding there, he was rescued by the Americans and mentioned in dispatches.

After the war John returned to King's, this time to read theology, and was subsequently ordained. He held a number of curacies and chaplaincies (as at Reading University for ten years from 1962), and after a period as priest in charge of St Peter's, Eaton Square, London, he became vicar of Houghton and Wyton in Huntingdonshire. By this time he had won an *Observer* competition for crossword setters two years running, and had been engaged by *The Guardian* to set crosswords for the paper about once a week. This began as a sideline but by the end of the 1970s became a necessity after his first marriage ended in divorce. Under the church's rules at the time, this disqualified him from continuing in the ministry. *The Guardian* then increased his quota of puzzles, and at present he sets six Araucarias for the paper monthly, as well as one in three of the quick crosswords. In addition he contributes cryptics to the *Financial Times* (as Cinephile, an anagram of Chile pine that also betrays a fondness for the silver screen) and the monthly 1 *Across* magazine, as well as one a month for *Homes and Antiques*. All of these he puts together at a desk upstairs in the cottage in Somersham in Cambridgeshire where he has lived alone since his second wife, Margaret, died some years ago.

He sends all his puzzles to be checked by a lady in Wiltshire, whose job, he says, is 'to be as critical as possible', though he does not always change clues she questions.

John specializes in themed puzzles, in which a central person, phrase, or idea informs much of the completed grid. One of his most famous was built round the heroes of South African resistance to apartheid, while another marked the 250th anniversary of the death of J. S. Bach. He also regularly sets 'alphabetical jigsaws', a type he invented, in which the clues are arranged in the alphabetical order of their solutions, with every different initial letter being represented, so that the solver must discover where each answer is to go in the diagram, like fitting together the pieces of a jigsaw.

John believes in bringing freedom of expression and fun to the business of writing clues, and is not too concerned about Ximenean strictures. In this he has inspired many younger setters, who see him as something of a mentor. He is particularly fond of long anagrams, his favourite being one he used in a Christmas puzzle: 'O hark the herald angels sing the boy's descent which lifted up the world', an anagram of 'While shepherds watched their flocks by night, all seated on the ground'.

After the death of his first wife, John resumed his priestly duties, and he is still in demand for occasional sermons and funerals. He is also called on to fill in during periods between the departure of one local priest and the arrival of the next one.

See the puzzle section for an example of this setter's work.

Armonie

John Dawson was born in Newcastle-upon-Tyne in 1946.
His pseudonyms, Armonie in the *Financial Times*, Chifonie in
The Guardian, and Symphonie elsewhere, betray his love of early
music, as they are all medieval names for the hurdy-gurdy.
He finds listening to the hurdy-gurdy, like solving crosswords,
highly enjoyable, though most satisfying when finished.

After attending Washington Grammar School in County
Durham and graduating from Nottingham University, John
worked as a chemical engineer. While working in a laboratory
in Birmingham in 1972 he was introduced to cryptic crosswords.
During the tea break each morning several lab staff, a secretary,
and the tea lady joined forces to attempt the *Daily Telegraph*
cryptic. Realizing that with a bit of thought and practice he could
progress, he was soon trying more difficult puzzles, though it was
some twenty years before he started setting his own. His first
published puzzle, based on the works of Aldous Huxley and
entitled 'Leda Writer', appeared on *The Independent's* Pursuits page
in 1992, and the first of his regular *Guardian* and *Financial Times*
puzzles followed in 1994. He has also had three puzzles in the
Times Listener series.

John prefers short, flowing Ximenean clues, and dislikes
those with an abrupt or nonsensical surface. These requirements
sometimes seem mutually exclusive and may lead to the occasional
compromise. While he enjoys a good anagram, the use of poor-
quality anagrams as a last resort for a word that is difficult to clue
is one of his pet hates, and he will sometimes recast a grid to
avoid resorting to it. He much admires the cluing technique of
Custos (the late Alec Robins), who has been criticized by some as
being undemanding but whose seamless constructions remind
John of the pianist Artur Schnabel's remark about Mozart: 'too
easy for beginners, too difficult for virtuosi'.

John is now semi-retired and lives in Kendal. He enjoys walking the Lakeland fells and, combining this interest with landscape photography and computing, he has set up the popular website *www.lakedistrictwalks.com*.

Ascot

Allan Scott was born in Southport in 1946, and was educated at Burnage High School for Boys in Manchester. After leaving school he worked in the insurance industry in Manchester, York, Norwich, and Colchester until 2000, when he retired to concentrate on setting crosswords full-time.

Allan began solving cryptics in the *Manchester Evening News* at the age of eleven and still enjoys the daily challenge (usually *The Times* or *The Independent*). His first published puzzle appeared in *The Listener* in 1977, and soon after that he met his mentor, MASS, with whom he wrote three crossword books for Marks & Spencer between 1984 and 1986. Mass had earlier compiled for M&S in tandem with Custos (the late Alec Robins), from whom Allan eventually took over *The Observer* Everyman series. Apart from his weekly Everyman puzzles, Allan compiles regularly for *The Times* and *The Spectator*, as well as the *Financial Times*, where he uses the pseudonym Falcon, after Robert Falcon Scott. He still has hopes of using Fitzgerald as his nom de guerre!

Allan dislikes crosswords with clue answers that must be treated according to a theme to be discovered before any entries can be made. He regards one of his best clues to be slightly risqué: 'Split personality? (5, 10)' for GORAN IVANISEVIC, the Croatian tennis player born in Split. Outside crosswords, Allan is a keen golfer, playing regularly at the North Wales golf club, not far from where he now lives with his partner Christina.

See the puzzle section for an example of this setter's work.

Auctor

Paul McKenna was born in Hertfordshire in 1961; in 1971 he moved to the south coast, where he has lived ever since. After leaving Eastbourne Grammar School and the local college of further education, he embarked on a career as a welder in the oil and gas industry, specializing in long cross-country pipelines. This enabled him to travel extensively throughout Europe and beyond. A natural proclivity for getting things done rather than doing things saw him rise through the ranks to more supervisory positions. In 2003 he completed a project in Yemen as assistant construction manager, but because of a slowdown in construction he decided to return to an interest retained since his schooldays, and is now reading for a degree in classics at King's College, London.

Paul's feet are firmly in the Ximenean camp when it comes to the writing of clues. This is due largely to a long epistolary relationship he had with Ix (the late I. C. Snell), through which he learnt the ability to analyse what a clue actually says, and how the grammar of cryptic and surface meanings works. His consistent success in the monthly AZED and other clue-writing competitions is testimony to the benefit of this rigorous grounding. Auctor, whose pseudonym is nothing more exciting than the Latin for 'composer' or 'writer', has puzzles appearing regularly in the *Times Listener* series, Enigmatic Variations in the *Sunday Telegraph*, and *The Independent* weekend magazine, as well as in *Crossword*, a classical society magazine, and two or three times a year (under his own name) in *Church Times*. He is also one half of Chubber (with Jeff Pearce, alias CAPER, who made up the pseudonym in reference to Paul's increasing waistline) and Panda (with Alan Donovan, alias Syd Lexis, i.e. P and A), joint partnerships which came into being following Gruntlings lunches (*see* OWZAT). Paul believes (but cannot prove) that he originated the 'decussated' technique for getting a message into a grid, i.e. supplying double clues where one answer belongs at the numbered across entry and the other at any of the crossing downs. He also finds grids in which each number refers to one clue only (thus obviating the need for across and down lists) fascinating and particularly tidy. Good clues, he feels, are at the heart of the best puzzles, and he is not tempted to add unnecessary thematic hurdles simply for difficulty's sake. If one can solve clues, albeit difficult ones, then Auctor's puzzles should never be too daunting.

Audreus

Audrey Young (née Jones) was born in north Wales in 1921 and grew up in Canada, where she was taken by her emigrating parents at the age of eight months. The family's return to the old country when Audrey was fifteen brought an abrupt end to her formal education: she went into service as a kitchen maid. The war, which started three years later, released her – into a factory – and after the war there were jobs in both town and country, from the comparatively genteel retail trade to an abortive attempt at pig farming.

When Audrey married in 1959 it was to a man who loved crosswords. Their evenings were spent happily poring over puzzles in the *News Chronicle* and *The Guardian*. Bill's work as a research forester made it necessary for him to make frequent trips around the country, often being away from home for up to six weeks. One evening, her husband away, the baby fast asleep in his cot, the puzzle of the day completed, and the prospect of a lonely evening ahead, Audrey had the idea of making up a puzzle of her own. Working casually at first, she became engrossed, and began taking pains. When Bill returned from his trip Audrey presented him with the finished puzzle. She also showed him a letter from John Perkin (late editor of *Guardian* crosswords), accepting the puzzle she had sent him and suggesting that she might like to 'try her hand' at one or two more. At that time *Guardian* setters were anonymous; pseudonyms were introduced a year or two later. 'Audreus' was an attempt at a classical approach!

In addition to her *Guardian* puzzles as Audreus, Audrey contributes crosswords to the *Financial Times* as Mutt. She admires the work and prodigious output of ARAUCARIA (her elder by six months), who always seems to come up with something new without apparent effort. She never knowingly misses a puzzle by BUNTHORNE, and admits to a partiality for SHED and Dogberry (the two pseudonyms of her son). But where, she wonders, are the women compilers? Why is crossword setting such a predominantly male preserve? The ability to think logically, allied to a quirky sense of humour, is not an exclusively masculine trait.

Audrey has a son in Sheffield and a daughter and grandson in London. Widowed many years ago, she now lives in a small town in France.

Auster

Shirl O'Brien grew up in Brisbane, Queensland. She always had a love of words and enjoyed solving 'orthodox' crosswords, but it was only when Brisbane's *Courier-Mail* began publishing cryptics in 1979 (first *Times* puzzles, then those from *The Guardian*) that she found her passion. She has been addicted to *The Guardian* puzzle ever since, but in 1984 decided that it was time Queenslanders had some local content and submitted eight puzzles to the *Courier-Mail*. The paper bought four for trial, subsequently offered her a year's contract, and twenty-one years later she is still setting a puzzle for the Saturday edition. She chose the pseudonym Southern Cross (the constellation on the Australian flag) because it begins with SO (her initials) and includes the 'cross' of 'crossword'. She is an original member of the Australian Crossword Club and her puzzles regularly appear in their monthly magazine.

In 1987, while visiting Manchester, Shirl met John Perkin, who recommended her to the late Alec Robins (Custos of *The Guardian*), who once described himself as 'a purist – oh well, a damned pedant if you must'. He became her mentor and friend and over the next ten years shaped her ideas on crossword setting. He encouraged her to submit a puzzle to *The Guardian* and suggested the pseudonym Auster (the south wind). She now contributes a few puzzles each year to *The Guardian*, which with her weekly *Courier-Mail* puzzles are about as much as she can fit into a busy life.

Shirl's favourite setters are RUFUS and CRISPA. They rarely use obscure words, yet their clues are usually succinct and clever. The use of ordinary words cleverly clued is what she aspires to, in puzzles that require little or no recourse to dictionaries of any kind. Her most memorable *Guardian* puzzles are ARAUCARIA's alphabetical jigsaws clued in rhyming couplets, a type she herself sets occasionally, though without the rhyming couplets!

As Southern Cross she has set many thematic puzzles, some relating to Australian subjects – state floral emblems, explorers, persons of note (on currency notes) – and others such as D-day, and the millennium year. One of her own favourite clues featured in the last of these. It was the end of 1999 and the millennium bug was feared. Planes, it was said, would fall out of the sky and money would disappear from bank accounts. Businesses did everything to ensure that their computer systems were date-compliant. Shirl wrote this down clue: 'You omit nothing, then Y2K turns up. It's horrible! (5)' for YUKKY.

Shirl had set her sights on completing 1,000 puzzles, but she has in fact passed that milestone and is hoping to go on for a bit longer. 'Lucky', she says, 'is the woman whose work is also her passion.'

See the puzzle section for an example of this setter's work.

Autolycus
See **TANTALUS**

Axe

Alun Evans was born on the last day of 1949 in the Rhondda, and was educated at the local county grammar school and Bedford College, University of London, where he obtained a degree in geography. After his career in financial services was cut short by an osteoarthritic ankle in 1992, Alun began peppering publishers with crossword puzzles and book ideas, as some may complain he still does. He had been hammering away for more than four years when the editors of *New Internationalist* were the first to give in, and he has been setting his unusual 2-in-1 'geographical' puzzles for them for nearly a decade, while picking up other commissions along the way. He took his pseudonym from his last company's three-letter password. Not having a middle name, he thought AXE would be a more appropriate mnemonic than, say, APE or ALE when advising on corporate finance. The 'X' was opportune too, alluding to both the 'Xword' and a missing letter indicator.

Unlike many other setters, Alun was not brought up on cryptic crosswords. He muscled in when his mother tackled the *Daily Mirror* crossword, but it wasn't until a fellow student introduced him to *The Guardian* in 1969 that he started to take an interest in cryptics, which was tepid at first but then obsessive enough for him to have a puzzle printed in 1973 in a doomed staff magazine published by his first employer, Abbey National. He admits that *The Guardian* of the 1970s was his main influence: he admired the widely varying techniques of Lavengro, BUNTHORNE, RUFUS, and of course ARAUCARIA. Ximenes remained undiscovered for several more years until he had perforce to take *The Times* and other broadsheets as business tools. *Ximenes on the Art of the Crossword* (1966) arrived too late to affect his clue-writing style, which owes more to the freer formed puzzles of *The Guardian* of the old days, sometimes at the expense of 'rules'. He believes that clues which are dogmatically correct, but clumsy or mechanical, leave the solver as dissatisfied as those classed as 'unsound'. His philosophy is therefore: 'Try to be different. If the clues make sense and are fair, use them; if they entertain, all the better.'

Today puzzles by Axe and those under his real name may be found in an eclectic range of publications. As well as being a member of the teams setting for the *Financial Times* and *Church Times* (where Don Manley regularly treats him to Ximenean tutorials), Alun's work may be found in *My Weekly* and the *BBC Wildlife Magazine*, and regularly in six regional newspapers and magazines. He also supplies Sudokus and other word puzzles (thanks to his invaluable Crossword Compiler grid-making software) to seven others, and half the 'Speedy' crosswords in *The Observer* are set by him. He is happiest when setting themed puzzles in tune with a particular specialist publication such as those mentioned above and (thanks to Rufus's recommendation) *Medical Laboratory World*. Despite this dubious privilege, Alun rates Roger Squires easily top of his list of mentors and supporters.

An avid sports fan, a former player of rugby, football, and cricket (and an administrator in the last two), Alun has also written books on golf history and, as ever hopelessly catholic, on war films. He and his wife live in Milton Keynes, and they have two grown-up daughters. Despite this plethora of interests, he finds time for others including music (liturgical, classical, and opera), France, wine, cinema, and good beer. He also runs his own courier company.

Azed

Jonathan Crowther was born in Liverpool in 1942, grew up in Kirkby Lonsdale in the Lake District, and was educated at Rugby School and Corpus Christi College, Cambridge (where he read classics and classical philology, and where his first puzzles were published under the pseudonym Gong, a family nickname, in the university weekly *Varsity*). He joined Oxford University Press in 1964 and worked for OUP in India, London, and Oxford for thirty-five years, latterly as a lexicographer writing dictionaries for foreign students of English, before retiring in 2000. He is married with two sons and lives in Oxford.

Having enjoyed crossword solving from an early age, encouraged by his father, Jonathan discovered Ximenes while still at Rugby and became an instant convert. After leaving university he started submitting occasional puzzles (sixteen in all) to *The Listener* as Gong and continued competing in Ximenes competitions until taking over from him after his death in 1971, when *The Observer* accepted and printed an X-shaped puzzle he had submitted in memory of X. Azed No. 1 appeared in *The Observer* in March 1972 and the series is still going strong, with monthly clue-writing competitions similar to those of Ximenes. The pseudonym Azed is a reversal of (Fray Diego de) Deza, a Spanish inquisitor general, preserving – if somewhat deviously – the inquisitorial tradition established by Torquemada and Ximenes. Jonathan also sets occasional puzzles under the pseudonym Ozymandias (from Shelley's poem: 'Look on my works, ye Mighty, and despair!'). Azed solvers congregate for dinners or lunches held every five years or so to mark the publication of each successive group of 250 Azed puzzles. They may also subscribe to the monthly 'slip', a newsletter in which Azed gives details of each monthly competition and discusses points of specific or general interest relating to his puzzles. Over the years AZ (as he likes to abbreviate his pseudonym) has made many friends among his regular solvers, and welcomes the dialogue on points of mutual interest carried on through the competitions and the slips.

Jonathan is unashamedly Ximenean in his ideas on the setting of crosswords (ideas which are expounded more fully in the introduction to this book), if anything regarding himself as even keener than his mentor on the importance of grammatical and syntactical soundness in clues. As a result he tends to prefer puzzles by setters who share these ideas – including COLUMBA, DIMITRY, DUCK, KEA, and PHI, among others – but is regularly amazed at the ingenuity of thematic construction displayed in the more specialized crosswords, such as those in the *Times Listener* series, the Crossword Club magazine, and 1 *Across*. He has himself created a number of new 'specials' which now appear regularly in the Azed series, including 'Cherchez la Femme', 'Eightsome Reels', 'Give and Take', 'Heads, Bodies and Legs', 'Left, Right and Centre', 'Overlaps', 'Red Herrings', and 'Spoonerisms'. New ideas may occur to him anywhere and at any time, but many of his happiest moments of inspiration seem to have been while out walking the dog, often along the banks of the Thames ('Aids theme, possibly?'). Jonathan's publications include *The Azed Book of Crosswords* (Latimer 1975, reissued by Pantheon in 1976 as *The World's Most Difficult Crosswords*), *Lost for Words* (Angus & Robertson 1988), *Best of Azed Crosswords* (Chambers 1989), *Observer Azed Crosswords* (Chambers 1991), *Book of Azed Crosswords* (Chambers 2005), and a series of four books of *Crosswords for Learners of English* (OUP 1980). His essay on 'The Art of the Crossword Setter' appears as part of the front matter in *Chambers Crossword Dictionary* (2nd edition, Chambers 2006) and in *Chambers Concise Crossword Dictionary* (2nd edition, Chambers 2005). In December 1991 Azed was voted best British crossword setter in a poll of crossword setters conducted by the *Sunday Times*, and in July 1991 he was chosen as the crossword compilers' crossword compiler in *The Observer Magazine* 'Experts' Expert' feature.

See the puzzle section for an example of this setter's work.

Bats
See **PAUL**

Beelzebub
See **CALMAC, COLUMBA, PHI**

BeRo

At the age of eight, in 1949, Barry Roe was introduced by his
father to the *Sunday Dispatch* crossword, from which he learned
many new words, like 'sockeye' and 'leister'. Education (culminating
in a BSc in industrial chemistry), social and home life, and work
(with a race to finish the *Daily Telegraph* crossword in the tea
break) meant little time given to serious crosswords, the existence
of which was unknown to him anyway. Some thirty crossword-
wasted years later he tackled an AZED crossword for the first time
(with predictably poor results) and, on looking at the solution,
could not believe that there was such a word as 'kgotla'.

At about the same time, Barry joined the Crossword Club,
using its magazine's comments to start solving *The Spectator*,
New Statesman, and eventually *Times Listener* crosswords. On the
principle 'If you can't beat them, join them', he submitted a
crossword to *The Listener*, which to his great delight was accepted
for publication in 1988. A few years earlier he had achieved his
only claim to clue-writing success, an Azed VHC (very highly
commended) which led to an also-ran appearance in the one and
only Azed *Observer*/Oxford Crossword Superbrain contest, whose
finals were held in the Oxford examination schools.

Since then, Barry has had about thirty thematic puzzles
published, mainly in the *Times Listener* series, the Enigmatic
Variations series in the *Sunday Telegraph*, and the Crossword
Club's monthly magazine. His aim in setting crosswords is
to provide entertainment with a penny-dropping moment,
through clues which may bend but never (well, hardly ever)
break Ximenean 'rules'. He gratefully acknowledges help given
over the years by various editors, including Mike Rich, John
Grimshaw (DIMITRY), Ross Beresford, Derek Arthur, James
Leonard (MR LEMON), and Brian Head, except when they publish
his pet hate: crosswords which require most of their clues to be

solved before a single letter can be entered with certainty.
The annual statistics relating to *The Listener* crosswords produced
by John Green add greatly to Barry's enjoyment of them as a
solver, and he has appeared regularly among the 100 most
successful solvers. He is continually amazed at the high standards
maintained in such 'serious' crosswords, both in their ingenuity
of construction and, perhaps more importantly, in their clues,
and he admires too many setters to pick out any individuals for
special mention.

Barry enjoys regular swimming and irregular walking to
counteract his more sedentary interests: red wine, crosswords,
an internet horse-racing game, and bridge, which he recently
took up again after a thirty-year gap. He also likes meeting fellow
setters and solvers, especially at the annual *Listener* crossword
setters' dinners.

Bower
See **RUFUS**

Bradman
See **DUCK**

Brendan
See **VIRGILIUS**

Browne, Richard

Richard Browne grew up in Cheam, Surrey, attended Epsom
College, and took a classics degree at Trinity College, Oxford.
He then spent twenty-five years with IBM, doing crosswords as a
hobby and graduating from joint compilation of the IBM house
magazine to an invitation to join *The Times* team in 1987. Having
taken (very) early retirement, he became a full-time compiler,
creating the *times2* crossword in 1993 (which he compiled for ten
years), and beating other applicants to join the *Daily Telegraph* in
1995 (appearing on Tuesdays for the next seven years). He also
joined the *Financial Times* (as Antares, a star in the constellation
Scorpio, his birth sign) and *The Independent* (as Victor, a family
name), but resigned from these papers on being appointed
crossword editor of *The Times* in 2002. Apart from occasional
appearances in 1 *Across* as Susie (picked at random), he now
compiles only for *The Times* (over 600 dailies and 50 jumbos so
far). He reckons that he has passed the mark of 1,000 puzzles
altogether in the quality press.

Richard's interest in crosswords started early, attempting the
junior picture puzzle in the London *Evening News* and helping his
grandfather with the *Sunday Express* skeleton puzzle – he filled in
the pattern and then grandpa solved the clues – before graduating
to his dad's *Daily Telegraph* and then *The Times*.

Richard lives on the Hampshire coast with Marilyn, his wife of
thirty-three years. He is a keen amateur singer of classical music,
performing regularly in Winchester with the Wayneflete Singers,
with whom he has made Prom appearances and numerous CDs
(one of which, *Belshazzar's Feast*, won a Grammy award). He also
performs with a smaller choir specializing in his favourite
repertoire, Renaissance sacred music. He attends as many concerts
and plays as possible, but is never without a card in his pocket
listing the words he is currently seeking inspiration to clue.

Richard is not a fan of burrowing through *Chambers*; he prefers the elegance of ordinary words clued simply but with originality, wit, and maximum sleight of hand – a far greater challenge to the setter, in his opinion, than anything permitting obscurities – and has always admired Brian Greer (VIRGILIUS) for exactly this. He admits to never having got the hang of Mephisto, AZED or *The Listener*. Although in principle a strict Ximenean (rigorously enforcing a similar approach on *The Times* team), he enjoys ARAUCARIA and BUNTHORNE for their sheer outrageous fun.

See the puzzle section for an example of this setter's work.

Brummie

Eddie James, Brummie of *The Guardian,* was born in (yes) Birmingham in 1941. Since taking early retirement from a middle management job with British Telecom, he has been pleasantly surprised to find that setting crosswords, intended as a paying hobby, has become a full-time occupation. He and his wife now supply crosswords to many publications, including *BBC History Magazine* and *Geographical,* as well as a monthly cryptic under the pseudonym Peebles on the Chambers Harrap website.

Eddie learned to do cryptics as a teenager, painstakingly working through the local paper's Reader's Crossword daily puzzles until eventually getting his own submissions published. It became clear that he was better at setting than solving, his below-average solving skills still being an embarrassment to him. This skill – plus gaining a place 'somewhere in the top thirteen' in a setting competition run by the former *Games & Puzzles* magazine (won, incidentally, by the incognito DUCK) – encouraged his hopes of becoming a professional setter, a notion that was shelved after a succession of rejections from the national broadsheets.

The advent of the microcomputer helped to revive Eddie's ambition. He wrote a crossword grid-filling program on a Sinclair ZX81 which made it much easier to produce themed puzzles aimed at specialist periodicals. Furthermore, puzzle grids could be printed out, giving submissions a distinctly professional look. He soon had monthly puzzles appearing in several magazines. More followed, but it was not until he was taken on many years later by *Private Eye* (having somewhat exaggerated his status as a setter to the editor Ian Hislop) that he felt he had arrived. Under the name Cyclops he has been setting the *Eye*'s fortnightly crossword for more than ten years. The crossword's scurrilous nature has brought him some notoriety but also many commissions he would not otherwise have had. It also led indirectly – the process was by no means an automatic one – to the achievement of his long-cherished ambition to become a *Guardian* setter.

Given that PAUL is one of his favourite setters, Eddie's flexible attitude to Ximenean principles will probably surprise no one. He does not mind standards being relaxed occasionally, e.g. in the misleading use of punctuation, if the aim is to enhance the solver's experience (rather than to make the setter appear clever or witty). However, he cringes at the likes of Peterhead = 'p' and feels that some setters often 'bend the rules' merely for the sake of a clue's surface reading, apparently without regard to its fairness to the solver. As a solver himself, Eddie's pet hate is the long anagram clue. As he puts it: 'All that tedious letter-crunching, at the end of which we're supposed to admire the anagram's 'apt' wording. What setter worthy of the name could fail to come up with an appropriate phrase, given twenty or more letters to play with?'

Bufo

Peter Rhodes celebrated his sixtieth birthday in 2005 on the same day that *The Listener* was seventy-five years old. His main pseudonym is the Latin word for a toad, though he does usually try to be a nice toad. For many years he has also collaborated with CORYLUS, using the pseudonym Peeper (another amphibian). This has been a very successful partnership, twice winning the Ascot Gold Cup for *Listener* puzzle of the year. Bufo has always specialized in thematic puzzles, for *The Listener*, *Sunday Telegraph* Enigmatic Variations, and the Crossword Club, among others, though he has more recently begun setting the plain puzzle in *Chemistry World*, the monthly magazine for members of the Royal Society of Chemistry.

As a boy, Peter was always interested in puzzles and got started in crosswords by solving those in the *Manchester Evening Chronicle* and *Daily Mail*. He went on to study chemistry at Leeds University, where he graduated to the crosswords in the *Daily Telegraph*, *The Guardian*, and *The Times*. Then, one very wet Sunday when there was nothing else to do, he attempted the Mephisto puzzle in the *Sunday Times*. After many hours' slog he almost completed it despite having a totally inadequate dictionary. That week he bought his first copy of *Chambers* and has never looked back since. Two of the words he learnt from that first Mephisto were 'igapo' and 'gat'. Those were the days, he recalls, before such aids as *Chambers Anagrams* and the puzzle-solving software *TEA* became available. Solvers had to make do with *Chambers*, though *Walker's Rhyming Dictionary* often proved useful.

During the Seventies Peter solved *The Listener* puzzle and Jac's puzzle in *The Spectator* each week with a work colleague. His crossword career received fresh impetus when he joined the newly formed Crossword Club, started by Brian Head, and his first puzzles appeared in the club's magazine in 1982. His first

Listener puzzle was published in 1984 and he has been a regular contributor ever since.

Though recognizing the importance of cluing, Peter is really more interested in gimmickry. He therefore appreciates most of all the work of setters who seem to him to show the greatest originality and ingenuity, such as DIMITRY, KEA, and Elgin (Glen Mullineux). His principal dislike is poorly constructed diagrams, especially those with a large number of interconnected bars. But he refuses to take crosswords too seriously, believing that their only purpose should be to provide entertainment for setter and solver. He feels that if he smiles when setting a puzzle then the solver might smile when solving it.

Bunthorne

Bob Smithies was born in 1934 at Middleton in Lancashire, and now lives in Westmorland (having no time for the modern Cumbria). He was broadly educated by his father, a knowledge-thirsty autodidact from that nineteenth-century tradition of the toiling poor, and at the local grammar school. His obsession with words began during childhood when he spotted the reversion of the manufacturer's name on the kitchen table vinegar bottle: Gartons. At sixteen, a darkroom apprenticeship led him to become a *Guardian* photographer for twenty years. They were followed by a further twenty as a Granada Television presenter.

Bob experimented for years before submitting puzzles to the then *Guardian* crossword editor John Perkin. He regards John, together with ARAUCARIA and Ximenes, as the major influences on his style, and is unhappy at seeing Araucaria and Ximenes represented as leaders of opposing factions. What matters, Bob feels, is that clues, however subtle, should be demonstrably fair. His first published puzzle, which provoked many letters of anguished complaint, appeared in the early 1960s. He sets occasional puzzles for 1 *Across* and the ENIGMATIST website, but is reluctant to compile for other newspapers, believing that there is a cultured, literate body of *Guardian* solvers who share his wavelength. He revels in the argument, wit, and vituperation that his and other setters' puzzles engender on the paper's website. His pseudonym was chosen because he had been singing in a series of Gilbert and Sullivan operettas and liked the association with 'Patience'.

Bob's method of working is to find a grid to fit a theme or one of the long anagrams for which he is notorious, or randomly to choose any of the fifty-odd *Guardian* prepared grids and see what happens. If a clue idea occurs during the grid filling he makes a note in the margin, although such inspiration more often strikes while he is sleeping, which drives Mrs Smithies to despair as he wakes up and reaches for his notepad. If cliché words like 'igloo', 'elemi', and 'Alamo' cannot be avoided, Bob spends hours seeking new ways to clue them; this led to perhaps his most famous clue: 'Amundsen's forwarding address (4)' for MUSH, the word the explorer might have used to send his dogs forward (it had to be Amundsen because his rival Scott used tractors).

The long self-defining anagram which began Bob's association with them about thirty years ago was: 'I.e. what oil-sheik said cheekily unto girl in gin palace', an anagram of 'What is a nice girl like you doing in a place like this, eh?'. Bob writes and photographs for a magazine to fund his other obsessions: fine wine and great music.

See the puzzle section for an example of this setter's work.

Calmac

Michael Macdonald-Cooper was born in 1941 in the rural west of Scotland, and educated there and in northern England before going to St Catherine's College, Oxford, to read modern and medieval languages and literature. His early career was spent in educational administration and university careers guidance. He was induced to try setting crosswords after meeting other setters at the final of the AZED *Observer*/Oxford Crossword Superbrain contest in 1984, which he won, being the only all-correct solver.

The 'superbrain' element in the contest's title gave Michael the idea for his first pseudonym, based on a laboured pun on Caledonian-MacBrayne (the Clyde and Western Isles ferry operator, invariably shortened to Cal-Mac in the Scottish media). His first puzzles were published in *The Listener* from early 1987. In the following year he became the first setter of cryptic crosswords in the newly launched *Scotland on Sunday*, and shortly afterwards became a regular contributor to *The Scotsman* (as Andrew Campbell, the paper requiring a different setter identity from its Sunday sister, which used Michael's real name). Meanwhile, more Calmac puzzles had already started to appear in *The Independent's Saturday Magazine* series.

Around this time Michael began to feature as a fairly regular finalist in *The Times* crossword championship, becoming national champion in 1991. From early in 1990 he had begun contributing cryptics to *The Independent* on a weekly basis, under the pseudonym Spurius. He was also prevailed upon to produce a copious supply of concise crosswords for both *The Independent* and *The Scotsman*.

After the untimely death of Richard Whitelegg (Beelzebub, Mephisto, Lucifer, Albipedius), Michael was invited to contribute Beelzebub puzzles to the *Independent on Sunday* in alternate weeks. In 1998 he assumed the role of crossword editor at *The Independent*, which he continued to hold until retiring early in 2005. During the same period he acted as crossword editor for *Oxford Today*, the thrice-yearly university alumnus publication, having been injudicious enough to venture a criticism of the quality of the magazine's earlier crossword.

Michael regards humour as the greatest asset in a setter, though soundness of cluing and fairness in grid construction are of almost equal importance. His favourite setters are Azed, COLUMBA, Dac (*see* SMOKEY), and MERLIN. Among his favourite clues are 'Unsuitable subject for oral examination? (4, 5)' for GIFT HORSE, 'Open course? Sometimes (8)' (SANDWICH), and 'Young man who found himself winning on the pools (8)' (NARCISSUS), this last being by the late Bert Danher (Hendra).

During the 1990s Michael produced around 225 cryptic puzzles a year and a further 400 or so of the definition type, finally achieving a total of roughly 6,200 published crosswords. He often had to take work on holiday with him. Once, after wrestling with the wording of a clue in a hotel lounge in Budapest, he permitted himself a nod and a smile of satisfaction, his unfocused gaze meanwhile roaming over the middle distance. Seconds later he was joined by a hooker who had been hovering at the bar and was evidently under the impression that an assignation had been made. The situation was too challenging for his limited knowledge of Magyar, but an explanation in German served to smooth over the misunderstanding.

See the puzzle section for an example of this setter's work.

Caper

Jeff Pearce was born in Blackheath in south-east London in 1957, and educated at Roan Grammar School and University College, London, where he tried but failed to get a chemistry degree. Jeff blames this on ARAUCARIA.

Much earlier, at his junior school, Jeff had looked forward to Friday afternoons, which were given over to 'mind games', including 'Animal, Vegetable, and Mineral', 'Twenty Questions', and a crossword. Each lunchtime his form teacher, Mr Charman, would copy out *The Telegraph* quick crossword on the blackboard, and an hour or so was devoted to solving it together as a class. Jeff wishes this practice continued today, not just in the office. It is his first memory of crossword solving, but he soon became hooked on the Pan series of crossword books and particularly liked the way in which each book was broken down into sections of increasing difficulty. AZED came rather later: Jeff has now been entering Azed's competitions for several years and can usually be seen in the HCs (those highly commended), with occasional appearances among the VHCs (those very highly commended) and prizewinners.

Jeff's first foray into setting was for the Department of the Environment's staff magazine, and shortly after that he responded to an advert by Tim Moorey (OWZAT), inviting attendance at the regular meetings of the Gruntlings in Covent Garden. There he met a number of brilliant setters, including Arcturus (Ross Beresford), DIMITRY, PHI, Pabulum (a.k.a. DUMPYNOSE), Hellebore (Daffydd Price Jones), and his particular friend Mike LAWS. He remains grateful to Tim for that opportunity and to Mike for all the advice and other help he has given. Jeff's first *Listener* crossword was published shortly after his first Gruntlings meeting, and his puzzles now appear regularly in the *Sunday Times* as well as many other periodicals (about ten a month).

He was part of *The Times* team in the early 2000s, and has also had puzzles in Enigmatic Variations (*Sunday Telegraph*), compiled jointly with his friend Paul McKenna (AUCTOR) under the name Chubber, a strange pseudonym but perfectly understandable, he says, if you've met Paul.

Casina

Wadham Sutton was born in London in 1935 and educated at
Chigwell School in Essex. Having picked up a couple of diplomas
and an external BMus degree from London University, he
embarked on a career in music, teaching and lecturing at all
levels from prep school to university, playing, writing, reviewing,
and conducting choirs and orchestras both small and large.

Brought up by parents who never so much as glanced at a
crossword, Wadham produced his first faltering efforts, for the
London *Evening News*, in the early 1960s, solely because he was
desperate for the two-guinea fee. He had never even heard of
Ximenes until he had been compiling professionally for several
years. In 1970 he sent two unsolicited puzzles to Edmund
Akenhead, then crossword editor of *The Times*, and in January
1972 he was taken onto *The Times* panel. In the autumn of the
following year he was invited to compile for *Country Life*, where
he was given the pseudonym Casina, the significance of which
he has been vainly trying to track down for over thirty years, and
which, rather illogically, he shared with another setter for the
same magazine. In the late 1990s he supplied puzzles for several
series of the Tyne Tees Television *Crosswits* programme, presented
by Tom O'Connor. By the end of 2005 he had set over 1,100
weekday puzzles and 40 jumbos for *The Times*, and about 670 for
Country Life. *The Times* marked the appearance of his 1,000th
puzzle, in April 2001, with a feature article by Alan Hamilton,
accompanied by the only stern, unsmiling photograph of himself
from among the thirty or so taken by the photographer.

When filling grids, Wadham starts with the longer words or
phrases and then generally works from the bottom up, though he
makes the point that different grids have different properties and
that setters become adept at recognizing this and varying their
approach accordingly. He has a fondness for clever anagrams,

his favourite being (someone else's) RACING TIPSTER/ STARTING PRICE, but has no time for slovenliness and inaccuracy or for clues that make no sense and, in Edmund Akenhead's words, 'could only be crossword clues'.

Wadham lives on Tyneside with his wife, an adult daughter (also a musician and crossword setter), two Chesapeake Bay retrievers (both of which have been exhibited at Crufts), and a couple of cats.

See the puzzle section for an example of this setter's work.

Charybdis

Chris Poole was born in Chingford, London, in 1951. His first half
term of education was spent at the primary school later attended
by David Beckham, their football abilities being, by a strange
quirk, exactly equal and opposite. He left school with a vague
secret wish to become a 'jack of all trades, master of one or two',
and is now astonished to be even halfway towards mastering one.
Having no idea how people ticked, he studied psychology at
Nottingham University, only later realizing that reading a few
classical novels and having a good time might have done the trick
just as well. For his PhD (in Nottingham's electrical engineering
department) he studied perceptual aspects of night vision image
intensifier usage, and particularly the unconscious eye–brain
strategies for detecting visual stimuli against a background of
0.01 mL. He wishes he could still remember what that means.

From an early age Chris immersed himself in dictionaries,
puzzles, and mythological tales, never suspecting that this might
one day prove useful for setting thematic crosswords. By chance
in his mid-teens he discovered Ximenes's seminal book and was
especially enchanted by the clue for HOUSEWIFE: 'I have most of
the time to stitch – then I iron'. His father also loved puzzles and
for a while he and Chris would attempt to scale the heights of a
Ximenes puzzle, a feat that could take months and entailed
numerous trips to consult *Chambers* in the local library.

Twenty fallow crosswording years followed, during which
Chris and his partner Karen took up teaching in Exeter and east
Devon. He only began solving seriously again in the late 1980s
with the arrival on the scene of the *Independent Magazine* puzzles.
He began setting similar thematics, at first just for friends.
The day that the late Richard Whitelegg (then Beelzebub and
Mephisto) accepted some of these for publication was one of the
happiest of his life. Chris has since set puzzles for the Saturday

Independent, Enigmatic Variations in the *Sunday Telegraph*, the Crossword Club, and *The Magpie*. The name CHaRybdIS refers to a 'sea whirlpool', which is a near-homonym of C. L. Poole. He also likes the classical reference and the suggestion of danger. In addition he has appeared (albeit rarely) as Little Eddy (a 'spin-off') and as Shrimp for South-West Water magazines.

Chris regards himself as more or less Ximenean in his clue writing, though his delight and obsession, as both setter and solver, is the weaving or unravelling of an interesting theme. At the time of writing he has set 110 thematic puzzles but still gets an endorphin rush upon devising a challenging thematic grid. Setting unthemed crosswords has never interested him. He prefers symmetrical grids, but is increasingly prepared to sacrifice symmetry for an interesting theme, particularly if the final solution reveals a new symmetrical element. He prefers his grid entries to be real words even (or especially) when they do not tally with their original clues for some thematic reason. His best ideas come unbidden and in the wee small hours, often on the night of a full moon. But he believes that careful research and a period of gestation give serendipity the chance to improve on an original idea before one plunges into the grid construction.

Chris's favourite setters include KEA, Bandmaster (Richard Morse), Ark (A. R. King), MR MAGOO, and MERLIN. He believes that above all crosswords should be fun and should never be taken too seriously. He therefore wishes it were not true that on two separate holidays he remembered to pack *Chambers* but forgot his pyjamas. He is passionate about art up to about 1950 and *some* rock music. He also enjoys comedy, coastal walks, the company of animals, and singing to his guitar (though the world is not ready for this).

See the puzzle section for an example of this setter's work.

Chifonie
See **ARMONIE**

Cinephile
See **ARAUCARIA**

CJM

Calum J. Macdonald was born in Aberdeen in 1961 and educated
at Aberdeen Grammar School and Aberdeen University.
Encouraged by his parents, he started tackling crosswords as a
teenager, *The Times* puzzle being the daily challenge. A journalist
since 1983, he is now deputy news editor of *The Herald* in
Glasgow, and began setting crosswords for the paper in 1994.
He has been crossword editor since 1996, overseeing the fourteen
puzzles that appear every week in *The Herald* and *Sunday Herald*.
He personally sets one cryptic and one general knowledge puzzle
a week, and in his spare time produces a weekly Glasgow-themed
crossword for *The Glaswegian*, under the pseudonym James
Jardine (his own middle name and his wife's maiden name).
In 1998 Calum devised and helped to produce a supplement
marking seventy years of daily crosswords in *The Herald*.
He has also edited two volumes of *The Herald Crossword Book*
(2004 and 2005).

Calum still uses blank grids and a pencil to build his puzzles,
but added a computer gizmo to his tools after realizing that an
apparently perfect solution could prove unworkable in relation
to others around it. He firmly believes that the essence of a good
crossword is its clues, which should be a mixture of the
straightforward, the teasing, and pure fun. An avowed non-
Ximenean, he likes clues to 'sing', so long as the solver is given
a fair chance. A major influence on his style has been MYOPS,
doyen of *The Herald* stable and creator of the infamous Wee
Stinkers. This has led to some of Calum's trademark delights/
horrors, in which a term for reform or change is implicit in the
solution, e.g. 'Condition of a new gite? (6, 8)' for EATING
DISORDER, or an old favourite, picked out by Sandy Balfour in
his review of *The Herald Crossword Book*: 'Ice with orange, OK?'
for THAT'S THE WAY THE COOKIE CRUMBLES.

As a crossword editor, Calum is acutely aware of the potential for howls of protest from solvers if mistakes occur, for example when LOCUM killed off the wrong wife of Henry VIII and Calum failed to spot it. (To his credit, Locum produced a very elegant *mea culpa* in a subsequent puzzle.) It is a truism that a higher premium is put on accuracy in a paper's crosswords than in its news pages, but he vividly recalls the occasion when the sports department managed, through technological ineptitude, to run two different back-page puzzles in different editions of *The Herald* on the same day. The next day's solutions section was packed – but Calum thinks the error went unnoticed (until now!).

See the puzzle section for an example of this setter's work.

Codex

Colin Dexter was born in 1930 in Stamford, Lincolnshire. In 1941 he won a scholarship to Stamford School, where he studied Latin and Greek in the classical sixth. He did his national service in the Royal Signals (as a high-speed Morse operator!) before going up to Christ's College, Cambridge, to read classics. From 1953 to 1966 he taught Latin and Greek in the Midlands, and in 1966 he was appointed to the Oxford University Schools Examination Board, where he supervised O, A, and S level exams in classics and English until his retirement in 1988. He still lives in Oxford.

Having had three school textbooks published in the 1960s, Colin began writing crime fiction in the early 1970s, and in subsequent years won two Gold Daggers and two Silver Daggers from the Crime Writers' Association. His novels, featuring Inspector Morse, were later successfully televised by ITV – thirty-three episodes in all – with John Thaw playing the part of Inspector Morse and Kevin Whately as Sergeant Lewis. The names of these two detectives were taken from those of Sir Jeremy Morse and Mrs B. Lewis (real name Dorothy Taylor), two of Colin's arch rivals as clue writers in the crossword world. Incidentally, the murderer in *Last Bus to Woodstock*, the first of the Morse novels, was the only named character whose alter ego had never won a first prize in Ximenes/AZED competitions. Some very familiar crossword worthies, including Crowther and Manley, have featured in the novels, usually as crooks!

Colin first became aware of cryptic crosswords in the war years, when a school friend introduced him to the wholly unremarkable clue, set by Hubert Philips in the now defunct *News Chronicle*: 'Ena cut herself (7)'. It is not the soundest clue ever written, with no definition in sight, but for him it was the introduction to the mysterious delights of playing around with the letters of individual words; and when the penny (ha'penny?) finally dropped, giving ENABLED, he knew he was going to be completely hooked. And he still is. He has never pretended to be particularly quick at solving crosswords, and even now it is rare for him to understand the rubrics of *The Listener* puzzles, let alone complete the grids, but over the years he has on several occasions been champion or joint champion in the Ximenes/Azed annual clue-writing honours list. Colin has ever been of the Ximenean ilk, never a 'libertarian', and he gladly confesses his addiction to the 'anagram & lit.' type of clue. Using the pseudonym Codex (first syllables of his forename and surname), he set cryptic puzzles for the *Oxford Times* for about twelve years. A selection of these, *Chambers Book of Morse Crosswords* was published in 2006. As a great Wagner fan, he thinks his favourite clue is Ximenes's 'We'll get excited with Ring seat (10)' (WAGNERITES); he also loves 'In autumn we're piling up the last of the leaves (8)' for FAREWELL, which won first prize in a Ximenes competition for H. S. Tribe.

Colin has been awarded many honours, including the coveted Diamond Dagger for services to crime writing, an OBE for services to literature, the freedom of the city of Oxford, and an honorary fellowship at St Cross College, Oxford.

See the puzzle section for an example of this setter's work.

Columba

Colin Gumbrell was born in 1961 at Barns Green, West Sussex, and educated at Collyer's Grammar School in Horsham. After several years as a bookseller he became a freelance writer, working mainly on historical and biographical books. He began submitting crosswords to magazines in 1991, and setting crosswords now occupies most of his time. As Columba (based on syllables from his forename and surname, and Latin for 'dove') he is a regular setter for *The Independent* and *The Spectator*, and has contributed to the *Times Listener* series and to Enigmatic Variations in the *Sunday Telegraph*. He also compiles one in four of the Beelzebub puzzles for the *Independent on Sunday*. In *The Oldie* his puzzles appear under the name Antico (suggesting antiquity, in keeping with the magazine's title), and he also sets puzzles for *www.AskOxford.com*, an Oxford University Press website.

Colin's interest in crosswords began at an early age. He did his best to help his mother and elder brother to solve the puzzles in the *Daily Telegraph* and *The Observer*, but had rather better luck with those devised specially for him by his father. As a teenager he began tackling the puzzles of AZED and learning about Ximenean standards of clue writing. He hopes his crosswords are challenging but not frustrating, his principal aim being to entertain. Having long resisted technological progress, he bought his first computer in 2004, and now finds it an invaluable aid to his work, though he continues to favour the use of graph paper and pencil in constructing grids. He considers the quality of the clues to be the most important feature of crosswords, especially those that lack a thematic element to provide extra interest. He most enjoys puzzles by setters who apply Ximenean standards with elegance and wit. As clue judge for the Crossword Club from 2000 to 2004 he discovered the difficulty of being dogmatic about clue writing, a field in which, along with plenty of rules which do need to be observed, there are many grey areas.

Outside crosswords, Colin's interests include music, art, reading, and helping as a volunteer with the local Talking Newspaper for the visually impaired.

See the puzzle section for an example of this setter's work.

Corylus

Chris Feetenby was born in York in 1940 and is a freeman of the city through his grandfather Alf Heselwood (derived from 'hazel', hence the pseudonym Corylus). His interest in crosswords was first aroused by his Latin and Greek teacher James Leitrim, whose heart was not in his teaching since, as a Jesuit priest subject to a vow of poverty, he was not paid. 'Big Jim' digressed on a variety of topics, including crosswords, and was easily distracted by a copy of the *Daily Telegraph* open at the appropriate page.

Chris's first Corylus crossword, 'Noms de Guerre' (based on Evelyn Waugh characters), was published in *The Listener* in 1980, but the real breakthrough came in 1983 when he started setting for the *Catholic Herald*. This puzzle still appears weekly but is now the responsibility of Mrs Chris, who shares his interest in crosswords, giving great back-up and support. He exchanged his twenty-four-year career as a teacher of physics for that of a self-employed crossword compiler in 1986, and since then he has worked freelance for a variety of periodicals, including *Computer Talk* and *Electronics Weekly*. He appeared weekly as Aelred in *The Independent* from 1987 to 2004 and in the ill-fated *European* throughout its existence.

Chris collaborated with Richard Whitelegg on *The Express* Crusader cryptic crossword in the early 1990s, before Richard's sad and untimely death. Through Richard he became one third of Mephisto from April 1995, and in April 2002 he moved to the *Mail on Sunday*, where he is known as the Puzzle Meister and has a column with his picture at the top, while continuing as Mephisto every third week.

Chris is reluctant to name any other setters as major influences, having never consciously sought to imitate anyone. He enjoys solving most of them and actively dislikes very few. A cryptic definition he and his wife both like is 'Ill-gotten gains?'

(8, 7)' for SICKNESS BENEFIT (clue by Michael Macdonald-Cooper, a.k.a. CALMAC).

See the puzzle section for an example of this setter's work.

Crispa

Ruth Crisp was born Margery Ruth Edwards in Middlesbrough on new year's day 1918, and attended the local high school until she was 18. She then entered the civil service, university having been vetoed by a domineering mother. She always felt much closer to her father, from an early age sharing his interests in all aspects of the natural world, and enjoying his stories of Greek gods, goddesses, and heroes. It was many years before she realized that she was being familiarized with Homer. These interests have often shown up in her crosswords.

Ruth's first husband was a Pole, who was conscripted in September 1939 when about to start university. Two weeks later he was a prisoner of war, forced to work in a Siberian coalmine. As a result of negotiations involving the British foreign minister, he and others were released three years later. After lengthy nursing in South Africa he arrived in Britain and joined the RAF. He met and married Ruth and the two were very happy until his early death at 32, the delayed result of the hardships he had endured in Siberia.

Ruth now found herself with neither a National Health nor a service pension, and no child-care facilities for her young son, so she looked for ways of earning from home. It was then that she tried setting crosswords, having for a long time enjoyed solving them in both *The Guardian* and *The Times*. Her first published puzzles appeared in *Radio Times*, and this emboldened her to approach *The Guardian* which, after accepting three of her crosswords, invited her to contribute one per week. She knew she had found her métier. Contributions to *The Field* and other periodicals soon followed, including *The Times* and puzzles which were used for the national crossword championships. Invitations came to join the *Sunday Times* and *Financial Times*, and then the *Daily Telegraph*, whose Friday crossword she set for many years.

When, finally, she joined *The Independent* team and set crossword No. 1 for the new paper, she was contributing to all five quality dailies and the *Sunday Times* simultaneously. This workload, however enjoyable, proved too heavy, and she steadily reduced it until the infirmities of age imposed reluctant retirement when she was almost 87. Her final puzzle appeared in *The Guardian* on 6 December 2004.

Ruth used a variety of pseudonyms: her favourite was Crispa in *The Guardian*, the feminine form of *crispus* (Latin for 'curly-haired'), 'Curly' being the name by which friends knew her, and Crisp being the surname she took after her unhappy second marriage, when she also started using her second forename Ruth. She opted for Circe (the enchantress) when pseudonyms for *The Times* were invited, though this was not followed through. In the *Financial Times* she was Vixen and in *The Independent*, Marcy (from her initials MRC), later adding Jiffy when the number of setters was greatly reduced.

In retirement, though she misses crossword setting, Ruth still keeps her wits well honed, thanks to Scrabble® evenings and Mensa fortnightly lunches, where kind fellow members offer a supportive arm, transport, and stimulating conversation.

See the puzzle section for an example of this setter's work.

Dac
See SMOKEY

Dante
See RUFUS

Darcy
See LAWS, MIKE

Derek

Peter Chamberlain was born in Finedon, Northamptonshire, in 1947, and educated at Wellingborough Grammar School, after which he qualified as a chartered accountant. He has lived all his life in Northamptonshire, for the last thirty-five years in Rushden. After working for a time for the Milk Marketing Board, he became a full-time crossword setter in 1988, working closely with his wife Jeannie.

As a boy, Peter was fascinated by the black and white squares on the back page of the *Daily Telegraph* which no one ever filled in. When he was fourteen, while staying at a guesthouse in Blackpool, he came across a completed *Telegraph* prize puzzle that someone had left in the lounge, but could see no correlation between the clues and the answers. Twenty-seven years later he would be setting prize puzzles for *The Telegraph* himself.

In 1978 Peter had his first puzzle published in the *Birmingham Post*, and also syndicated to the *Glasgow Herald*. In 1986 he became an occasional setter for the *Daily Telegraph*; he took over the Saturday slot in 1988 and has set almost every Saturday puzzle ever since. In addition to the *Daily Telegraph*, Peter currently compiles the *Sunday Telegraph* general knowledge crossword, which also appears throughout the world in the *Weekly Telegraph*.

Derek (his younger son's name) is the pseudonym Peter used for a *Listener* puzzle in 1983, and is also used by him for some of his work in trade magazines, etc. He sets puzzles for a number of agencies under the pseudonym Pegasus. His work has appeared fortnightly in *Scotland on Sunday* since that paper started in 1988. More recently he has become a regular in the *Yorkshire Post*, and he also contributes to *Woman's Weekly* and the *Puzzler Collection*.

Peter's hobbies include travel, photography, and country music, and he is also involved with his local church. He also loves solving crosswords. Among his favourites are those by TANTALUS,

Peter Bee in *The Scotsman*, and Ann TAIT in *The Telegraph*. He admires the grid construction of the Beelzebub puzzles and the thematic concoctions of ARAUCARIA. His pet hates include 'bit of' meaning 'first letter of' in clues, and the overuse of plurals. His all-time favourite clue is 'Nuclear rabbit? (4-7)' for FAST-BREEDER.

Peter's special crosswords have included one for *The Telegraph* which appeared on the 51st anniversary of D-day and contained all the D-day code-words. More recently, also in *The Telegraph*, he paid tribute to his mother in a puzzle which contained the words ELIZABETH (BESSIE) CHAMBERLAIN (née) REYNOLDS, NINETIETH BIRTHDAY TODAY. His mother-in-law AGNES also managed to creep into the same puzzle.

See the puzzle section for an example of this setter's work.

DGP
See **LOGODAEDALUS**

Didymus
See **DOC**

Dimitry

John Grimshaw was born in Fulham, London, in 1950 (by a strange coincidence next-door to the pub where he now meets quarterly with a group of other crossword setters). He was educated at St Clement Danes School and St Catherine's College, Oxford, where he read engineering science and subsequently gained a DPhil in studies in hypersonic aerodynamics. He feels he has been slowing down ever since and now pursues a career in the Ministry of Defence, but claims to be quite sane in other respects and is eagerly looking forward to retirement.

John has solved crosswords for as long as he can remember, since first being introduced to definitional puzzles by his mother. An abiding first memory of cryptic puzzles is solving what he thinks was *The Times* crossword with his (probably more experienced) cousin, at about the age of fifteen, in a rain-bound car in Glencoe. He graduated to barred cryptics at around the time when AZED's series in *The Observer* began, since he distinctly recalls a couple of the 'in memoriam' puzzles to Ximenes the paper printed before Azed's debut.

Apart from one (unpublished) joint effort submitted to the London *Evening News* with a fellow sixth-former whose mother was also a keen puzzler, John's own puzzle debut was in *The Listener* series in 1981, and since then he has had over thirty *Listener* puzzles published. Other outlets for his barred cryptics include the *Sunday Telegraph* Enigmatic Variations series (around forty puzzles), the Crossword Club, and *The Magpie* magazine. He also sets for *The Times* (both daily cryptics and cryptic jumbos with over 100 of the latter), the *Times Online* monthly puzzle, the *Financial Times* (a few dailies and about thirty Polymaths), but by far his biggest contribution to the art has been the daily *times2* puzzle, which he has set single-handedly since March 2003, his 1,000th puzzle appearing in May 2006. He has also provided all the Saturday *times2* jumbos since they began.

From 1984 to 1994 John was co-editor (with Mike Rich) of the *Times Listener* crossword, having been offered the job as the only all-correct solver in the preceding two years. He resumed this editing task for a second stint in 2005. Also with Mike Rich, he ran a series of word game weekends until Mike's death brought them to an end. He has also been a clue judge for the Crossword Club magazine and the *Times Online* website.

John chose Dimitry as his pseudonym mainly because of his love of the music of Shostakovich (whose musical motto, written into many works, inspired a surreptitious 'signing' of barred cryptics with a hidden pseudonym in contiguous squares), but also because of an imagined cryptic significance of Dimitry the False Pretender from Russian history, and its potential for interpretations as '(being) dim, I try' and 'I'm into dirty tricking'. John is quite pleased that his full name is an anagram of 'charming, if shrewd, joker'. His favourite clue of all time is Les May's 'Bust down reason?' for BRAINWASH in an Azed competition. Setters he admires include SABRE, KEA, MACHIAVELLI, Ark (A. R. King), and many more. He hopes to be solving for long enough to add a few more new names to the list.

John enjoys walking, canal boating, and, above all, music. For many years he has been chairman of the Havergal Brian Society, a registered charity that promotes the music of this underrated composer.

Dinmutz
See **MUTCH, JEREMY**

Diplodocus

Roy Dean was born in Watford in 1927, the youngest child of
a railway signalman, and was educated at Watford Grammar
School. He joined the RAF in 1945, serving mainly on airfields
in northern India. After his demobilization in 1948 he became
a publishing executive in the Central Office of Information,
working mainly on international magazines in three languages,
and later handling domestic publicity campaigns for various
government departments. In his spare time he gained diplomas
from the London College of Printing and Graphic Arts and the
College for the Distributive Trades.

In 1958 Roy moved to the Commonwealth Relations Office
(later subsumed into HM Diplomatic Service), which led to
postings in Sri Lanka, Canada, Nigeria, and the United States.
After a long spell as director of the Foreign and Commonwealth
Office's (FCO) arms control and disarmament research unit, in
his final posting he was acting British high commissioner to
Ghana. Married with three sons, he now lives in Bromley.

Roy's mother introduced him at an early age to crosswords
of the straightforward definition type in the *Evening News*. While
still at school, in the sixth form, he had his first encounter with
a cryptic crossword (in *The Spectator*), which baffled him until he
saw the answers and realized dimly how the system worked. But
he did not become a regular solver until 1954, when he became
hooked on Ximenes in *The Observer*. He started entering X's
monthly clue-writing competitions, with considerable success,
and in 1958 he organized the dinner for Ximenes No. 500 at the
Café Royal in London, three weeks before going overseas for ten
years during which he rarely saw a crossword.

Back home in 1968, Roy started regularly solving *The Times*
crossword (on the train to London), and in 1970 he won the first
Times national crossword championship. He then set a record for

the fastest verified solution, in the *Today* studio on BBC Radio 4. This led to an entry in the *Guinness Book of Records* and a rather spurious reputation as the 'world crossword champion', an appellation which nevertheless proved very valuable in some diplomatic situations. At this point he was best known as a solver, but in 1972–3 he set simple cryptic crosswords as a cultural contribution to 'British weeks' in the USA. In 1999 he was invited to set puzzles for *Password*, the journal of the FCO association of retired diplomats. As an antiquated setter, without recourse to modern technology such as computers, he chose the pseudonym Diplodocus. He began setting for *Church Times* in 2002, *The Times* in 2003, *Quest* in 2004, and *Plain English* in 2005. His puzzles are still handmade.

Roy believes that constructing a barred grid would be beyond him. He reckons to backfill a *Times* diagram in two hours, and writing the clues takes him a week. His main influence has been the paper's crossword editor Richard BROWNE, whose puzzles he admires and whose advice on how to meet the required standard has been invaluable. He recognizes that the more difficult Ximenes/AZED type of clues (which he relishes) would be inappropriate for a daily paper. His special dislike is *The Listener* puzzles, which at his age he cannot tackle because of their often complex preambles. His favourite of his own *Times* clues is 'Silicone valley (8)' for CLEAVAGE, and from the Azed series he particular likes 'Bust down reason (9)' for BRAINWASH by Les May, and Colin Dexter's '(M)urine extraction (6-6)' for MICKEY-TAKING.

Since his retirement in 1987 Roy has developed a new career as a writer and composer. In 1989–90 he wrote and presented three series of programmes on 'The Poetry of Popular Song' on Radio 4, and in 1996 he published *A Century of Song*, a collection of his own compositions representing different styles of twentieth-century popular music. *Mainly in Fun*, an anthology of his prose and verse, including several articles on crosswords, appeared in

2002. He is vice-president of Bromley Arts Council, and writes a regular column for *Words & Music*.

See the puzzle section for an example of this setter's work.

Doc

Tom Johnson was born in Birmingham in 1947, where he attended King Edward's School and Birmingham College of Commerce. After a year in teacher training at the University of Keele, he spent thirty-three years teaching modern languages at Malbank School in Nantwich. He retired in 2002 to devote his time to freelance crossword compiling and proof-reading. He works from his home in Nantwich in partnership with his wife Jean. They have a son and a daughter.

Tom learnt about crosswords from his grandfather and his parents, who introduced him to the Reader's Crossword in the *Birmingham Evening Mail.* From 1961 onwards he had about 200 puzzles published in that paper, either under his own name or as Didymus, and he set the very last Reader's Crossword in September 1982. While he was still a teenager, his puzzles appeared in *Radio Times*, and under the pseudonym Twudge (a rough pronunciation of his initials TWJ) in *The Listener*.

In 1971 Tom discovered Jac's series of thematic crosswords in *The Spectator*. Jac's approach to cluing and compiling generally influenced Tom's own career as a setter. In 1981 he was invited to join Jac (J. A. Caesar) and MASS as *The Spectator*'s regular compilers, and since then he has produced a thematic cryptic every third week, under the pseudonym Doc. He became *The Spectator*'s crossword editor in January 1999.

In 1995 Tom was asked to join *Prospect* magazine, for which he sets the challenging Generalist puzzle, as Didymus. This series of puzzles led to his being invited by Colin Inman to contribute to the Saturday Polymath series, which was introduced in the *Financial Times* in 1999. Here he uses the pseudonym Gozo, reflecting his love of the islands of Malta and Gozo.

Tom's freelance work consists of regular commitments to many monthly periodicals. He has set for *Puzzler* magazine since its first issue, and he produces crosswords for six other magazines in the Puzzler Media portfolio. The founder and first editor of *Puzzler* was Alfred Guttman, who insisted on several quirky rules for setters: plurals, adverbs, and botanical terms were all taboo, along with past participles. One of Tom's puzzles was rejected because Guttman thought QUADRUPED was a past participle.

ARAUCARIA of *The Guardian* has been another strong influence on Tom's style. In 2000 Tom became editor of Araucaria's 1 *Across* subscription magazine. Though heavily committed to many varied publications, Tom enjoys full-time crossword work, finding the variety challenging and stimulating. When not compiling he enjoys classical music, painting, photography, cricket (as a supporter of Warwickshire), and buses in Britain and abroad. His Gozo connections led to the publication of his *Malta Bus Handbook* in 2003.

See the puzzle section for an example of this setter's work.

Dogberry
See SHED

Dogop
See LOGODAEDALUS

Duck

Don Manley (whose various pseudonyms are mostly famous Dons or Donalds) was born in 1945 at Cullompton, Devon. After a short-lived career in research he was an editor in academic and educational publishing for over thirty years. Married with two grown-up children, he now lives in Oxford and works more or less exclusively as a crossword setter, but also finds time for interests that include the church, cricket, singing, cycling, drinking decent beer, walking, and reading, when he is not tied to his computer.

Don's commercial traveller father bought the *Daily Express*, *Daily Mail*, and *Daily Telegraph* mainly for the crosswords, so Don caught the crossword bug at an early age. After exhausting the possibilities of the children's crossword books published by Wheatons, he was allowed to help with the quick puzzle in *The Telegraph*. He graduated to cryptic crosswords in his teens and to barred cryptics (Ximenes and *The Listener*) in his early twenties. He developed his clue-writing skills by entering *The Observer* competitions (Ximenes briefly, then AZED), in which he has become one of the most successful competitors. He is a firm believer in the Ximenean principles set out in *Ximenes on the Art of the Crossword* (1966), but accepts that the fringes of what is regarded as acceptable may be somewhat blurred, and therefore prefers not to name favourite (or unfavourite) setters and clues. He thinks that some of the output in national dailies is terrific but is dismayed by clues that appear unsound in construction and have no 'surface meaning'. He recognizes that there is a strongly anti-Ximenean school, but can still enjoy some of the output from non-Ximenean practitioners. He regrets that newspapers seem uninterested in printing 'junior' crosswords and that, perhaps as a result of this, the younger generation shows little interest in cryptic crosswords.

Although conceding that compiling crosswords can be a solitary occupation, Don has made many friends with fellow solvers and setters. In his first job (at a physics laboratory) he was soon banned from the lunchtime solving group for being too quick, but in his second (in publishing) he became a close friend of Richard Palmer (MERLIN), who proved, as he still does, a worthy adversary both as a setter and as a solver.

One of Don's best clues resulted from a happy accident. After a fruitless Sunday evening working on TOLERABLE for an Azed competition, he woke to the realization that the word could be formed from an anagram of ALBERT and LEO, which immediately brought to mind Stanley Holloway's monologue (written by Marriott Edgar). Finding the poem on a top shelf, he discovered that the lion's name was Wallace (sadly not Leo), but on reading further he also noted that the lion 'swallowed the little lad 'ole'. This was enough to spark off his prize-winning clue about the intolerable youngster: 'Being otherwise, Albert's swallowed 'ole'. For him, this is a great example of the 'Aha!' moment in clue writing that makes the whole crossword enterprise such a joy despite the many hours of slog.

Don's puzzles appear in many periodicals: he is Duck in the *Times Listener* series, Quixote in *The Independent* and the *Independent on Sunday*, Pasquale in *The Guardian*, Bradman and Polymath (one of several) in the *Financial Times*, and Giovanni in the *Sunday Telegraph*. He also sets for the *Daily Telegraph* and edits the *Church Times* crosswords, setting six puzzles a year under his own name. He is the author of *Chambers Crossword Manual* (4th edition, 2006).

See the puzzle section for an example of this setter's work.

Dumpynose

Chris Brougham (whose pseudonym is an anagram of 'pseudonym') also sets *Listener* puzzles in *The Times* as Pabulum, a more dignified name (suggested by his wife) with a pleasant sound and an ambiguous definition in *Chambers*. He was born in London in 1947 and educated at Radley College and Worcester College, Oxford. Called to the bar in 1969, he was appointed a deputy high court bankruptcy registrar in 1984 and QC in 1988. He is a practising barrister and writer of legal textbooks. Married with four children, he lives in London.

Chris began solving cryptic crosswords, with his mother's help, in 1961, and has been a keen solver ever since. He began solving AZED's puzzles in 1980 and remains a regular entrant in Azed's monthly competitions. His first puzzle was published in the Crossword Club magazine in June 1989, and his puzzles now appear regularly in *The Spectator* (since 1996), the *Times Law* (since 2000), the *Times Listener* series, and *Church Times* (since 1990). His puzzles all contain themes. His ideas may come from anywhere: noticing, during a tedious sermon, that 'Thou art the King of Glory, O Christ' divides into four seven-letter groups produced the central columns of *Church Times* No. 48; seeing a factory sign 'SUNGLASSES' produced a puzzle (No. 1,391 in *The Spectator*) whose answers included ANNIE LAURIE and ELEANOR RIGBY. He uses a computer and Ross Beresford's Sympathy program to construct a grid and fill it with words, carefully selecting those best suited to the intended difficulty of the puzzle. He finds clue writing hard work, but regards the writing of good, interesting clues as the setter's main function. The easier a puzzle is intended to be, the harder he finds it to write good clues. Two of his favourite clues are 'It's this Littlewoods could make you' (WELL-TO-DO) by Colin Dexter and 'Given unconventionally for Jack's head' (VINEGAR) by J. P. H. Hirst, both winners in Azed competitions. His two major influences have been Azed and DUCK, and he has also been inspired by DIMITRY, PHI, and SALAMANCA. Other setters he admires include BUFO, COLUMBA, KEA, MACHIAVELLI, MASS, SABRE, Samson (Max A. Taylor), and VIRGILIUS. He dislikes puzzles with sloppy or dull clues, however brilliant the theme.

See the puzzle section for an example of this setter's work.

EB
See **QUARK**

Enigma

Simon Martin was born in Egypt in 1950, where his father was serving in the Royal Air Force. Educated at Dean Close School, Cheltenham, Warwick University, and the RAF College, Cranwell, he followed a career in the RAF as a fast jet and weapons engineer before taking early retirement in 1990 with the rank of wing commander. He is now overseas director for the Royal Air Forces Association. Simon is married with two grown-up children, and lives in Malvern. His pseudonym derives from the dictionary definition of the word (as well as being a rather feeble anagram of 'I am Eng.').

Simon first became involved in crosswords in the mid 1960s, when he started solving the *Daily Telegraph* puzzle. After joining the RAF in 1972, he began setting crosswords for RAF stations' monthly magazines. The first published puzzle for which he received payment appeared in 1990, a thematic puzzle in the *Stamford Mercury* (the oldest newspaper in England). After leaving the RAF, he spent time in the crossword department of *The Independent*, working closely with Louise Devine and the late Richard Whitelegg (Beelzebub), and later with MASS and Michael Macdonald-Cooper (*see* CALMAC). While appreciating that crossword cluing and complexity must vary in different publications, his own personal style (typified by 'elegant' clues such as 'Response to Warne's spinners' for ANSWER) is founded on the advice he received from Whitelegg and Mass, and on ideas gleaned from puzzles in the daily broadsheets. More recent advice from Val Gilbert, editor of *The Telegraph* puzzles, has also been helpful and welcome.

Since 1990 Simon has set occasional thematic puzzles for *The Independent Saturday Magazine*. He joined the *Daily Telegraph* team in 2005. Over the years, he has set puzzles for many local newspapers, magazines, and military publications. He has also raised money by setting puzzles for a number of different charities. He is pleased that his son Christopher, a cancer research scientist, has started setting *Guardian*-style crosswords to carry on the family tradition.

Enigmatist

John Henderson was born in 1963 and grew up in Cornwall, where his mother (a *Daily Mail* solver) and his father (a *Daily Telegraph* solver) shaped his interest in crosswords from an early age. He submitted his first puzzle to *The Telegraph* at the age of eleven. 'Please contact us in ten years' time,' he was told, which he duly did, but received no response from the same editor. He was first published by *The Guardian* in 1979, at the age of fifteen, as a result of his correspondence with his idol ARAUCARIA and with John Perkin, then the paper's crossword editor.

John has been setting crosswords for various outlets ever since. He graduated in, acted as an examiner in, and published books and articles on psychology between 1985 and 2003, before becoming a full-time setter of quizzes and crosswords. He now has his own crossword and quiz website (*www.enigmatist.com*). He won *The Times* crossword championship in 1996 and lays claim to the title of quickest *Times* crossword solver with a time of two minutes and fifty-three seconds.

John is a fanatical Arsenal supporter, loves cricket (from which he recently had to retire), and lives in north London, regularly meeting up with PAUL (another 'Araucarian') to discuss the qualities of real ale in London. He is Enigmatist in *The Guardian*, the *Times Listener*, and 1 Across, Nimrod in *The Independent*, and Io in the *Financial Times*.

See the puzzle section for an example of this setter's work.

Esau
See **LAWS, MIKE**

Goldman, Hazel

Hazel Goldman, née Damant, was born in London in 1929. She was educated at Queen Elizabeth's Girls' Grammar School, Barnet, where she learnt the use of the apostrophe (of which Lynne Truss would approve), and St Anne's College, Oxford, where she read history.

After university, Hazel had jobs at (among other places) the BBC, Courtaulds, and the John Lewis partnership, as well as becoming enmeshed in the fascinating world of local government. As a Middlesex county councillor, she was appointed a trustee of Alexandra Palace, and met and married a fellow trustee, Leonard Goldman, with whom she now lives in Oxfordshire.

Hazel's introduction to crossword solving came through her grandfather, an irascible plus-fours-wearing Scot who could not bear to lose any game, even to his youngest grandchild when playing Beggar My Neighbour. It was Grandad Macdonald who one day showed her a *Daily Telegraph* crossword and asked if she could suggest an answer to the clue 'Elizabethan dress is small beer (11)'. She couldn't, but when given the answer (FARTHINGALE) was so thrilled by the double meaning that she was soon badgering her mother to let her solve the 'difficult clues'.

It wasn't until many years later that Hazel started setting her own crosswords. For some years she contented herself with making themed puzzles to mark significant dates in the lives of her friends. Her husband was not best pleased when, in a St Valentine's day card, his name appeared in the anagram of AN OLDER man. Hazel's first published puzzle appeared in 1976 in the *John o' Groats Journal*, a periodical that was a favourite with the late Queen Mother (along with the *Racing Post*). To this day Hazel contributes a 'twin set' of cryptic and simple puzzles to a group of Scottish newspapers. She has also been setting puzzles for many years for the *Financial Times* (as Adamant, an adaptation of her maiden name) and more recently for *The Guardian* website (as Hazard, which combines her name and that of her husband).

Hazel's style of cluing is (she believes) straightforward and correct, without too much cryptic variety, though she admires this in other setters, her aim being to achieve a mix of well-known and less familiar words in any one puzzle. One of her favourites remains Edmund Akenhead's 'Cinderella's midnight music' for RAGTIME. She enjoys constructing puzzles with a theme, and for this reason one of her favourite commissions is for the NADFAS (National Association of Decorative and Fine Arts Societies) *Review*, which features a different artist or school of painting in each issue. She also has a fan base among members of the Women's Institute movement, for whose magazine, *WI Home and Country*, she produces a monthly puzzle page.

Gordius

David Moseley, a man of Kent, was born in 1930, and educated at Maidstone Grammar School, University College, Oxford, and Wells Theological College. After ordination he served as an assistant curate in Lancashire, and subsequently as a vicar of parishes in Trinidad, Bristol, and east Devon, where for the last ten years he has continued to live with his wife in retirement.

David took relatively little interest in crosswords until after his return from the West Indies, when he began solving those in *The Guardian*. He became a setter quite by accident: probably the only time *The Guardian* has been so short of setters, the crossword editor John Perkin devised a competition to find a few more during Christmas 1966. In the slack days following Christmas, David was foolhardy enough to submit an entry, and the rest, as they say, is history. At some point in the next few years it was decided to ask setters for pseudonyms, and David responded to this knotty problem with Gordius.

Lacking the inspiration of some of the more eminent setters, ARAUCARIA in particular, David finds it as much as he can do to fill a grid at all, and seldom manages an integrated theme. However, he takes the view that the important thing is the clues, and with *Guardian* readers in mind he tries to concentrate on entertainment rather than erudition. As an amateur in setting, he regards it more as a not unprofitable hobby than as a chore, and in particular holds that the ephemeral nature of a crossword affords a welcome opportunity for topical and satirical comment. So the temptation of a clue such as 'Transport unfortunately isn't arriving (6, 6)' for VIRGIN TRAINS is hard to resist, as (bearing in mind George Orwell's real name) is 'Blair's authoritarian character (3, 7)' for BIG BROTHER.

Gozo
See DOC

Grant, John

John Grant was born in 1923 in Burnley, and educated at Giggleswick School in Yorkshire. He served for five years as a wartime officer in the Royal Artillery, between spells at Balliol College, Oxford, reading classics and then English. He started as a trainee journalist with the *Liverpool Daily Post* and then spent five years as a reporter on the *Manchester Guardian*. He moved to *The Times* as defence correspondent in 1955, and retired as deputy editor in 1983. He spent the first twelve years of his retirement as editor of *The Times* crossword, to which he still contributes. A career in journalism has left him with a mind well stocked with half-forgotten facts that come in useful for crosswords. He feels the aim of *The Times* crossword is to amuse and entertain rather than to baffle. He looks for elegance and wit, and recoils from laboured build-ups that result in something that could only be a crossword clue. His favourite clue is 'Herodias danced here under the British' for RHODESIA (Herodias being the mother of Salome).

Hall, Barbara

Barbara Hall has, for the last thirty years, been puzzles editor and a crossword setter for the *Sunday Times*. She was born in 1923 in Derby, and now lives in London. Her first puzzle, published by a London newspaper in 1938 when she was fifteen, earned her two guineas.

An only child, Barbara played word games such as Lexicon with her parents. During the Second World War she devised crosswords using the names of British and German planes for an aircraft spotters' magazine. Her father, who had flown seaplanes in the First World War, trained the spotters. They sat on rooftops or telegraph poles and signalled for the sirens to be sounded when they spotted German planes approaching. Barbara meanwhile enlisted in the WRNS and worked with codes. Later she set puzzles for the Oxford University magazine *Isis*, then for the *Yorkshire Post* and *World Digest*. With her husband Richard, a newspaper editor, and their five sons, she lived for fifteen years in Zambia, expanding her twin careers of journalism and crossword compiling. She provided weekly puzzles for the *African Mail*, *Central African Examiner*, *Broken Hill Observer*, and Gemini Commonwealth News Services. For the Zambian government papers she devised simple puzzles in three African languages (Tonga, Bemba, and Nyanja) to encourage literacy.

Barbara's earliest crossword collections were published by Mayflower and then Fontana. In the 1960s the *Daily Mail* commissioned her to produce what was claimed to be the world's biggest cryptic crossword, with a Christmas theme. Thereafter she concentrated on thematic puzzles and produced scores of these on a wide range of subjects. There were series for *Banking World*, *Executive Travel*, and in-flight magazines, and puzzles on railways, yachting, wine, food, gardening, and one on medicine for the *Times Health Supplement*. In 1984 *The Times* commissioned from her a puzzle based on Orwell's novel.

Barbara lists all her clues, alphabetically and numerically, in notebooks, consulting them regularly to avoid repeating herself. She does not use a computer when compiling, preferring paper and pencil, dictionaries and a thesaurus, and the *Longman Crossword Key*. Her aim is to appeal to the average solver, so she does not attempt to emulate the more demanding clues of AZED and Mephisto (setters she nevertheless holds in high regard). A humorous element is essential, she believes, so after the rather serious series she produced for *Mechanised Handling*, she enjoyed writing spicy clues for the sex journal *Forum*, e.g. 'Voluptuous girl, reason enough for crime?' for BIGAMY. *Woman* commissioned her thematic puzzle entitled 'Jokes Against Gentlemen': a typical clue was 'Washing powders that scare the men?' (DETERGENTS). One of her own favourites is 'Contralto bursting out of lace bra – it's wired for uplift' (CABLE-CAR), and in a puzzle in the *Weekend Australian*, for which she sets regularly, she particularly liked 'The last, lone frog in a polluted marine park' for NINGALOO REEF, until an indignant solver down under protested that 'our reef is not polluted'.

After compiling non-stop for about sixty-five years, Barbara has lost count of the number of puzzles and puzzle books she has published, but reckons it must be several thousand.

See the puzzle section for an example of this setter's work.

Hesketh, Bob

Bob Hesketh was born in 1952 in Prestbury and educated at
Manchester Grammar School. He has been a civil servant for
the last twenty-five years, after earlier jobs in the rag trade and
Amnesty International. He is married with three daughters and
lives in Bath.

Bob started solving *The Guardian* crossword in 1975 and still
remembers the feeling of achievement when he completed his
first puzzle. He bought *Teach Yourself Crosswords* by Alec Robins
(Custos of *The Guardian*) and became hooked. In the late 1970s
he began solving *The Times* daily puzzles and competing in the
annual crossword championships.

Bob's first puzzles as a setter were published in the early
1980s in *Motor Transport*, a weekly paper for the haulage industry.
The attempt to include as many trucking-related references as
possible was a demanding but valuable experience. In the early
1990s he set monthly puzzles for *BBC Worldwide Magazine*, as a
result of which he received correspondence from many solvers
around the world for whom English was not their first language.
During this time he broadened his experience as a solver,
tackling *The Listener* puzzles for a year and entering AZED's
monthly competitions, which taught him much about the art of
setting. He found Don Manley's *Crossword Manual* (*see* DUCK)
enormously helpful and received much useful feedback and
encouragement when he sent Don one of his puzzles. At the
third attempt one of his puzzles was accepted by John GRANT,
crossword editor at *The Times*, and Bob now has a puzzle a month
in *The Times* and has begun setting jumbo puzzles also.

Bob believes that clues should be technically sound, should
entertain, and should require the solver to think creatively.
Among literary influences he cites Roald Dahl and Myles na
Gopaleen. He admires the brilliant work of many of his fellow

setters, but would choose Gemini as having provided him with the most pleasurable challenges. He remembers in particular a puzzle of theirs in which the same clue led to two different solutions, e.g. 'Boast about what one may be wearing' for SABOT and BRAG. Other favourites include (from *The Times*) 'Of which bird-watching is an example' (SPOONERISM) and 'What I must be when small' (DOTTED); also Colin Dexter's 'A kick in the pants' (HIP-FLASK) in one of the Inspector Morse novels. Of his own clues, he was especially pleased with 'Cabinet fought over housing repeatedly' for OFTEN (a down clue). On holiday in France he looks out for place names which might be used misleadingly in clues, such as Nice, Tours, Angers, Nancy, and Dole.

Hodge
See RUFUS

Hypnos

Philip Marlow was born in 1965 in Leicester, and educated at Repton School and St John's College, Oxford. He now lives in London and works as a freelance producer in the television industry, specializing in documentaries and drama documentaries about politics, current affairs, and history for British, American, and European broadcasters. His other interests include art, films, football (he is a long-time supporter of Leicester City), tennis, table tennis, cycling, and travel.

Philip first learnt the joy of crosswords on his grandmother's knee, with the *Daily Telegraph*. His fascination grew when, as a schoolboy, he started tackling *The Times* crossword. In his twenties he graduated to the more advanced cryptics, including AZED and *The Listener*, and in the late 1980s he began entering the Azed clue-writing competitions. His first puzzle appeared in the Crossword Club magazine in 1994. As Hypnos, a literary pun equating the Greek god of sleep with *The Big Sleep*, Raymond Chandler's novel and his namesake, Chandler's fictional detective, he has appeared in the *Independent Magazine* and Enigmatic Variations in the *Sunday Telegraph*. He appears regularly as Sleuth (maintaining the Chandler link) in the *Financial Times*, and is one of the main setters for *Church Times*. His puzzles have also been published in *Magistrate*, *Verbatim* (a UK/US language magazine), *The Complete Book of Sporting Crosswords*, and the Crossword Club magazine.

Philip is a firm believer in Ximenean principles of clue writing and enjoys precision, elegance, and imagination in clues over gimmicks in themes or devious or unusual grid construction. He has been influenced most by Azed and DUCK but also admires COLUMBA, MASS, and MERLIN. His first prize-winning clue in an Azed competition (in December 2001) was 'Page, say? Such works acquiring rupees' for CHUPRASSY; this was about his fourth attempt at a competitive clue and hence a lesson in the value of patience, open-mindedness and, above all, persistent honing in clue construction. A good clue is a bit like a work of sculpture, needing to be constantly chiselled and refined, sometimes over several days.

Philip finds it fascinating that individual cluing styles can differ widely within the constraints of the Ximenean framework, and thinks that there are perhaps unexplored parallels between literary and clue-setting styles. Might crossword setters and setting itself, he wonders, enjoy a higher profile if compilers used their real names as bylines, like print journalists, instead of lurking behind anonymity or pseudonyms? Philip's dislikes include mathematical puzzles and needlessly complex or ambiguous preambles. He is somewhat pessimistic about the future of crosswords, given the current obsession with Sudoku and a catering in the media generally for puzzles requiring an ever shorter attention span, but he remains hopeful of realizing a long-held wish to see the joy of crosswords translated into a watchable televised format.

Icarus
See RUFUS

Ikela
See LAWS, MIKE

Impromptu
See LYDIAN

Io
See ENIGMATIST

Jago

Jim Coulson was born in 1951 in High Wycombe, and was educated at the local technical school and technical college, where he trained as a polymer chemist. He later returned to the same college to retrain as a wood scientist. After seven years in the rubber and plastics industry he joined the Timber Research and Development Association in 1975, remaining there until 1990 when he set up his own practice as a consultant timber technologist, based in Ripon. He lives in Bedale, on the edges of Wensleydale, with two grown-up sons and two grown-up daughters (both police detectives).

Jim began solving crosswords during his 'polymer days', joining the canteen crowd who attempted the *Daily Telegraph* puzzle during coffee breaks and initiated him in the subtleties of cryptic clues. He began setting as a result of a chance conversation one evening in 1974 over a pint with Michael Freeman (a friend of his brother-in-law), who revealed that he was SALAMANCA of *The Listener* and suggested he try his hand at compiling. His first *Listener* puzzle as Jago was published the following year, when he was still only twenty-three. The pseudonym derives from Diego de Deza, a cardinal of the Spanish Inquisition (*see also* AZED), Jago being an alternative Spanish spelling of Diego and cognate with 'James'. He began attending the annual *Listener* crossword setters' dinners, then held in the Old Cock Tavern, Fleet Street, and organized by the late Mike Rich (Ploutos), who became a friend and later settled, like Jim, in Ripon.

The mid 1970s to the late 1980s were Jim's most productive period as a setter: in addition to becoming a *Listener* regular, he had puzzles published in local papers and national technical magazines as Rook; in the *Timber Trades Journal* as Woodworm; in the *Architects' Journal* as Anobium; and in *Building Magazine* as

Xestobium (the latter two names being Latin for 'woodworm' and 'deathwatch beetle' respectively). After a relatively fallow period in the 90s because of business commitments and personal problems, the new millennium has heralded a new spate of setting, with puzzles for the Crossword Club and the Enigmatic Variations series in the *Sunday Telegraph*, as well as the *Times Listener* series again. Jago also now organizes *The Listener* crossword setters' dinners.

Jim is a fairly staunch follower of Ximenean cluing principles. He dislikes all mathematical puzzles (in which he now includes Sudoku), unfair or unsound clues and those with no 'surface reading', however well constructed. He particularly dislikes pedantry and lack of humour in crosswords. His *Listener* puzzles have included some unusual grid features: hexagons, split squares, a church tower, and a pocket watch, both with their hands missing. His favourite from among his own clues is 'Fish and chips cooked with lard' for PILCHARDS. His favourite setters include SABRE, PHI, and Ark (A. R. King); perhaps heretically, he is not a fan of ARAUCARIA's long and complex anagrammatical clues, for the reason that they make little sense when read on their own.

In his professional life, Jim now earns his living as a wood science tutor and an expert witness in timber technology, helping to run the Institute of Wood Science (of which he was president from 2002 to 2004). In his spare time he collects, learns, and writes English folk dances and mummers' plays. As a guest on *Midweek* on Radio 4 in the late 1980s he was introduced as 'probably the only morris-dancing, crossword-setting wood scientist in the country'.

See the puzzle section for an example of this setter's work.

James Jardine
See CJM

Jem
See MUTCH, JEREMY

Jiffy
See CRISPA

Jude
See LAWS, MIKE

Kcit
See PHI

Kea

Roger Phillips was born in 1960 in the small New Zealand town of Pahiatua and grew up in Wainuiomata, a suburb of Wellington that has since produced its fair share of All Blacks. After a BA in mathematics and English at Victoria University, he trained as a teacher but ended up programming computers instead. He emigrated to the United Kingdom in 1983, reversing the journey his father had made thirty years earlier, and spent a few 'wilderness years' squatting in London before returning to writing software. He is currently a happy bachelor living in central London.

As a teenager, Roger solved mainly American crosswords until his father introduced him to a British cryptic puzzle syndicated in a local newspaper. Shortly before he left New Zealand, a friend gave him a stack of old copies of *The Listener*, whose crosswords Roger found impenetrable. Once in London, he spent much of his time ensconced in reference libraries, scouring *The Chambers Dictionary* and plugging away at *Listener* and AZED crosswords. When he reached the point of being able to solve occasional *Listener* puzzles, he soon began to think about setting them. Now he is one of the team setting for *The Times*, and sets themed puzzles for the *Times Listener* series, the Enigmatic Variations series in the *Sunday Telegraph*, *The Independent Saturday Magazine*, and *The Enigma* (the magazine of the US-based National Puzzlers' League). He sets mostly as Kea, a pseudonym chosen not only to signal his New Zealand background, but also because of the parrot's engaging habits, such as chewing car windscreen wipers and reputedly attacking sheep for their kidney fat.

Roger remains fascinated by elegance in grid construction and, though he initially found writing clues a chore, he has come to enjoy the challenge of finding a neat, entertaining clue pitched at the right level for the target audience. The entire solving process must be designed to make a puzzle challenging yet fair, and fun, and the same considerations apply in microcosm to each clue. Roger counts himself a Ximenean, though he never knew Ximenes's puzzles, being influenced more by the clues of Azed and SABRE. The Ximenean precepts seem simply to encapsulate common sense, and are far from a straitjacket for the imaginative setter. For thematic ideas, Roger likes to draw on the differences in his background from that of the majority, but he has found the styles of DIMITRY, LAWS, PHI, Ploutos (Mike Rich), and Sabre inspirational.

See the puzzle section for an example of this setter's work.

Kruger

Tom Reynolds was born in Durham in 1952 and educated at Chester-le-Street Grammar School and the University of Wales, where he graduated in statistics and computer science. After working continuously for thirty years in the energy sector under various guises, he is now retired and lives in Leicestershire.

Although interested in solving crosswords from his early teens, Tom had no inclination to try his hand as a setter until he became engrossed in the early 1990s in the newly created Enigmatic Variations series in the *Sunday Telegraph*. He subsequently had his own puzzles published in the series, as well as in *The Independent* and the Crossword Club magazine, under the pseudonym Kruger, the name of his golden retriever that died while he was constructing his first puzzle.

Tom accepts and adheres to Ximenean principles, but feels that it is acceptable to push the boundaries from time to time if the context is right, and that crossword compilation should be an evolving technique. He has no favourite setter, but particularly dislikes puzzles with long or poorly explained (sometimes just incomprehensible) preambles, and anything involving a Playfair theme (*see* page 7). He finds the hardest part of setting to be thinking of a relatively original theme or gimmick to base a puzzle on.

Tom believes that a setter's objective should be to entertain the highest possible proportion of solvers while still being challenging to the majority, and not to be over-elaborate, obscure, or self-gratifying in the formulation of clues. He is not averse to using computer technology to help in grid construction but does strive to minimize the number of less common words used. He is also grateful for the clue-writing opportunities presented by the wonderful diversity of the Scottish dialect.

Outside crosswords, Tom enjoys long-distance walking

(an excellent environment for switching off and thinking of themes and clues), chess, golf, cricket (he is a qualified umpire), football, and real ale – not necessarily in that order.

Laws, Mike

Mike Laws was born in London in 1946 and educated at Whitgift School and Christ's College, Cambridge, where he graduated in classics. He married his first wife, Judy, in 1973, was divorced in 1990, and remarried, to Julie, in 1996. He has a son and a daughter from his first marriage. He was a teacher of Latin and English for twenty years, after which he became a postman/driver for eight years, and since then he has been a full-time crossworder.

A tentative teenage foray into cryptic solving (a Corgi book, price 2/6) petered out, and it was not until 1973 (too late to discover Ximenes at first hand, a source of lasting regret) that the efforts of a *Times*-solving staffroom trio inspired Mike to a fevered summer holiday progress through *The Times* and *The Guardian*, then Mephisto and AZED, and finally (in November) a jumping-jack-shaped *Listener* puzzle by SALAMANCA. Having by now become omnicruciverbivorous (his own term), he was one of the first quartet of all-correct solvers to be invited to the annual *Listener* crossword setters' dinner. He later (in the early 1980s) organized this event, inviting Azed and Colin Dexter as guest speakers, and was the first to take it out of London, where it had always previously been held. Meanwhile, a fellow Sunday lunchtime drinker had introduced him to Don Putnam's crossword section in *Games & Puzzles* (*see* LOGODAEDALUS) and *Ximenes on the Art of the Crossword* (1966), the principles of which have suffused all his subsequent crossword activities. Don took him on as a vetter, and published his first crossword, 'Plain Prize Puzzle' by Jude (as in 'the Obscure'), in the September 1975 issue. He later edited this section, always insisting, as he still does, on solving submissions from scratch.

Jude's next appearances were in *The Listener* (from 1977), the *Hamlyn Book of Crosswords* series (five volumes, 1978–80), and other more obscure outlets, before a long domestically-induced setting hiatus. Eventually Fawley (Jude's surname in Hardy's novel) seemed appropriate for a revival, appearing first in the short-lived *Country Week* (1991), then in *The Guardian* (from 1992, helped by a testimonial from Alec Robins), as one of James Leonard's original team (*see* MR LEMON) for the *Sunday Telegraph* Enigmatic Variations series (from 1994), and in the rescued *Listener* series in *The Times*. The year 1992 also saw Mike's anonymous debut in *The Times*, and his first puzzle as Ikela (hidden in his real name, nothing to do with scouts or Kipling) in *The Independent Saturday Magazine*. His three-weekly crosswords in the Mephisto series began in 1995, as did a run of fortnightly contributions to the *Weekend Australian* (via the *Sunday Times*), and in 1997 he added to his portfolio the *Financial Times* (as Darcy, to commemorate his get-up at his second wedding), the editorship of the new weekly series of *Times* jumbos, and the daily *Independent* (as Esau, a 'hairy man').

Mike became *Times* crossword editor in 2000. He strove to maintain the standards set by Brian Greer (*see* VIRGILIUS), and overhauled, with many new additions, the set of grids available for setters' use. A condition of his taking on the job was that he withdraw from all but News International publications, so when his contract was not renewed in 2002 he found it very difficult to pick up the pieces of his career. He became disillusioned and depressed, missing a number of opportunities as a result, in particular the chance to be promoted from occasional to weekly status as a *Telegraph* setter. He eventually resurfaced as Yorick ('Alas ...', and possibly the only pseudonym beginning with a Y) in *The Independent*. Mike still appears in the Mephisto series, and now edits the Weekend Crossword in the *Independent* Magazine, using Eddie (echoes of 'editor', the winter sporting Eagle, and the paper's masthead logo) and other previous pseudonyms, ad hoc, for his own contributions.

See the puzzle section for an example of this setter's work.

Little Eddy
See CHARYBDIS

Llig

Jack Gill was born in 1930 in Atherton, a town at the heart of the Lancashire coal-mining and textile industries, where every view was a Lowry. He was educated at Bolton School and then joined the civil service in the Manchester office of the Export Credits Guarantee Department. He later transferred to the London office and retired as chief executive in 1987. His career also included spells in the Department of Trade and Industry and the Monopolies and Mergers Commission (of which he was secretary). Jack was made a Companion of the (Order of the) Bath in 1982. He has been married for more than fifty years and has three married daughters.

From an early age Jack was intrigued by logic puzzles, and soon developed a lifelong interest in chess. Serious crossword solving began during his national service in the Royal Electrical and Mechanical Engineers when he started buying the *Daily Telegraph* and *The Observer*, whose Everyman puzzle was an inevitable stepping stone to Ximenes, with its unfamiliar grid matched only by its even less familiar vocabulary and seemingly insoluble clues. Solving Ximenes was at first slow and intellectually demanding, but irresistible and ultimately successful and addictive, an addiction that was fed by occasional prizes and commendations, and encouraging comments from X himself. These puzzles paved the way in turn for an attachment to *The Listener* thematics.

Primarily a solver, and somewhat in awe of regular setters, Jack was inspired by one of them whom he met at a Ximenes dinner (J. Brock, a.k.a. Badger) to plunge in at the deep end. He submitted to *The Listener* 'Half Seas Over', which was based on the origins of pub signs. It attracted two pages of trenchant criticism ('unruly unching and weak clues') from the solitary checker, who nevertheless liked the theme and accepted the puzzle with a number of amendments. Jack followed it with a steady series of crosswords, mainly for *The Listener* and the Crossword Club, with a wide diversity of themes, including the gates of old Jerusalem, Goethe's last words, *The Tempest*, heroes and their shields, Saint Cecilia, and the classical names of court cards. He also celebrated twenty-five years of the Crossword Club, run by Brian Head, with 'A TV (Theme and Variations) Life of Brian'. A more specialized circular puzzle for the Friends of Wigmore Hall drew on the texts of Schubert's song cycles, marking the composer's bicentenary in 1997. The puzzle which gave him most pleasure was 'Ring the Changes', based on Wagner's *Ring* cycle.

Jack selects his themes and topics with special care, his aim being to entertain solvers and to extend their knowledge in interesting if useless directions. If the puzzle can raise a smile or two in a wicked world, so much the better. His cluing is informed by Azedian/Ximenean criteria without being overly didactic. Where necessary he will bend the 'rules' slightly in favour of humour and fluency. Though he tends to forget clues and puzzles once solved, he well recalls Jeremy Morse's inspired winning clue to THOUSAND in the competition to mark Ximenes No. 1,000: 'Up-to-date product of X and C'. For conventional cryptic crosswords he regards Ximenes and AZED as keepers of the sacred flame; in the case of thematics his laurel crown would go to DIMITRY for his imaginative and innovative ideas, impeccably exploited while at the same time scrupulously fair. He also admires certain puzzles of MACHIAVELLI which cleverly use all the letters of the alphabet. Jack is sometimes frustrated by obscure themes based on inaccessible reference works, and remembers combing London to establish whether the final (of course unchecked) letter of a Venetian doge ended in 'i' or 'o', a task to which even the extensive library of the Italian Cultural Institute in Belgrave Square proved unequal. His preferred solving aid is the indispensable *Bradford's Crossword Solver's Dictionary*.

At seventy-five and with an understanding wife, Jack is still an avid solver, striving as yet in vain for *The Listener* solvers' silver salver and hoping for a few more visits from the setters' muse to help him entertain the long-suffering addicts of this extraordinary pastime.

Locum

Geoff Adams was born in Birmingham in 1943 and grew up in Nuneaton, where he attended King Edward VI Grammar School and learned a bit of French, a bit of Spanish, and rather less Latin. He was often in trouble for writing bawdy verses in class (notably 'The British Bum Ubiquitous', a quasi-Chaucerian epic, now sadly lost, which included a rather fine Christmas sonnet on the subject of St Cupro-Nicholas). He claims to have learnt four things from his schooldays: that doggerel is hard to write well, that précis-writing is, after all, a useful skill, and that he was no good at maths.

Geoff married his wife Ann in 1966; they have two sons, both musicians. After a working life as a librarian in Kettering, Solihull, Birmingham, Manchester, and Oldham, he gratefully took early retirement in 2004 and moved with Ann to a bungalow by the sea at Knott End, barely a stone's throw from BUNTHORNE's more upmarket abode.

Shortly after a six-year spell as the city's librarian, Geoff became crossword editor of the *Birmingham Evening Mail* in the 1980s. The paper had for many years run daily crosswords submitted by readers, as a spawning ground for new talent. Geoff introduced a weekly prize crossword set by invited contributors, including a very youthful Guy Haslam (Aldhelm) and a fairly youthful Don Manley (*see* DUCK), and enjoyed a regular correspondence with Tom Johnson (DOC) which has developed into a long, though always argumentative, friendship. Geoff's pseudonym dates from this time: though he was living in Rochdale at the time, he was a stand-in for the then crossword editor who had been suddenly taken ill.

Apart from keeping his cryptic hand in with a bi-monthly armed services magazine, and an occasional one for 1 *Across*, Geoff has contributed all the daily 'quirky' quickies for *The Herald*

(Glasgow) and will soon be celebrating his 5,000th. They are quirky because he enjoys taking words apart and linking bits all over the grid, and because of his dreadful puns in the first two or three across lights, which are now always themed in sets of five, thus inviting solvers to guess the theme as the week progresses. He once managed the German titles of ten Wagner operas over the course of a fortnight, finishing with *The Ring*, in sequence.

Geoff dislikes over-generalized or otherwise sloppy definitions (the easiest way to making a clue difficult being to fudge the definition) and padding. He likes '& lit.' clues, cognate anagrams, and, above all, wit. His favourite compilers are AZED, Bunthorne, PAUL, and ARAUCARIA. Of the quickies he most enjoys the *times2* crossword. When not compiling (or solving Sudoku or writing very bad Killers) he will either be pottering in his garden, walking by the sea, or ranting about something or other. In his younger days he was a useful baritone, and he still enjoys choral singing, which reminds him of his favourite clue from among his own: 'O trilling chorus?' for LUTON GIRLS' CHOIR.

Loda

Geoffrey Loder traces his lifelong addiction back to a memory of sitting on his father's knee while being taught how to solve the London *Evening News* picture crossword. Ever since then 'the grid', in all its forms, has continued to fascinate and frustrate him in equal measure, initially as a solver and then when setting (which he describes as 'solving in reverse').

Geoff was born in Egham in 1947 and educated at the local secondary modern school, where his love of English and sport developed. He now lives in rural Oxfordshire. His early career required a half-hour train journey to one of London's leading advertising agencies, just right for honing his skills on the daily offerings of *The Times* and *The Telegraph*. Over the next twenty-five years or so his career progressed through various marketing management positions in manufacturing and retailing companies. Gradually his addiction demanded the harder stuff, and Mephisto and AZED became weekly challenges, with Azed's eagerly awaited 'specials' providing a range of new and different experiences. He often exchanged phone calls with his father to compare notes on these puzzles, and always regretted that his father never got to solve one of his (Geoff's) own puzzles in print, the first of which was 'Cricket Match', published in the *Independent Magazine* in 1991.

It seemed a natural progression for Geoff to move into setting puzzles, but it also required a lot more spare time (which a recent redundancy provided) and an encouraging and supportive editor (in the person of the late Richard Whitelegg). He now spends much of his time setting themed puzzles for *The Independent* (Weekend Crossword), the Enigmatic Variations series in the *Sunday Telegraph*, the *Times Listener* series, and the Crossword Club magazine, as well as specially commissioned work. Some of his puzzles have appeared under his alternative pseudonym LODgER. Geoff's other interests, which include the stock market, sport (especially cricket), and films, have all provided inspiration for a number of his crosswords. He admits to having no idea where some of his ideas originate or how they mysteriously twist, grow, or mutate. A favourite starting point is one or other of his many quotation dictionaries. Wit in theme and wordplay are all-important since the setter's first responsibility should be to entertain: the pleasure of the chase (however long and tortuous) and the satisfaction of the kill should be an appropriate reward for the successful solver.

Geoff tries to ensure that his themes are accessible to all; he deplores self-indulgence or elitism in setters. His major hobby-horse is the pitiful remuneration paid for such piecework, especially in light of the fact that, for many, the crossword is their main reason for buying a particular paper. He sees this as exploitation of a largely amateur activity. For years he bought *The Guardian* purely for the tussle with ARAUCARIA, so he feels he speaks from experience.

Logodaedalus

Donald George Putnam was born just off Baker Street in London in 1930, and grew up in Harrow, where he attended Harrow Weald County School (1942–49). Despite the paper shortage, crosswords were published throughout the war, and Don's parents, both in the ARP (Air Raid Precautions), did the quickies in the *Daily Telegraph*. Don had only a slight interest in crosswords then, but he clearly remembers the occasion on which a possibly war-weary setter wrongly interlocked a T with a Y. He waited in vain for an apology, much later realizing how easily such mistakes can be made.

Don was called up for national service when he left school. He dismally failed a practical test, and can still hear the invigilator's sniggers at his frustrated attempts to assemble a bicycle pump, but then scored 98 per cent in an English synonym test, so was transferred to the intelligence corps in BAOR (British Army of the Rhine). Here he joined a group of conscript crossworders who each week tackled the Ximenes puzzle in *The Observer*, though he doesn't remember them ever finishing one, let alone submitting a clue. While still with BAOR, Don bought from forces' welfare bookshops copies of *Chambers's Twentieth Century Dictionary* (the original 1901 edition with its huge and irritating appendix) and Afrit's *Armchair Crosswords* (1949), which contains some golden rules for compilers and a favourite two-meanings clue: 'Come nice and close, like the milk man (6)' for NESTLE.

After national service Don began solving Ximenes puzzles on his own. Each attempt took a whole day – he has always been a slow solver – but, for such labours of love, time was not important. Helped by the useful hints for solvers in X's monthly slips, he won second prize in Ximenes No. 647 (June 1961) and equal first prize in No. 989 (January 1968) with perhaps his best ever clue: 'Pineapple rings in syrup' for GRENADINE. Inspired by a Penguin collection, he submitted 'For Connoisseurs', his first barred puzzle, to *The Listener*, using the pseudonym Dogop, based on his initials; it was accepted and published as No. 2,011 in October 1967. There were 107 entries, and it yielded a number of helpful and encouraging comments from top setters. In one of Don's most treasured letters Ximenes wrote of 'An Unconsidered Trifle' (*Listener* crossword No. 2,030 in April 1969): '... your puzzle, which I have just finished (2 hours) and greatly enjoyed and even more greatly admired as a truly remarkable performance. I would hardly have believed it was possible, and certainly would never have thought of attempting it.' In all Don set twenty-three *Listener* puzzles.

Wanting to get more crosswords published, Don turned from barred to blocked grids with 'normal' cryptic clues. He had 100 of these (under the name DGP) printed in the *Birmingham Post* and 89 (as Don Putnam) in *The Puzzler*. Two collections of miscellaneous and reprinted puzzles, *Crosswords for the Enthusiast* and *Crosswords for the Devotee*, were published in 1972 and 1974 respectively, and he also set for *The Guardian* as Logodaedalus ('one who is cunning in words'). He got himself made crossword editor of *Games & Puzzles* magazine, simply by telling the publishers that they needed one. He was asked to write three articles on cryptic crosswords, and then given the job. He soon found that he did not enjoy scrutinizing other people's crosswords, but he was able to provide a launch pad for new setters who went on to greater things. His eight-page section in the magazine enabled him to include in-depth features on aspects of the crossword contributed by a number of well-known setters.

In 1976 Don learnt that his wife was terminally ill, and he disappeared for a time from the crossword scene. After her death, and two breakdowns, he married again and eventually, after an absence of twelve years (during which he took early retirement from the civil service), he rejoined *The Guardian* team in 1988. Since then more than 150 Logodaedalus puzzles have appeared in

The Guardian and more than 50 Quiptics (simple cryptics by Don Putnam) on the *Guardian Unlimited* website. Of his varied output Don has had perhaps most satisfaction from compiling acrostic puzzles and others clued with rhyming couplets or half-couplets. Afrit (A. F. Ritchie) approved of these types ('the composer often brings off something really good … after failing to incorporate his first merely good idea'), whereas Ximenes did not ('I prefer prose clues: verse ones seem a needless handicap to the composer.'). While acknowledging that verse clues double the setter's task, Don has found *Chambers Rhyming Dictionary* (2003) an excellent aid, in addition to the other useful titles for setters and solvers in the Chambers list.

See the puzzle section for an example of this setter's work.

Lydian

Jason Lyon was born in London in 1968 and educated at Westminster, the Polytechnic of Central London, and London University. He holds a degree in English and Russian and a masters in international relations and law, and has worked in a wide variety of jobs from cocktail barman to journalist. He is currently deputy production editor of *The Business* newspaper and is also reviving an earlier career as a jazz pianist.

It was Jason's father who got him started on crosswords, with *The Telegraph* puzzle, and he was later introduced to those in *The Guardian* and *The Times* by his university sweetheart. He rarely meets anyone of his own age who is interested in crosswords, and finds this sad. An ARAUCARIA devotee, he particularly admires the great man's alphabetical jigsaws, and began setting syndicated puzzles for the Press Association in 2002 and joined *Country Life* as a regular setter in 2004 under the byline Lydian, a reference to modern jazz harmony, with pastoral connotations, as well as a play on his surname. (He also uses the pseudonym Impromptu on the internet, reflecting his musical interests.)

Crossword setters, Jason believes, are first cousins to newspaper subeditors, in that they must exercise the same precision with words and structure and a flair for arresting imagery and double meaning in order to entertain. A clue will often occur to him as he is working on a headline. He aims to be firm but fair, loves anagrams and topical references, and enjoys themed puzzles (themes he has used include Santa's reindeer, Miles Davis, Beethoven, and Ealing comedies). Jason uses Anthony Lewis's Crossword Compiler software and works by 'seeding' a new grid with strongly clued entries that have occurred to him in advance, and then filling in the edges. The knack of grid filling, for him, involves an instinct for choosing words or phrases that will yield good clues. And there is always a better clue to be found if one only has the time to find it.

While finding it hard to single out favourite clues, Jason feels that his own proudest moments came from 'Diabolical help is in this poem' (MEPHISTOPHELIAN), 'Girls aloud? How mawkish?' (MAUDLIN), and 'Suspicious deaths and stern crook in classic film' (KIND HEARTS AND CORONETS).

Machiavelli

Joyce Cansfield (née Patrick) was born in 1929 in Surrey, grew up
in Lewes, East Sussex, and was educated at Lewes Grammar School
for girls (with a period during the war at Greenhead High School,
Huddersfield), and London University (Westfield College and the
London School of Economics). She worked as a statistician in the
National Health Service until her marriage in 1974, taking a year
out in the late Fifties to go round the world (in those days with
two cabin trunks rather than a backpack), working in Canada and
also staying for a while in Australia and Malaya. She now lives in
Yorkshire, where she has had various part-time jobs in addition
to assisting in her husband's printing business.

In 1942 Joyce found a Ximenes puzzle in a newspaper lining
a drawer, and immediately became hooked, though it was many
months before she actually finished a Ximenes puzzle, and years
before she won a clue-writing competition. She started compiling
for annual competitions in the National and Local Government
Officers' Association (NALGO) magazine. When a friend became
editor of the *Mensa Journal*, he asked her to produce barred
puzzles for it. She sent her first effort to Ximenes to ask for his
opinion (which was flattering), and also for suggestions for a
suitable pseudonym beginning with M, and has used his offering
of Machiavelli ever since. She entered a clue-writing competition
in a short-lived crossword magazine which brought her into
contact with Edmund Akenhead, then crossword editor of
The Times, who was one of the judges. The next time they met,
at *The Times* crossword championship (Joyce qualified five times
for the national final, after moving away from London for the
northern regional final), he invited her to compile for *The Times*,
which she has been doing ever since, passing the 1,000-puzzle
milestone in 2003. She also compiles *Listener* puzzles. Her
favourite compilers are DIMITRY and SABRE (who used to submit

entries for her Mensa puzzles from school), and her major influence was, of course, Ximenes. She was delighted when *The Observer* published her puzzle in his memory. She admires symmetry in crosswords, but deplores the increasing tendency to add further tasks for the solver (such as highlighting parts of the completed grid), which are merely hinted at in the preamble, once all the clues have been solved.

Joyce's major interests outside crosswords are Scrabble® (national champion in 1980, sixth in the first world championship in 1991); skiing (she met her husband Mike in St Moritz, and they still ski every year); the Royal Naval Volunteer Reserve (long since retired, after twenty-two years' service); and television game shows (she was the first champion of *Countdown*).

See the puzzle section for an example of this setter's work.

Marcy
See CRISPA

Mass

Harold Massingham was born on St Crispin's Day 1932 in Mexborough, a town in south Yorkshire surrounded by a Lawrentian landscape of collieries and coalfields. He is married, with three sons and one daughter. His pseudonym is a diminutive nickname from his schooldays. He was educated at Mexborough Grammar School and then read English language and literature at the University of Manchester. He recalls his degree course as 'honours in penury' because of all the temporary jobs he had to do to float his studentship and repay his debts. He had already worked in Northern Dairies near Rotherham, done some stooking and harvesting at a local farm, had menial jobs in hotel kitchens, tried strawberry farming near Driffield, and spent a claustrophobic week as an ice-cream vendor in a beach kiosk before being fired for refusing to make hollow wafers. His university vacation jobs included fourteen dehumanizing weeks in a Wall's ice-cream factory in Hyde, working as a milk roundsman, and a fortnight of ten-hour shifts counting and weighing nuts and bolts in the Massey-Harris industrial complex. The latter gave him the opportunity to muse on language and literature, to whistle his beloved Beethoven, Wagner, and Vaughan Williams, and think up pretty subtleties for two-mover chess problems.

After graduating, Harold taught for about fifteen years in secondary schools and a tutorial college, during which time his first volume of poems was published, his first puzzles appeared in *The Listener*, and many of his chess problems were printed in *Chess, The Guardian, The Observer*, and *The Times*. He became a freelance operator as poet-in-residence in the University of Manchester extramural department and as a team member in the British Council's 'Poetry in Schools' programme. He toured Tennessee and Virginia as a visiting poet; his poems were published in the UK, USA, and Canada, and he received three national poetry awards. It's resources that matter, he says.

Harold found his way into the mysterious world of crosswords through solving the puzzles of the late Alec Robins (Custos in *The Guardian*, Zander in *The Listener*, part of the Everyman team in *The Observer*, and author of the pioneering *Teach Yourself Crosswords* (1975)). Thanks to Alec's patient encouragement, Harold was invited to compile, with Alec, three crossword books for Hamlyn, followed by a book of his own thematic puzzles. All of these were retailed by Marks & Spencer. Harold is also indebted to Charles Seaton, former crossword editor of *The Spectator*, for at least one rigorous guideline: he insisted that only recognizable words should appear in the grid, whatever transformation devices had been applied to clued answers. Harold set about 200 puzzles for *The Spectator*. For many years these had been set by Jac (J. A. Caesar) on his own, until he was joined by Harold and DOC , and the team was later expanded to include ASCOT, COLUMBA, and DUMPYNOSE. Harold now lives in semi-retirement in Spain with his wife Pat, who needed a change of climate while she did the groundwork for the *Daily Star* weekly jumbo, Harold helping with the clues.

Harold regards grids as either 'organic' (i.e. evolutionary, with selected words forming a symmetrical pattern at the setter's command) or 'inorganic' (i.e. fixed, thus conditioning or limiting the selection of words). He prefers the former, but is happy to adapt to the latter if required. His real bugbear is having to clue words so intractable that they take a maddeningly long time to deal with satisfactorily. Then there are circular grids, for which Harold is renowned (though he didn't invent them), with entries running radially and circuitously. He regards those he did for *The Spectator* ('Song Cycle', 'Helm', 'Potter's Wheel', etc.) as his best, if not his most ambitious, puzzles. And while he is a firm believer in the aesthetic importance of symmetry, he did once deviate from it deliberately in a puzzle for *Crossword* magazine called

'Amorphous (by) Mass', which called for shapelessness in every respect, an appallingly messy grid, and a clue gimmick echoing the theme.

Among setters, Harold appreciates the old masters Ximenes, Zander, and Apex (*see* page 3), and from those still at work AZED, Centigram (Chris Millin), and Samson (Max A. Taylor), as well as Hex (Henry Rathvon and Emily Cox) in the US. Among his favourite clues he likes to quote Dr E. Young's Azed prize-winner 'Style me Hitler's man – I could die for the bully of Europe' for SIMMENTHALER. He personally likes his own clue to the (difficult) idiom AS THE ACTRESS SAID TO THE BISHOP: 'You worship God, but the gods worship me ...', which unashamedly eschews Ximenean structure and lets the dots provide their own hint. His (shared) prize-winning clue for Azed No. 250, an anagram of the quotation 'Stands the church clock at ten to three?', was in the form of a tribute: 'To CCL, then! – He's the hardest nut to crack'.

Apart from his Hamlyn books, Harold co-compiled *100 Puzzles* by Mascot (Mass and Ascot). His puzzles have appeared intermittently in *The Guardian*, the short-lived American *Four Star Puzzler*, the *Sunday Telegraph* Enigmatic Variations series, the *Times Listener* series, and *Crossword* magazine. For the last twenty years his work has appeared mainly in *The Independent* – the daily cryptic and the *Saturday Magazine* puzzle (which he edited for a few years after Richard Whitelegg's death) – and the *Independent on Sunday*, for which he regularly sets a concise thematic.

See the puzzle section for an example of this setter's work.

Mawby, Ian

Ian Mawby was born in Newcastle, Tyne and Wear, in 1942, and grew up in Cambridgeshire. He began his working life as an apprentice draughtsman and soon embarked on a sales career, opening his own Lotus dealership in 1971. He became a professional racing driver in 1972, racing formula Atlantic and formula 2 Lotus cars, but his promising career, watched over by the Lotus boss Colin Chapman, came to an abrupt end when his brakes failed at 130 mph and the car bounced 30 feet in the air end over end, breaking his neck in the process. Though paralyzed and confined to a wheelchair, Ian still drives his 200-mph Mercedes and lightweight BMW M3 CSL.

Ian came quite late to crosswords. When he first attempted the *Daily Telegraph* puzzle he was instantly hooked, and in 2003 he began setting. Looking back on his early efforts he considers them dreadful, though with the odd clue that smacks of professionalism. Compiling two or three puzzles a day, each taking about ninety minutes from blank grid to completion, he quickly improved his quality and technique, and in mid 2004 he sent some sample puzzles to the *Daily Telegraph*, whose assistant editor Anne Campbell Dixon forwarded them to the crossword editor Val Gilbert with her personal recommendation. He was taken on as a 'floater' straight away and his first puzzle appeared in February 2005. Four months later he joined the regular team. *Telegraph* setters are not named, so Ian has no use for pseudonyms, though he has ambitions of compiling for other broadsheets. If he had to choose a pseudonym, it might be Pitstop or Speedy (he works fast), though Cabalist (an expert highly skilled in obscure, difficult, or esoteric matters) might be more suitable.

Ian enjoys solving puzzles that are interesting, witty, and elegant, fair but with subtle deceit. He has no favourite setters but is impressed by the work of Don Manley (*see* DUCK), whom he feels to be on his own wavelength. When a word strikes Ian as offering the basis for a good clue it is quickly jotted down, and he begins his grid with several words selected in this way. He insists that puzzles should be solvable with the help of a good dictionary but no other reference books. He tries to test the solver with everyday words, deliberately avoiding those that are more obscure, even if this means abandoning an almost completed grid. His puzzles include a number of simple clues to get solvers started and to encourage new solvers. Using a team of experienced broadsheet solvers to give him feedback, he likes to explore new techniques to entertain solvers, especially in the adroit use of synonyms.

Mephisto

See **CORYLUS, LAWS, OWZAT**

Merlin

Richard Palmer first took a serious interest in crosswords after starting work at the Institute of Physics publishing office in Bristol, where he was much encouraged by Don Manley (*see* DUCK). After reading *Ximenes on the Art of the Crossword* he started solving X's puzzles shortly before the latter's death (in 1971). In his own clues, Merlin has always aimed to keep to Ximenean standards. Since AZED took over from Ximenes in *The Observer*, Richard has been a regular competitor and has won several prizes. He was the first to win the coveted prizewinners' cup two months running (in 1975), given the added incentive of wanting to keep it as an embellishment to his wedding cake.

Richard chose his pseudonym for the prosaic reason that he was then living in Merlin Street. Early setters (notably Torquemada) took pseudonyms implying that their puzzles provided some sort of mental torture (and having attempted some of their puzzles Richard can see their point), but he thinks that the magician's art of misdirection is the most important aspect of clue writing so would rather be thought of as a magician than as an inquisitor. He noted that all the letters of Merlin occur in his real name and hoped to find an apposite anagram, but the J of his middle name (John) proved problematical.

In the 1970s Merlin had three puzzles published in *The Listener*, and his work also appeared in now defunct magazines such as *Games & Puzzles*. From the mid 80s to the mid 90s he contributed puzzles to *IEE News*. These were mostly 15 x 15 blocked puzzles using everyday vocabulary but with a *Listener*-style twist. Puzzles of this type, providing a bridge for solvers of plain cryptics who want to move on to more sophisticated puzzles, are almost unheard of. Richard would like to see them included in the quality dailies on a regular basis.

Richard has contributed crosswords under his own name for Christmas editions of *Physics World*. After an absence of twenty-five years, he returned to the *Times Listener* series in 1999 and has made further appearances there since then. In 2003 he joined the team of setters for *The Independent*, where he contributes two or three puzzles a month. Two of his favourite clues are: 'Relations are finally over for them (4)' (EXES) and 'One who thrived on turning wicket scoring century (11)' (WHITTINGTON).

In the 2006 Queen's birthday honours list, Richard received an MBE for services to scientific publishing.

See the puzzle section for an example of this setter's work.

Miguel
See **SALAMANCA**

Moodim

Alix Jagger sets for the *Financial Times*; her puzzles have also appeared in *The Independent*, *1 Across*, and the now defunct *Punch*. At thirty-seven she is a relative youngster. Her pseudonym is an amalgamation of the names of two of her cats. One of them has now gone to the great litter tray in the sky but lives on in Alix's pseudonym since she did not wish to reduce this to a less than flattering three-letter word.

A friend introduced Alix to cryptic crosswords about fifteen years ago. Her first foray into cluing was while waiting for a delayed flight with the said friend; she cannot remember the actual wordplay, but 'terminal boredom' was much in evidence. She now keeps a note of clues as they come into her head (she finds bus journeys particularly productive) and uses these as the basis for her next puzzle. She uses a computer program to compose grids, but tries not to rely too much on the anagram finder. She admires clues that raise a wry smile.

Alix works for the council. She lives in a village south of Bristol with her partner and remaining cat, Moo.

Mordred

Derrick Knight was born in Leicester in 1942 and grew up in Wimbledon. He was educated in Wimbledon, where he developed an obsession with cricket, fostered by his uncle Bill Burdett, who also introduced him to *The Times* crossword. Early bereavement led him to abandon marine insurance for a career in social work and personal counselling.

Derrick moved to Newark in 1987 and began commuting to London. Boredom during the train journey prompted him to set a crossword, which he sent to his friend Mike Kindred. Mike solved it and retaliated. Regular commuters asked Derrick to help them with their daily puzzles, and this led to *Cryptic Crosswords and How to Solve Them* (1993), written jointly with Mike and published by Chambers.

The first barred puzzle by Mordred, 'Hits', appeared in the *Times Listener* series in May 1994. It was set jointly with Mike Kindred, and the pseudonym combined an evil Knight and the second part of Kindred. Though the two stopped setting together in 1996, Derrick retained the pseudonym, and in 2005 the partnership produced *Chambers XWD – A Dictionary of Crossword Abbreviations*.

In addition to *The Listener*, Derrick sets for the Enigmatic Variations series in the *Sunday Telegraph*, the *Sunday Independent Magazine*, the Crossword Club magazine, and *The Magpie*, the successor to the late Mike Rich's *Tough Puzzles*. Derrick admired Mike, whose belief that crosswords should be fun, and preference for real words in the grid, have remained Derrick's own abiding principles, along with accuracy and tightness in cluing, in line with the stringent advice he received from the late I. C. ('Jim') Snell. His favourite setters, among many, are (for sheer fun and elegance of cluing) Samson (Max A. Taylor) and (for ingenious complexity) SABRE, MR MAGOO, and DIMITRY.

In March 2004 Derrick's son Samson (Sam) won a transatlantic solo rowing race. Four weeks before Sam was expected to arrive in Barbados, Derrick had the idea of setting a celebratory puzzle. He submitted it to *The Magpie*, stressing the importance of meeting the deadline. The editors, Mark Goodliffe and Simon Anthony, accepted it, emailed a proof to Barbados, and published it on the day of Sam's arrival. Derrick was particularly pleased with his clue for 2004, which solvers were required to enter in Arabic numerals in four symmetrically placed single cells in the grid. The clue was 'The court of mad French king' i.e. t'woo o' fou R (TWO O O FOUR, 2004).

Mr Lemon

James Leonard was born in Barnstaple in 1940 and educated at Eton and Christ Church, Oxford, where he read mathematics. After a brief period with the Clerical Medical & General Life Assurance Society he moved to Lloyd's, where he worked as both a broker and an underwriter from 1964 until he retired in 1989. He was, however, soon brought back into the field of insurance and reinsurance as an expert witness in several court actions involving various 'names' disgruntled by the large losses they incurred in the late 1980s.

James enjoyed solving crosswords from an early age, his skill at tackling *The Times* puzzle honed with the help of Mickey Jones, then bursar of the Dragon School in Oxford and rackets and tennis correspondent for *The Times*, on many car journeys between Oxford and the Queens Club in London. He discovered *The Listener* puzzles in about 1975 and managed, a few years later, to solve correctly a whole year's puzzles, on the strength of which he attended the setters' dinner, where the late Michael Rich introduced him to Les May (Eel, who lived nearby in Oxfordshire). This led to his successfully submitting puzzles to both *The Listener* and the *Saturday Independent* under the pseudonym Mr Lemon (*see below*).

For a short while James produced puzzles for *Country Week*, his team of four being Michael Rich (as Dives), Sylvia Jordan (Warbler), Mike LAWS (Jude), and himself as Rustic. The magazine folded after little more than thirty issues, but James managed to persuade the *Telegraph* group that they needed a quality barred puzzle each weekend. Thus the Enigmatic Variations series was born, in October 1992, originally with the *Country Week* team, though this rapidly expanded to about twenty-five setters, including some of the best known in the field. The series has survived a recent threat to axe it, thanks to the rapid and vocal response from setters and solvers alike. No. 700 in the series appeared in April 2006.

James is most at home with barred grids, but dislikes sloppy ones containing words that have either no unchecked letters or too many. As editor of the Enigmatic Variations series he has stopped accepting or using puzzles whose preamble includes such wording as '... each clue contains a surplus word, the initial letters of which spell ...', regarding this method of conveying a message as now overused and making life too easy for the setter.

Mr Lemon was originally a corruption of Mr Leonard, used as a form of address by some young friends, and Rustic seemed an appropriate name for a setter in *Country Week*, as well as being a serendipitous anagram of 'citrus'.

See the puzzle section for an example of this setter's work.

Mr Magoo

Mark Goodliffe was born in Carshalton in 1965, grew up in Cheam, and was educated at Epsom College and University College, London, where he read linguistics. He is a finance director at London International Financial Futures Exchange (LIFFE), and lives in London with his wife Anna and their daughter Emma.

Ever since his parents introduced him to *The Guardian* puzzles, Mark has had a passion for crosswords. He won *The Times* crossword championship in 1999 and a prize for the quickest individual solution in the final of the same competition in 2000. It was at this event that he was encouraged, by John Henderson (ENIGMATIST), to start setting puzzles. The latter, remarkably, could recall Mark's first compiling attempt, sent eighteen years before to ARAUCARIA and forwarded to John with the perceptive comment: 'He seems to lose interest after construction of the grid.'

Mark began setting for various websites, his increasing interest in *The Listener* crossword leading him to concentrate on themed puzzles. After the death of Mike Rich (Ploutos), Mark and Simon Anthony (PIEMAN) took over Mike's monthly subscription magazine *Tough Crosswords*, rechristening it *The Magpie*, to provide a serious challenge for mainly *Listener* faithfuls. Each issue usually contains five crosswords and a numerical puzzle, graded from A (harder than a *Times* crossword) to E (extreme). As one of the puzzles each month is normally by Mr Magoo, Mark has been highly productive since 2001, also appearing in *The Listener*, the *Independent on Sunday*, and 1 *Across*. A regular starting point is wondering whether a certain type of grid is possible, and then straining to achieve it, the successful efforts then demanding to become puzzles.

Since Araucaria's remark about his youthful effort, Mark has learnt much about cluing from a setter's (and an editor's) point of view, and his ideas on soundness largely overlap with those of Ximenes, AZED, and their 'school'. Mark loves variety, respects innovation, and dismisses few puzzle types or styles, even enjoying numericals (and Sudoku!). Solving remains his passion (he managed to submit correct solutions to every *Times Listener* puzzle in 2003 and 2004). The moments of discovery are always for him the most exciting part of the solving process: this may be encapsulated in fine clues but is more likely to be memorable in a theme. His favourite setters include DIMITRY, Elgin (Glen Mullineux), SABRE, and Ark (A. R. King).

Other 'surprise' appearances in Mark's life have included the *Daily Mail* schools bridge final (in 1982), *University Challenge* (1986), Murray Cricket Club record score (140) in 1998, appearing as an extra in *Bridget Jones's Diary* (2001), and travelling as a passenger on Concorde's last commercial flight (2003).

See the puzzle section for an example of this setter's work.

Mudd
See PAUL

Mutch, Jeremy

The son of a veterinary surgeon and a doctor, Jeremy Mutch was born in Liverpool in 1947 and brought up in the Wirral. He left Manchester University in 1970 with a degree in Spanish and Portuguese, and spent many years in the tourism industry as a contracts manager, travelling widely and seeking new destinations and products for Wings/OSL until the company was taken over and closed down in 1988.

In 1997, after an ill-fated attempt to run his own business (a gift and card establishment in the Wirral), he entered the world of crossword compiling. In this he was much influenced and helped by his good friend, the now sadly departed Bert Danher, who set puzzles for five of the quality newspapers: as Hendra in *The Guardian*, Aquila in *The Independent*, and Dinmutz in the *Financial Times*. Bert set the Thursday puzzle in the *Daily Telegraph* for many years, a slot which Jeremy has filled since Bert's death in 2002. In addition to *The Telegraph* he sets for the *Financial Times* as Orense (a city in north-west Spain where he spent a year as part of his degree course), *The Herald* in Glasgow as Jem, and the *Yorkshire Post* under his own name. He has also had occasional puzzles in *The Times*.

Jeremy believes that crosswords should provide a fair and enjoyable challenge, and that clues should be amusing whenever possible. He dislikes assumptions about the solver's familiarity with literary references and deliberately avoids these, seeing them as something of a throwback to the days when 'cryptic' clues took the form of quotations to be completed. He does admit to occasional lapses in his overall aim, but will always ensure that there is an alternative route to solution. He also believes that rules are made to be broken, and has occasionally created clues which others might consider unacceptable, e.g. '4t + 4e + a = 121?' for TETE-A-TETE, which he likes despite its lacking both anagram and homophone indicators. His favourite clues, however, are those which read as statements in their own right, e.g. 'Calls to support union pledges' (WEDDING RINGS), 'Labour betrays small manufacturing units' (WORKSHOPS), or 'Point conceded – the hippo did it!' (WALLOWED).

Jeremy is single, still living in hope and the Wirral, where he enjoys golf, wine, and travel. He supplements his crossword income with work as a freelance interpreter, principally for the Home Office.

Mutt
See **AUDREUS**

MynoT

Tony Martin was born in London in 1929 and educated at
Marlborough College and Trinity Hall, Cambridge, where he read
mathematics and law. He then became a chartered accountant
and after a variety of jobs with IBM UK had a career in commerce,
specializing in automated accounting systems. He has been
divorced for many years and has four grown-up children, none
of whom does crosswords.

Tony himself first became aware of crosswords in the 1930s
when he saw his grandfather solving *The Times* puzzle each day.
Later he did the same puzzle himself while commuting to work.
He discovered the *Times Listener* series and thematic puzzles
generally at around the time of his retirement, getting the hang
of them after an initial struggle. A visit to one of *The Listener*
setters' dinners, and membership of the Crossword Club, also
opened his eyes to the opportunities for aspiring setters. After he
discovered thematic puzzles, he largely lost interest in ordinary
cryptics. Now he likes puzzles which reveal layers of complexity,
his favourite being 'New Year Resolutions' by DIMITRY, though he
was unable to complete it.

Tony's first published puzzle was in *Crossword*, the magazine
of the Crossword Club. Having to find a pseudonym in a hurry,
he simply reversed his real name, the M being the initial of his
surname. Subsequent MynoT puzzles appeared in the Enigmatic
Variations series in the *Sunday Telegraph*, *The Independent Saturday
Magazine*, *The Listener*, and *The Times*. He now sets regularly for all
of these publications, as well as for *The Magpie*, to whose editors
he is grateful for their encouragement and constructive criticism
of his work. He is famous (or infamous) for having set *The Listener*
puzzle ('Take Turns') with the fewest entries since the puzzle
moved to *The Times*. He tries to vary the style of his puzzles and
keep his preambles and clues succinct. He once submitted a

thematic puzzle to *The Independent* with no preamble at all ('Self-contained', in which the preamble was to be contained within the grid), to which the crossword editor added one, saying, 'If there isn't one, everyone will ring up the switchboard and ask where it is.'

Tony now spends part of the year in London, where he plays tennis regularly, and the rest in south-west France, where he skis in the winter and tries to control his garden. He is also an opera-lover and likes fine wine and good food, which he often cooks for himself and his friends.

Myops

John McKie was born in Innellan in 1939 and has lived in Glasgow since 1943, having been educated there at Hutchesons' Grammar School and the university. He returned to Hutchesons' in 1967 to teach classics and retired in 2004, in the meantime marrying and fathering five children. His earliest attempts at crossword solving were as part of a huddle over the back page of the Glasgow *Herald* during the morning break and subsequently under the desk to while away the boredom of Latin lessons. By his late teens he was enjoying the puzzles in *The Times*, the *Sunday Times* and *The Observer*, in the days of Dilys Powell and C. A. Lejeune. At first he preferred *The Observer* Everyman puzzle but later 'discovered' Ximenes. Here was a treat to savour – slowly – for though he entered *The Times* championships it was for the fun of meeting other devotees rather than to ruin the pleasure of wasting time.

John's summers were spent on Arran and during one particularly wet week, with no puzzles left to solve, he turned to compiling; the Glasgow *Herald* invited him to contribute a weekly puzzle, which he still does. His first published crossword was in Latin, for a trade magazine, and over the years he has devised occasional special puzzles: for *The Herald*'s bicentenary, as a celebration of its editors; for Glasgow's garden festival; and for its year as city of culture, among others. His pseudonym Myops recalls Socrates' description of himself as a gadfly (and a memory of the Arran midge), and acknowledges his own short-sightedness.

John usually uses stock grids, thus avoiding expense (his first puzzles having required hot metal and copper plates) and error: he still remembers the unnumbered light in his first big (41 x 41) puzzle and the panic in the case-room two hours before the presses rolled. Later jumbo puzzles, for Christmas or Hogmanay or both, have been thematic and mostly on a 31 x 31 grid. An even larger crossword, with 2,000 clues, was wanted for the millennium and appeared on a two-page broadsheet spread, including the gutter. When a small puzzle, with definition-type clues, was added to *The Herald*'s back page, the then editor Arnold Kemp asked for something to give readers a Monday-morning feel: 'Make it more challenging than the cryptic crossword.' So the Wee Stinker (as it came to be called) offered such clues as 'Polo Park (8)' for EXPLORER and 'G-GAG (5, 8)' for HAPPY BIRTHDAY, the latter causing some readers to complain, even after they tried it on the piano. Myops cannot claim to have produced anything approaching the brilliance of Ximenes's 'Important city in Czechoslovakia' (OSLO), but he still strives to be fair, which means being syntactical: who is to say what is hard and what easy? A good crossword is a language puzzle and, one hopes, literary; it will include words our grannies used and look to appeal to readers who enjoy the same authors as its compiler.

See the puzzle section for an example of this setter's work.

Nibor

Robin Baxter (whose pseudonym simply reverses his forename) was born in west London in 1937. He was educated at Aldenham School and New College, Oxford, where he read classics. Between school and university he did national service, during which he became a Russian translator, but his Russian is now long forgotten. By profession a chartered accountant, he retired in 1999. He is married with two grown-up children (neither of them interested in crosswords) and lives in south-west London, close to Clapham Common.

Robin became interested in crosswords partly through his father, who did *The Times* puzzle daily, and partly as the result of being given, while in his teens, *The Observer Second Crossword Puzzle Book*, which contained a mixture of Ximenes and Everyman puzzles. While still at Oxford, he had his first puzzle published (No. 10,271 in the *Evening News*). He soon started solving Ximenes in earnest and then (from 1973) *The Listener* puzzles. In April 1975 his first *Listener* puzzle appeared (No. 2,257, 'Reason It Out'), and since then he has had thirteen more published, six of them with musical themes. His puzzles have also appeared in the former daily *Today*, *Crossword* (as Robax), and *Church Times*. It was only when he started setting *Listener* puzzles that he discovered that his uncle, A. O. Baxter, had also done so, having set twenty-one puzzles (as Jabberwock) between 1939 and 1951.

Having learnt about crosswords from Ximenes's puzzles, Robin is essentially Ximenean in his views, though he does occasionally stray from the path (as did X himself in his early days with such clues as 'Wolf! Wolf!' for EBBS). Robin's favourite setter is SABRE, but he enjoys the work of most setters and never ceases to be amazed by their seemingly endless inventiveness in *The Listener*. He even likes mathematical 'crosswords', though with no formal maths training finds that they can take a whole week to complete. Since he hardly speaks to his wife until he has finished the Saturday puzzle, she has good reason to dread the mathematical ones. His pet hate is any puzzle in which a considerable number of clues have to be solved blind before anything can be entered in the grid.

Since his retirement Robin's interests have been mainly sedentary: listening to classical music and jazz, playing the piano, exploring the internet, and watching sport on television. He and his wife have also started going on cruises.

Nimrod
See ENIGMATIST

Obiter

I. Torbe (of which his pseudonym is an anagram) was born a true cockney on 2 February (Groundhog Day) 1918, and brought up and educated entirely in the east end of London, from elementary school to university (Queen Mary College). He graduated with a first-class degree in mathematics in 1939. Instead of proceeding to a higher degree, for which he had won a scholarship, he was directed to work in the aircraft industry: first at Rolls-Royce in Derby and then at Airspeed in Portsmouth, where he worked on the design of the gliders used during the D-day landings.

When he arrived at the design office he was asked what his first name was. For some reason Isaac (a suitable name for a mathematician) was unacceptable and he was called Charlie. When the production blueprint of the component he had been checking was brought to him for signature as 'approved for strength' he signed, as usual, 'I. Torbe'. 'I thought your name was Charlie,' said the draughtsman. 'What's the 'I' for?' 'I for Charlie,' he replied, and from that moment he was universally known as Ifor, despite repeated, and largely unsuccessful, attempts to get himself called by his real name, Isaac.

After the war he remained for a while in the aircraft industry, eventually becoming assistant chief designer in the helicopter division at Fairey Aviation in Hayes, Middlesex, a position largely concerned with administration, for which he did not care much. Consequently he left the industry and took up teaching, first (from 1949) at Loughborough Technical College, where he taught aerodynamics, and then, from 1957 until his retirement, at Southampton University, where he taught structural design in the department of aeronautics and astronautics. While at Loughborough Isaac studied part-time at Leicester University and in 1956 he obtained a PhD with a thesis entitled 'The Geometry of Contact Transformations'. (He came across a copy of this recently and couldn't understand a word of it!)

Isaac became a crossword addict while at university, where students could get *The Times* at concessionary rates. He cannot remember when his first puzzle was published, only that it was in the Crossword Club magazine and long ago, before the advent of the PC. Grids were drawn by hand and clues keyed on a typewriter. Nor can he remember the date and title of his first *Listener* puzzle. [It was No. 3,232 on 11 December 1993 – Ed.] There have to date been ten of these in all. Isaac regards himself as a tolerant chap, whose only major dislike is of thematic puzzles whose preambles are harder to solve than the puzzles themselves.

Orense
See **MUTCH, JEREMY**

Owzat

Tim Moorey was born a man of Kent in 1940 and now lives in London. His pseudonym derives from his love of cricket (once a player, he now umpires regularly). As a schoolboy he started solving puzzles in the *News Chronicle*, *Radio Times*, and the *London Evening News*. He progressed from the dailies and the standard Sundays to Ximenes in *The Observer*, and thence to AZED, whose monthly competitions he has missed only when living abroad. His first puzzle was published in the *Evening News* when he was fifteen.

Tim's first career was with BP, with whom he worked for thirty-two years at home and abroad, including postings in Bahrain and Helsinki, ending as finance director for several BP companies. In 1991 he joined the civil service and for ten years worked at the Centre for Management and Policy Studies, an arm of the Cabinet Office, before becoming self-employed as a lecturer and business consultant. He now sets the Mephisto puzzle in the *Sunday Times* with Mike LAWS and Chris Feetenby (CORYLUS), contributes to the *Sunday Times* standard crossword, and is sole setter for *MoneyWeek* and *The Week*, for which he inaugurated the 'clue of the week' chosen from the weekly press. His puzzles have also appeared in the *Independent Magazine*, the Enigmatic Variations series in the *Sunday Telegraph*, and *Church Times*. He was the first 'cluru' (clue guru) for the Crossword Club and the club's clue judge for four years.

Tim dislikes long, complex preambles, mathematical puzzles, and any puzzles in which cleverness of grid construction takes precedence over good cluing. His guiding principle is fun, and to this end he has been the first setter regularly to invite comments from solvers at his email address, resulting in many rewarding dialogues with his 'customers'. One email he received, from a Belfast subscriber to *The Week*, read: 'My wife is such a fan of yours that she gets withdrawal symptoms if I hide *The Week* to have first go at the crossword. Please keep going as I do not want my wife to descend into depression for want of your weekly offering.' Tim's favourite clue types are those with nicely misleading definitions, such as 'Mum, listen for a change' for SILENT, and 'Eggs on toast' for CHEERS. Unfavourites are numerical puzzles: as a not very numerate accountant he gets little joy from figures. Among major influences he acknowledges *Ximenes on the Art of the Crossword*, and Azed and his monthly slips (*see* page 6). His favourite contemporary books include Brian Greer's *How to Do The Times Crossword* and the reference works of Anne Bradford and Herbert Baus. His favourite setters include MERLIN, Bandmaster (Richard Morse), and VIRGILIUS. His setting method is to start filling a blank grid with two or three words for which he has already written fun or special clues, stored as they occur on a pocket computer. He then uses software to take the hard work out of grid composition, leaving time to enjoy clue writing. He is usually most creative early in the morning.

In 1985 Tim (with Colin Clarke, a.k.a. Buff) founded the Gruntlings, a group of crossword enthusiasts who meet monthly in London, sometimes with guest celebrities. In recent years he has given over 200 talks and after-dinner speeches on crosswords; he also runs workshops for those wanting to improve their solving skills. These invariably show that the only essentials for enjoying crosswords are a modicum of intelligence and a love of words.

See the puzzle section for an example of this setter's work.

Oxymoron
See SCHADENFREUDE

Ozymandias
See **AZED**

Pabulum
See **DUMPYNOSE**

Pasquale
See **DUCK**

Paul

John Halpern writes as Paul for *The Guardian* and as Mudd in the *Financial Times*, and also sets for *The Times*. He believes that, at thirty-seven at the time of writing, he is the youngest setter on the broadsheets. Paul was the name of his late brother, while Mudd replaced his former *FT* pseudonym Bats (named after an ex-girlfriend with a similar surname). Since the breakdown of that relationship his name is, he says, most definitely Mudd!

Having attended Sackville School Comprehensive, East Grinstead, and gained a BA in music and maths at Canterbury, John found work in varying roles as banker, laboratory technician, journalist, and English teacher, among others. He is now a full-time crossword setter, living happily in south London.

John regards ARAUCARIA as his chief mentor, 'the most generous of men with advice and with friendship'. He sees crossword setting as, first and foremost, a form of entertainment. 'Once we start taking ourselves too seriously,' he says, 'we are writing only for ourselves. We should be providing a bit of fun for others, nothing more. Technically, we can still make progress while being fair. Sometimes it is instinct that tells us something is right, and fair.'

See the puzzle section for an example of this setter's work.

Pedro
See PHI

Peebles
See BRUMMIE

Peeper
See BUFO

Pegasus
See DEREK

Phi

Paul Henderson was born in Darlington in 1959. He took a degree in astronomy at St Andrews University. After a short period with Oxfam he worked for the UK Home Office from 1988. In January 2006 he moved to New Zealand to work for that country's Ministry of Justice.

Paul's father introduced him to crosswords, and he started solving those published in puzzle magazines before stumbling on Alec Robins's *Teach Yourself Crosswords* (1975). Finding Alec's views on fairness much to his taste, he has espoused them ever since. His interest gradually widened and he started solving AZED and *Listener* puzzles.

For Paul, crossword clues should give an immediate picture (which may or may not be relevant to the solution), should read well, and should be grammatically sound. Beyond that, he feels, the setter can do what he likes, and the apparent restrictions of soundness are nothing of the sort. It is all too easy to write a clue that looks good to the setter, but is almost impenetrable to the solver. A few ground rules make the battle even, but that doesn't mean that the clues cannot be harder or easier, depending on the subtlety and vocabulary used. One of Paul's own favourite clues ('This word's not right for "shy"!' for BRASH) relies on what is effectively an antonym, an unusual implied subtractive process, and the realization that 'shy' and 'bash' are synonyms for 'attempt', all of which is indicated, albeit obliquely, by the clue's wording.

Phi appears regularly in *The Independent* (including the magazine puzzle) and *The Listener* (for which he produced a series of twelve puzzles based on the labours of Hercules). Puzzles under his own name appear in *Church Times* and *BBC Music Magazine*. For the *Sunday Telegraph* Enigmatic Variations series he is Kcit (if HP = Tick, then Kcit = PH) and he also uses the pseudonym Pedro (alternate letters of P. hEnDeRsOn, which he sometimes wishes he'd thought of first). He is an anonymous contributor to *The Times*, and also runs 'A Puzzle Every Xmas', an annual puzzle circulated to a small group of aficionados, in succession to Apex (*see* page 3).

Paul has arranged several of the annual *Listener* crossword setters' dinners, including the seventy-fifth anniversary one in 2005 and the only (to date) overseas one in Paris in 2000, the planning of which allowed him to visit Rouen for the 1999 eclipse, only to find that the sun chose Paris. Outside crosswords, Paul's chief interest is music, especially contemporary classical music, and quizzes (he reached the semi-finals of *Mastermind* in 1987).

See the puzzle section for an example of this setter's work.

Phiz
See QUARK

Piccadilly

Mick Willey was born in Oxford in 1949, and educated at Chipping Norton Grammar School, Lancaster University, and Queen's University, Belfast. His parents showed him the basics of cryptic crossword solving when he was about fourteen. He became proficient at solving the *Daily Mail* puzzles and later enjoyed tackling ARAUCARIA's bank holiday double crosswords in *The Guardian*. At university he encountered a broader range of puzzles but could make nothing of Ximenes or Mephisto. In the late 1970s he started buying *The Listener* and gradually made progress with its crosswords. Those by Leon (Noel Longmore) probably had the most influence on his own mathematical creations. His solving rate improved dramatically when he bought a Chambers dictionary.

In 1980 Mick tried his hand at setting crosswords. At that time he was living in Salford and enjoyed listening to Piccadilly Radio; since the station's name rhymed with his own he adopted it as his pseudonym. He sent ten of his puzzles to *The Listener*, nine of which were deservedly rejected, but the tenth, a mathematical puzzle called 'Primes', was published in 1985. Since then he has had about ninety puzzles published, in the *Times Listener* series, the *Independent Magazine*, Enigmatic Variations, *Tough Crosswords*, and *The Magpie*.

Mick finds all aspects of crossword compiling – thinking of a theme, constructing the grid, composing the clues – difficult but ultimately rewarding. The theme sometimes determines the size of the grid. Mick enters the thematic elements and tries to position at least two long words, then builds up the symmetrical bar pattern and completes the diagram, with much rubbing out and redrafting along the way. Coming finally to the clues, he aims for a good mix of clue types. In his mathematical puzzles he tries to supply one or two easy clues as an entry for the solver.

Mick hopes that solvers find his puzzles entertaining rather than difficult. He dislikes puzzles that appear to have been set with the intention of making them as difficult as possible, and those that require extensive searching in reference books. Perhaps surprisingly, he dislikes most mathematical puzzles, except those by Oyler (Alastair Cuthbertson).

Crosswords aside, Mick enjoys gardening, though he prefers sitting in the garden with a crossword on a sunny day to digging and weeding. He makes and drinks his own wine, blackberry being his favourite tipple.

Pieman

Simon Anthony was born in 1973 in Carshalton, and was educated at Dulwich College and Queen's College, Cambridge, where he represented the university at bridge and golf, winning blues for the latter. He is currently employed in Canary Wharf, London, where he fights a natural tendency towards indolence by working for an investment bank. He is married to Anna, possibly the most tolerant person in the world.

Simon's first themed crosswords appeared on Derek Harrison's website (*www.crossword.org.uk*) and were generally thought to be fairly difficult, encompassing themes such as the albums of Dire Straits. Clearly dissatisfied with this verdict, he has over time produced steadily harder puzzles, appearing regularly in the monthly *Magpie* magazine, which he co-edits with Mark Goodliffe (MR MAGOO). Themes have ranged from Da Vinci's Vitruvian Man to the geography of the Old Course at St Andrews. Feedback on Pieman puzzles suggests that they may be the most consistently tough available today. If they are, it is probably because he is attempting to outdo his co-editor, who is too clever by half (and was born in the same hospital as himself though a decade or so earlier). His puzzle 'Dates' appeared in the *Times Listener* series in June 2005, marking the end of what may have been a record number of consecutive rejections.

Simon considers his own best clue to be 'Heroin with E, possibly (9, 2 words)' for SNOW WHITE, but he wishes he could write clues like SABRE. He thinks there are too many 'rules' governing the setting of crosswords today. Puzzles, he thinks, can still be wonderful if they are not symmetrical, if their answers are 'over-unched', or if they are presented carte blanche. His passion remains solving, especially *Listener* puzzles. He won *The Listener* silver solver salver in 2004.

Plausus

David Dare-Plumpton was born in 1943 in Lincolnshire, where he now lives. He showed an early interest in words and language, and gained triple BA honours in modern languages and classics, and an MA in classics, at Sheffield University. The first clue he can recall was heard in a chemistry lesson at school: '50s band leader's gone US (4, 4)' for DEAD LOSS. He taught classics for a while, and was intrigued to stumble on a *Listener* puzzle in the school library reading room, but it was only after a climbing accident led to wheelchair life (and the abandonment of his hopes of captaining England at cricket) that he started setting crosswords seriously. He no longer teaches and wonders how he ever did or wanted to.

David's pseudonym has appropriately Latin connotations: Pl (first two letters of his nickname Plum + *ausus* (Latin = dare); and *plausus* = cheers!). His crosswords have appeared in *The Listener*, the Enigmatic Variations series in the *Sunday Telegraph*, and Crossword Club, and he has set Latin ones for *ad familiares* (the biannual journal of Friends of Classics, edited by Peter Jones and Jeannie Cohen). With the writer and broadcaster Peter Jones he published *Latin Crosswords* (Constable & Robinson, 2000). He reached the final of *The Times* crossword championship in the halcyon days of old, and even once won first prize in an AZED competition. He likes solving crosswords on various levels of difficulty, especially those where 'the penny finally drops long and low'. He admires most setters but hates mathematical 'crosswords'.

See the puzzle section for an example of this setter's work.

Polymath

See DOC, DUCK, QUARK

Pundit

See XMAS

Putnam, Don

See LOGODAEDALUS

Quantum

See QUARK

Quark

Eric Burge was born in 1926. He retired some years ago from his job as principal education officer for further and higher education in Gloucestershire. He worked for many years as a physics lecturer at various colleges and polytechnics in London before moving into educational administration. Sport of all kinds has featured strongly in his life, especially cricket. He has been a member of MCC for over thirty years and has spent many pleasurable summer days at Lord's.

Eric's interest in crosswords began after he left university in Bristol, where he graduated in physics. He enjoyed solving a variety of puzzles, none more so than Ximenes in *The Observer*. He has followed the AZED series from the start, and over the years has gained several prizes and commendations in AZ's monthly competitions. This encouraged him to start setting and successfully submitting his own puzzles, principally to the *Financial Times* and *The Guardian*, where his pseudonyms (Quark and Quantum respectively) betray his physics background. He has also had crosswords published at various times in the *Birmingham Post*, *The Listener* (as Phiz), *Country Life*, the *Independent Magazine* (as EB), the *Sunday Telegraph* Enigmatic Variations series (as Quota), and the *Financial Times* Polymath series.

Eric's guiding principles are based on the standards set by Ximenes and Azed, with occasional deviations depending on the publication in question. He would welcome more feedback from solvers generally, setting being a lonesome pursuit. Among his favourite clues is Mrs L. Jarman's 'I provide something you can rattle up and down in a box' for CHEMIST, a first prizewinner in a Ximenes competition in April 1963, soon after the opening of the M1 motorway. He was also pleased with his own 'E.g. ... "delivery a *brute*" (when one's out)?' for BALLYHOO, reflecting his love of cricket.

Eric has given many talks to groups of retired professional and business people, under the title 'Getting a Word In'.

Quixote
See DUCK

Quota
See QUARK

Robax
See NIBOR

Rook
See JAGO

Rover

Ian Morgan was born in 1932 in Monmouthshire, and was educated there and at St John's College, Cambridge, where he read English literature and theology. His favourite study at school (Bassaleg county secondary school in Monmouthshire) was Latin composition, and he was taught English literature by the late D. P. M. (Parry) Michael, the crossword setter Egma.

After graduation Ian taught at Preston Grammar School until his retirement. While clearing his personal possessions on being seconded to take up the presidency of the National Union of Teachers, he came across a copy of *The Hoghtonian*, the school magazine, dated January 1957. In it he recognized a story he had written, 'The Man who Found Himself'. 'He was a maker of crossword clues. That is to say, of course, that he was a poet. He enjoyed all the types of ambiguity that poets enjoy; he was thrilled at the sight of similarity in things dissimilar; he loved, as though they were sleek cats, words, and the poise of words and letters.' The story ended with a contract for him to submit clues to a newspaper and have them edited into poetry; he had found himself.

Until that serendipitous find, Ian had not set a single crossword, but he was now given the opportunity to contribute regularly to *The Teacher* and *Education*. He adopted the pseudonym Serendip, the name he and his wife Edith, liking the word 'serendipity', had chosen for their house, and under this name had puzzles published in the *Times Listener* series and in *1 Across*. He was encouraged by ARAUCARIA to send some samples to *The Guardian*. When the crossword editor there asked for a different pseudonym, Ian chose Rover, a good name for a setter, particularly one who drives a Rover and supports Blackburn Rovers. In 1990 he published *Cracking the Codes: A Guide to the Cryptic Crossword* in a limited edition.

Ian likes his clues to be terse and tightly packed, while acknowledging that all too often words are difficult to clue except by a measure of prolixity. In compiling the grid and the clues he tries to ensure that the solver is given a fair indication of the register of the vocabulary used. Given, say, the word MERCURY to clue, his first thought is of the messenger of the gods; then of thermometers and Hg; then of newspapers and the planets. (He had not heard of Freddie Mercury until his death.) What would *Guardian* readers think of first? Which clue would they most appreciate and relish: 'The Daily Planet'; or 'Queen's lead, a metal hard to get hold of'; or 'A messenger poisoned me with curry'? Whichever it is, crossword solving has to be an entertainment. If the vocabulary is too precious, if the knowledge required is not general enough, if the wit is too self-indulgent, the setter has failed. After a time the solver needs to feel a sense of achievement: that is entertainment enough.

Rufus

Roger Squires was born in 1932 in Tettenhall in what is now West Midlands and educated at Wolverhampton Grammar School. During the war he acted as a messenger transferring the D-day wounded, and as a member of a Gang Show entertaining war workers in factories. From an early age he had wanted to see the world, so after gaining his school certificate he joined the Royal Navy at fifteen as a boy seaman. At twenty, as the youngest ever seaman petty officer, he moved to the Fleet Air Arm and flew as a lieutenant for eleven years. During the Suez Crisis his was the first aircraft to land at El Gamil, Port Said, then still under fire, with urgently needed medical supplies. He joined the 'Goldfish Club' (for survivors of crashes in the sea) in 1961 when he survived a ditching off Ceylon, escaping from his aircraft sixty feet below the surface. In fifteen years he visited fifty different countries.

When ashore in bad weather, aircrews played cards for money but, as a member of the Magic Circle, Roger was barred from taking part, so he began solving crosswords instead. At sea, without newspapers, he started setting puzzles, and his first appeared in *Radio Times*. Meanwhile his hobbies kept him busy. He organized variety shows – known as 'sods' operas' – taking them to hospitals in Cape Town, Rio, Singapore, etc; ran the television station on the *Ark Royal*; and represented the navy at cricket and football, having qualified as a Football Association coach and referee. He also appeared in nightclubs around the world under the stage name El Squalido.

Roger left the navy in 1963 and became entertainments manager at Butlin's shortly before turning freelance with magic, acting, and crosswords. His TV and film appearances have included 5 *Crackerjacks*; 26 *Rolf Harris Shows* (BBC1) as a comedian and magician; and over 250 dramas, including *Doctor Who* and

War and Peace; and *Crossroads*, where he played the character Harold Brackett for several months. Celebrity crossword solvers he met between takes included Alec Guinness, Anthony Hopkins, and Wendy Craig. Roger joined Mensa and captained the Great Britain team in the international crossword marathon in Yugoslavia (1989), the Wolverhampton crossword team on *Crossword on Two* (BBC2), and the Wolverhampton IQ team on *Pencil & Paper* (ITV), as well as competing on *Countdown*, *CrossWits*, and *Catchword*. He recently provided a Rubik's Cube crossword for an internet competition.

In 1977 Roger's marriage foundered and he gave up show business to look after his two young boys at home. In 1978 he became the world's most prolific compiler in the *Guinness Book of Records*, a record he still holds, with over 64,000 published puzzles in over 470 publications (some of which have printed his work illegally without permission). In 1981 he completed twenty-two years as crossword editor for the *Birmingham Post*, and he sets regularly for *The Guardian*, the *Financial Times* (as Dante), and the *Times Educational Supplement*. In 1986 he added the *Daily Telegraph* and *The Independent* (as Icarus, with extras as Hodge and Bower) to his list of credits, and in 1993 *The Times*. He has also had stints on *The Sun*, *Daily Mail*, *Mail on Sunday*, *Sunday Correspondent*, and *The Observer*, as well as forty years in the *Evening Standard*, plus numerous provincial papers and magazines. His millionth clue appeared in *The Telegraph* in 1989.

Roger likens his crossword work, now all cryptic, to that of magic, 'trying to entertain by misdirection'. He avoids obscure words, aiming to provide accurate clues with good surface reading that occasionally elicit smiles. He is pleased when he receives letters from readers who have started solving his puzzles before progressing to harder puzzles, and from setters who have, with his help, progressed to the nationals. He particularly likes cryptic definition clues, like Alec Robins's 'A stiff examination' for POST MORTEM, and apposite anagrams as in 'All of a tingle.

Perhaps, from such beating' for FLAGELLATION. He was the
first to use the anagram 'Presbyterian' for BRITNEY SPEARS
(in *Church Times*). His specials are now limited to regular jumbos
at Christmas with seasonal clues and solutions.

Of Roger's various pseudonyms, Rufus derives from his
initials (RFS) and Dante from an American magician of the 1940s;
Hodge (a rough peasant) is an alternate name for Roger, and also
appears in his address, as does Bower. Icarus came from his
aircraft ditching. He believes that he owes his love of words to
his grandmother, a Victorian poet, and to his father, who often
won prizes in competitions. Roger's hobbies now include theatre,
films, reading, football, and photography. Now remarried (and
still setting crosswords at 73) he lives with his wife Anna, a
voluntary worker, at Ironbridge in Shropshire, and with his
children Simon (a property developer), Michael (a vet), and
Tamsin (a doctor).

See the puzzle section for an example of this setter's work.

Rustic
See **MR LEMON**

Sabre

Andrew Bremner was born in 1951 in Lancashire and grew up
in Yorkshire, then studied mathematics at the Queen's College,
Oxford. His doctorate was at Cambridge, and he became a
research fellow at Emmanuel College, specializing in number
theory. From 1976 to 1977 he spent a year as a visitor to the
University of Michigan, followed by a tour of the US which
resulted in a lifelong love affair with the desert south-west.
He returned to Emmanuel as official fellow and tutor in 1977,
but moved permanently to Arizona State University in 1984.
He served as head of the mathematics department there from
2001 to 2005.

Andrew's earliest memories of crosswords are at his
grandmother's knee, but he discovered *The Listener* in his school
library, with much furtive time spent transcribing the puzzle in
order to study it at home. It took him well over a year of
frustratedly comparing puzzles with solutions before that magical
day when he was able to submit an entry. Setting puzzles proved
an enticing challenge. His first submission to *The Listener* was of
the 'unclued thematic' type, and absurdly esoteric. He owes a
great debt of thanks to Jim Evans, then vetter of *The Listener*
puzzles, for a wonderfully polite rejection, accompanied by the
encouragement to 'have another go'. His next submission was
accepted and appeared early in 1970. Andrew finds time to be a
regular solver only of *The Listener* puzzles; he has witnessed over
the years a mutation of the puzzle into its current form, where he
finds the ingenuity of some of the newer setters truly impressive.
At the same time he deplores the trend towards arch preambles
and themes that can leave the solver unsure what is required. Of
the older generation of setters he has the highest admiration for
DIMITRY's constant excellence. A current project is putting into
electronic form the complete *oeuvres de Sabre*, and he is suffering

intense embarrassment at some of the terrible cluing devices he has encountered. The use of 'in' as the imperative form of a transitive verb was not uncommon (so 'X in Y' would really mean 'Y in X'). Fortunately, he last used this device, which he now abhors, in 1982, indicating that he does try to learn from solver feedback.

Andrew relishes the challenge of paper and pencil composition, and rarely resorts to the use of computers, which almost inevitably diminishes the sense of accomplishment. After completing a puzzle, he will lay it aside for at least three months before re-inspecting it with a fresh eye: clues are often then amended. His main dislike in crosswords is sloppy clue writing. His other recreations include classical music, exploring desert slot canyons, the study of minerals and meteorites, and trying to grow (with partial success) unusual succulents. His boojum tree is thriving.

See the puzzle section for an example of this setter's work.

Salamanca

Michael (preferably Mick) Freeman was born in Buckingham in March 1948, a typical Aries. Attempts were made to educate him in a small C of E primary school and later at Wycombe Royal Grammar School, where he did moderately well in literature and languages. Most of his end-of-year reports stated 'could do better'; a typical comment was 'I'm tired of seeing the back of his head in my lessons. He always seems to be holding a class of his own.'

Mick came to a fascination with the concept of crosswords through the daily papers. With a like-minded friend at school he regularly tried during free periods to crack the *Daily Telegraph* puzzle in the school library, much to the disapproval of those who required silence to study. One day this friend opened the gates to a whole new and unimagined world – *The Listener* crossword – by showing him a puzzle called 'Diametricode'. They were so intrigued that, although they couldn't finish it, they determined to climb on the ladder. Meanwhile Mick made two other crucial discoveries: the original Mephisto (in the *Sunday Times*), which he ploughed away at, grateful to solve three or four clues each week, and the fact that his primitive dictionaries were not sufficient for the task. Having eventually mastered Mephisto, he discovered another new world, that of Ximenes in *The Observer*, sadly only in X's later years. He mastered Ximenes's puzzles well enough and really appreciated their cleverness, which was only surpassed by X's successor AZED. He then learnt about Torquemada, the predecessor of Ximenes, like him named after a Spanish grand inquisitor. Having acquired a book of Torquemada's puzzles he discovered that times had changed radically – i.e. he found them impossible to solve – but they *did* provide some valuable inspiration.

Determined to be a setter himself, Mick submitted puzzles

to *The Listener* in the early 1970s, some of which were accepted, and to the now defunct *Games & Puzzles*, whose crossword section was then edited by Don Putnam (*see* LOGODAEDALUS). He now sets puzzles for the Enigmatic Variations series in the *Sunday Telegraph*, and for the Crossword Club magazine. For twenty-five years he set a monthly puzzle in the *New Statesman*, only to be dropped because the magazine needed 'more advertising space'. His first and main pseudonym was taken from the University of Salamanca (founded by the original Ximenes). He also sets under the names Aelfre (i.e. [Mich]ael Fre[eman]) and Miguel (preserving the Spanish idiom, with which he helped to enthuse his friend JAGO).

Mick's favourite crosswords are probably Torquemada's 'Knock Knock' and Ximenes's 'Legsin Cricotas'. His favourite among his own puzzles, 'Weather Report' in *The Listener*, was also the one that unintentionally caused him the most grief. During a visit to his local library he discovered a new edition of *Webster's New Collegiate Dictionary*: its appendices included a list of 'internationally recognized' weather symbols. He innocently devised a puzzle over a map of England in which weather features within words (e.g. bRAINless) were to be replaced with the appropriate symbols. Unfortunately the source of the symbols was omitted from the preamble, and it transpired that in any case they weren't internationally recognized at all. In fact hardly any agency had ever heard of more than a few of them. The puzzle provoked about 160 complaints (to all of which Mick replied apologetically), not only from solvers but also from the BBC weather service and the Met Office, which had both been snowed under (so to speak) with calls from irate solvers. He can laugh about it now. He couldn't then.

Mick's all-time favourite clues include (from *The Times*) 'Bacon saver (5, 4)' for PIGGY BANK and 'The one to put your shirt on? (7-5)' for CLOTHES-HORSE; and from Eel (Les May) in *The Listener*, 'My chains are gold (4)' for MAYOR. Of his own he would choose 'What dogs do round trees (4)' (BARK), 'In which knight and mount tear recklessly (10)' (TOURNAMENT, *anag. incl. n*), and 'In mucky gloop has bed? (11)' (BOG-ASPHODEL).

See the puzzle section for an example of this setter's work.

Satori
See **TAUPI**

Schadenfreude

John Harrington was born in 1944 in Hertfordshire but has lived mostly in Surrey. He was educated at Hampton School and graduated in mathematics from RMCS Shrivenham before following a thirty-one-year career in radar system development. He moved to Cornwall soon after taking early retirement to live a life of leisure.

John caught the crossword bug from his father, who had been spending his Sundays immersed in Ximenes for as long as John can remember. He started as a young boy on the picture puzzle in the *Evening News*, and progressed via various dailies to Ximenes, AZED, and most recently *The Listener* and other thematic puzzles.

Over the years John has built an extensive library of reference books to cater for esoteric crossword themes, but he realizes that they could all be dispensed with if he connected his computer to the internet. So far he has resisted the urge to do this, though on one recent occasion he found it necessary to use his local public library's online facility to research the work of an author unknown to him (and to his library).

John's interest in setting coincided with his retirement: his first puzzle appeared under the pseudonym Oxymoron in the *Sunday Telegraph* Enigmatic Variations series in August 1998. Since then he has also had puzzles published regularly in the *Times Listener* series, *Independent Weekend Magazine*, *The Magpie*, and *Crossword*. He chose his pseudonym Schadenfreude because the word held some fascination for him and was both memorable and nastier than any Spanish inquisitor. He wishes there were more outlets for thematic puzzles to keep up with his output: he has a steadily growing number ready for submission. His greatest fear when solving is that the unfolding theme will mirror one in his own stockpile, something that has already happened more than once. Inspiration for his themes usually comes serendipitously, sometimes from questions on *University Challenge* and once from revisiting a Pink Floyd record sleeve.

John's favourite setters are those who consistently produce crosswords with technically correct clues with good surface readings and no superfluous words, symmetrical grids with few connected bars, no grid entries without unchecked letters, innovative themes, and unambiguous preambles. He aspires to all these things (and would like to see the end of 'definition and letter mixture' clues). His favourite puzzles are both from *The Listener* series: 'New Year's Resolution' by DIMITRY and 'Carte Très Blanche' by Elgin (Glen Mullineux).

John is now largely reclusive, spending most of his time walking the footpaths, setting more crosswords, and keeping an extensive garden under some sort of control. He was once a half-decent squash player and poor runner until recurring back problems put paid to those activities. His current interests include the turf (once as a regular gambler, now only as a spectator), and cricket (as a spectator), and he is not averse to a glass or two of Clos de Vougeot.

See the puzzle section for an example of this setter's work.

Serendip
See ROVER

Shed

John Young was born in 1959 in Farnham, Surrey, and educated at the local grammar school. He was introduced to crosswords by his mother, herself a setter (*see* AUDREUS). After studying French and German at Durham University, he spent a footloose decade working mainly as a holiday rep and teaching English in Spain, Austria, Morocco, and Germany. In 1996 he completed a PhD at Sheffield (where he now lives), and since then he has worked as a transcriber and researcher on various text-encoding projects, an electronic edition of John Foxe's *Book of Martyrs*, and the online publication of Isaac Newton's theological manuscripts, his current day job. His book *Faith, Alchemy and Natural Philosophy* (1998) is about the seventeenth-century German preacher Johann Moriaen, and he is co-editor and co-translator of *Jan Jonston's Letters to Samuel Hartlib* (2000), which also deals with the intellectual cross-currents of seventeenth-century Europe.

John's first published crossword appeared in *The Guardian* in 1984. The pseudonym Shed is an undergraduate nickname inspired by his sloping and ramshackle appearance. He also sets for the *Financial Times* as Dogberry, after the incoherent constable in *Much Ado About Nothing* who is 'too cunning to be understood'. As a setter for non-specialist dailies, John tries to avoid making unreasonable demands on solvers' literary and general knowledge. He aims to follow three guiding principles. The first is that a puzzle should, from the solvers' point of view, be more like fun than hard work (though the two are not mutually exclusive). The second is that it should be possible to show that a given solution is the only possible valid solution to its clue. And the third is that solutions, once arrived at, should be self-evidently right.

John fills grids in at home, by hand, using the Chambers and Collins dictionaries, *Pears Cyclopaedia*, and the *Longman Crossword Key* as the chief tools of his trade. Clues are written in periods of enforced or voluntary idleness – in queues, on public transport, in the bath, or (most often) in the pub. He sees nothing wrong with using computers as a setting tool but seldom does so himself, since he has more than enough to do with them in his professional life and regards setting as a paid hobby. His most embarrassing mistake to date was a published clue to the Norwegian explorer 'Admundsen'.

John's favourite setter is ARAUCARIA, for his inexhaustible wit and maverick ingenuity, and he much admires PAUL and TAUPI for their similar knack of bending rules without breaking them. He has been accused of being 'anti-Ximenean', so it came as a surprise to him to find that he agreed with almost everything in X's book *On the Art of the Crossword*. Ximenes himself wrote: 'Many ... do not subscribe to the principles I am going to lay down ... and no doubt they will continue to ignore them – why shouldn't they?', and John thinks that X would agree that the language of crosswords, like any living language, must evolve if it is not to become extinct.

As a solver, John likes best clues that make him laugh and kick himself (at the same time), his favourite example being Araucaria's 'Impossible to express in a four-letter word?' for INEFFABLE. He is deeply annoyed by anagrams in which only two or three letters need to be rearranged, by clues in which the subsidiary parts simply break their answers down into their etymological or syntactic components, and above all by clues that bear at best a tenuous relationship to their ostensible solutions.

Shrimp
See CHARYBDIS

Simplex

Mary O'Brien compiles a straightforward, though not always
simple, crossword six days a week for the *Irish Times*. She was
born in Dublin in 1944, was educated at a convent school, and
obtained a BA degree in English and sociology at Trinity College,
Dublin, in 1999 (as a very mature student). She is currently
studying for a PhD in literature. She was still a young schoolgirl
when she became a fan of the previous Simplex. When she joined
the staff of the *Irish Times* in 1970 she was delighted to meet
Mr Simplex (Basil Peterson), an ex-army man who had introduced
the crossword in 1951 in response to impassioned pleas from
readers wanting something less challenging than Crosaire (whose
puzzles had been appearing once a week since 1943). At that time
Simplex and Crosaire puzzles were published on alternate days,
though they both became so popular that, from the 1970s, the
paper included both of them each day.

When Basil Peterson died in 1986, Mary became Simplex
and for a time also held the part-time post of crossword editor.
Over the years she has met many Simplex-solvers whose stories
sustain her whenever she grows weary of deadlines. Perhaps the
most heartening story was from a daughter who phoned to
express her thanks for the comfort the crossword had given her
very ill father. When he had lost interest in everything else, she
said, he still looked for his Simplex and had asked for it even on
the day he passed away. There have been complaints too. With
worrying frequency, callers grumble that they have never heard of
a particular word – a sign perhaps of the diminishing vocabulary
of modern school-leavers. Another indication of changing
educational standards is the wrong use of words. For example,
few now seem aware of the 'true' meaning of 'fulsome' or
'decimate'. But possibly Mary's biggest bugbear is the confusion
that arises from the ubiquity of American spelling in global

communications. A young puzzler recently was convinced that 'programme' (of events) was a misspelling.

Mary took early retirement from her job as readers' desk executive and deputy letters editor of the *Irish Times* in 2002 but continues to set the crossword. Now in her twentieth year as Simplex, she plans to continue as long as health allows.

See the puzzle section for an example of this setter's work.

Sleuth

See **HYPNOS**

Smokey

David Crossland, born in Lancashire in 1948, first began solving cryptic crosswords as a teenager. His school's 'newspaper club' subscribed to a number of publications which included *The Listener*, and as a sixth-former he was both fascinated and flummoxed by its crossword. His solving developed through a fairly predictable route: first the local evening paper's syndicated cryptic puzzle, then via *The Guardian* and the *Sunday Telegraph* to Ximenes and *The Listener*. He remembers winning a 'first-out-of-the-hat' Ximenes prize after delivering his entry to *The Observer* by hand during a postal strike.

David's first published puzzle was in the London *Evening News* in 1971 (non-cryptic, fee £2); his cryptic setting career began during his first teaching job, in a London comprehensive; he produced half-termly puzzles for fellow addicts among the staff, mainly thematic and often imitative of Ximenes/AZED themes. Encouraging comments from colleagues persuaded him to submit a puzzle to *The Listener* in 1976, and this was followed by several others both there and in the short-lived puzzle magazine *Games & Puzzles*. He was then invited to be one of the four setters for a series of Hamlyn paperback crossword books, the others being Don Manley (DUCK), the late Eric Chalkley (Apex), and Mike LAWS (Jude).

Over the course of two decades, David's puzzles appeared in *The Listener*, the *Independent Magazine*, the Enigmatic Variations series in the *Sunday Telegraph*, and *The Spectator*. In 1998 Mike Laws asked David to become one of the setters of *The Times* jumbo puzzles and, soon after that, one of the team setting *The Times* daily crosswords. He joined *The Independent* daily team (as Dac, representing his initials) in 2002, and now sets regularly for both *The Independent* and *The Times*, including the occasional double holiday jumbo for both. (Smokey puzzles – the pseudonym

was taken for sentimental reasons from the name of a much
loved family dog – have gone on hold for the time being.)
David has also compiled unattributed puzzles, both cryptic and
non-cryptic, for magazines and book collections, including many
of the Past Times crossword books. He continues to admire the
ingenuity of compilers whose puzzles appear in *The Listener*, the
Crossword Club magazine, etc., but these days finds some of
them impenetrable.

David moved from teaching to teacher training in 1993.
He is married with two grown-up children and lives near York.
His interests include bridge, wine, and travel.

See the puzzle section for an example of this setter's work.

Spurius
See CALMAC

Tait

After graduating in economics and politics from Durham University in 1990, and without a job to go to, Roderick Easdale started writing articles about cricket, his great love, and selling them to magazines. This led eventually to his becoming a journalist, not his expected career path. He also answered an advert for crossword compilers and got work setting for an agency. Such was the secrecy surrounding the project that he only found out years later, and quite by chance, where his crosswords had appeared. He also at this time produced puzzles for a business-to-business newsletter contract publisher who had spotted 'crossword compiler' on his CV. The publisher asked him how much he charged for a crossword, so he told them (basing his figure on what the agency paid him, plus a bit). The publisher replied that this didn't seem to be enough, and offered him four times the rate he had quoted.

Both Roderick's parents were keen solvers of *The Telegraph* crossword, and they taught him the knack. He now tries out all his own puzzles on his mother before submitting them.

Some years later, by now working as a freelance journalist after a spell on the staff of the Press Association, and not having compiled a crossword for more than a decade, he found himself editing crosswords for *Country Life*. He was asked to bring in a younger compiler, and did so. When another vacancy arose, as he was about to give up editing the puzzles, he took over the setter's role instead. He chose the pseudonym Tait, a family name and also one of his own forenames.

Roderick's favourite clue is probably the well-known 'Gegs (9, 4)' for SCRAMBLED EGGS. He paid homage to it with 'Tom Sharpe and Thomas Rep harm poet's trash poem (5, 9)' for MIXED METAPHORS. His interests include cricket and golf. He is the author of *The Novel Life of P. G. Wodehouse* (2004).

Tait, Ann

Ann Tait was born in Surrey in 1941, the only child of a regular
RAF officer and his wife. Because the family moved frequently,
her early education was much disrupted. She started school in
Germany at the age of six, and was a poor reader even at seven.
Contrary to expectation, she passed the 11-plus exam and
completed her education at a boarding school in Devon and at
Pate's Grammar School in Cheltenham. She then read classics
at Bristol University, and did a postgraduate teaching diploma
at Nottingham University. Her teaching career began with two
years at Cheltenham Ladies' College, and this was followed by
many years at Ribston Hall High School in Gloucestershire,
where she was also head of careers. She derives much pleasure
from continuing contact with ex-pupils.

Ann was a stranger to crosswords until her early twenties,
though both her parents were keen solvers, her father being a
finalist in the first *Times* national crossword competition.
Her initiation began when she met Douglas St P. Barnard, then
senior setter for *The Telegraph*, and became his protégée. She
began compiling for the paper on a regular basis in 1987, four
years before she left teaching. If she needed a pseudonym, her
choice would be Pythia, after the priestess of Apollo who spoke
in riddles.

Though the object of crosswords is to challenge as well as to
entertain, Ann tries to avoid abstruse words and redundancies,
while at the same time being fair to the solver. She feels, however,
that the desire for brevity and crispness can sometimes lead to a
clue giving insufficient information. She finds setting a difficult
and often lonely job, but has been sustained by her friendship
with Ruth Crisp (CRISPA), whom she met in 1990. Both Ruth and
Douglas Barnard have been major influences, and she likes their
respective clues: '"Men's my one failing" – mother of nine'

(MNEMOSYNE), and 'No adequate description of father's cuemanship' (FAIR, i.e. Fr with A1 break). Her favourite clue of her own is 'Lots of lucre, but little luck' (SMALL FORTUNE).

Unexpected coincidences can beset a compiler. A horrific one for Ann occurred in 1990 when this clue of hers appeared in the *Daily Telegraph* two days after the murder of Ian Gow by the IRA: 'Outcry caused by Tory assassination' (BLUE MURDER). The crossword editor Val Gilbert regularly checks clues against current news items, but on this occasion she happened to be away on holiday.

Ann's interests are largely academic: she attends classes in French, German, and the history of art, and has long been a student of history, religion, and the Middle East. She also enjoys classical music and foreign travel, especially in the company of her daughter, and best friend, Helena. She regularly attends the large Anglo-Catholic church directly behind her house.

Tantalus

Donald Yerrill was born and educated in Brighton. At school, he developed a taste for crosswords – mainly those in *The Spectator* – and he fondly recalls 'Bocatots (4, 2, 5)' for PUSS IN BOOTS. He early formed the ambition to write, and began with reviews for *Sight & Sound*. He soon found, however, that a 'writing career' consisted largely of sorting rejection slips, so he got a job as a copywriter at J. Walter Thompson, sharing an office with Joyce Lustgarten (wife of Edgar, the author, broadcaster, and criminologist) and Alastair Buchan, which involved solving a great many crosswords, liquid lunches, and last-minute rushes to make deadlines. This period, spent working in the two-column-inch spaces available in the relatively small newspapers of the time, taught Don the necessity of carefully assessing every written word to ensure that it carried its weight in context, a discipline that later proved valuable to a budding crossword setter, together with the guiding principle that 'brevity is the soul of wit'.

A business career followed, graduating to creative management, marketing management, and general management in several multinational companies, and culminating in five years as a management consultant. Parallel to this, Don followed a career as a writer, with over 400 radio and television scripts (mainly documentaries), reviews of French books for the *Times Literary Supplement*, short stories, miscellaneous journalism, and one novel which was mentioned in dispatches in a *Sydney Morning Herald* competition, though never published and quickly consigned to unmourned oblivion.

After taking early retirement Don started setting thematic puzzles for bridge and chess magazines, soon branching out into specialized puzzle magazines. His big break came when he was taken on by the *Birmingham Post*, whose crossword editor at the time was Roger Squires (*see* RUFUS). Roger became his mentor, guiding him through Ximenean principles and the art of accurate yet entertaining cluing, and finally entrusting him with the Autolycus puzzle. This cryptic had been, for more than fifty years, a prize puzzle with the distinctive characteristic of using the most recondite (and least tractable) words in *Chambers*. Seven years later, however, the *Post* changed its puzzles policy, but Don (as Tantalus) has continued to offer the crossword by direct mail to a circle of enthusiasts. In 1993 he started setting for the *Times Literary Supplement* (all clues on the editorial theme), providing forty-eight crosswords and four seasonal acrostics a year. He also does cryptics for a range of regional and local papers, as well as *Choice*, and general knowledge puzzles for *Gulf News* in Dubai.

Don's leisure pursuits include tournament bridge, reading, online bridge, rereading, and social bridge. His pet hates are 'long, clunking clues, hernia-inducing surfaces, anagram-rash' and (possibly in common with others in this book) Sudoku.

Taupi

Albie Fiore was born in 1946 at Southend-on-Sea, Essex, and educated at Southend Grammar School, Southend School of Architecture, and the Architectural Association in London. After working initially in architecture, he has been, variously, an antiques dealer specializing in old slot machines, editor of *Games & Puzzles*, production designer for Games Workshop, and a freelance writer and designer. He has written game and puzzle-related books, contributed to television programmes including *The Crystal Maze*, advised on the development of Rubik's puzzles, and written storylines for a children's comic.

While he was working on a French farm in his student days, Albie was nicknamed Taupi ('Moley') by the locals. When he first submitted crosswords to *The Guardian* in 1992, he adopted it as his pseudonym. Similarly Satori, his pseudonym in the *Financial Times*, is based on the Basque word for 'mole' but also means 'sudden enlightenment' in Zen Buddhism. He also sets for the *www.enigmatist.com* website as Taupi.

As a schoolboy Albie was interested in word, mathematical, logic, and mechanical puzzles. His first memory of a cryptic crossword is from the early 1960s. While he was camping with friends at the Battle festival, one of them produced *The Guardian* bank holiday double cryptic. Oblivious to the festival's events, he and others spent days trying to solve it. *The Guardian* puzzles were then uncredited, but he is sure it was by ARAUCARIA. After that, he was hooked; he began regularly solving cryptics and setting them for the amusement of his friends.

Albie tends to compose his crosswords on the hoof, usually waiting in a café or a pub while one of his three children is involved in some extracurricular activity. Consequently, he uses a pad of squared paper, a pencil, an eraser, and his own vocabulary. He finds this an enjoyable mental exercise, one best suited to standard cryptics and the occasional themed puzzle. Crosswords with complicated preambles irk him, as he feels that any special instructions should be inherent in the puzzle or its title, without additional explanation. For example, in one Taupi puzzle the answer to 7 Down was ONGOING; several other answers, e.g. B(ON)EHEAD, SEMIT(ON)E, and DEM(ON)ISE, were clued to be entered 'with 7'. He prefers clues that are fair to the solver and nicely worded in both surface and cryptic interpretations. While he acknowledges Ximenes's exemplary principles that brought order to a chaotic field, Albie feels that one must look to what, in jurisprudence, is called 'the golden rule': that, to inform a judgment, one must determine exactly what that law was intended to prevent. So a law may be technically breached, so long as that breach is not what the law was meant to prevent, which allows for flexibility and progress. In his view, the ultimate judge of the fairness of a clue is the solver. Hence, one of his favourite clues is Araucaria's 'Of of of of of of of of of of (10)', where the solver knows when he has the right answer, OFTENTIMES. Of his own clues, he was pleased with 'Heady stuff that's said to precede highness (4, 3)' for HAIR OIL, which sprang to mind after many other failed approaches to an uninspiring answer.

Albie enjoys solving crosswords for fun: he admires Araucaria, AZED, the late Apex, and MACHIAVELLI for their sustained ingenuity, wit, and originality; ENIGMATIST, PAUL, MR MAGOO, Cyclops, and COLUMBA for their humour and inventiveness; and Jude (Mike LAWS), BUNTHORNE, DIMITRY, SHED, and many others whose every crossword inevitably includes some brilliant clues that raise a smile.

Terrell, Ray

Ray Terrell was born in 1956 and educated at Pocklington School before attending York Art College. He spent many years in a variety of run-of-the-mill jobs before moving to Paris, where he now lives with his partner and their son. When not chained to his computer he teaches French journalists and broadcasters the finer points of the English language.

Having been introduced to crosswords by a *Guardian*-reading colleague, Ray was inspired by the puzzles of ARAUCARIA and rapidly became hooked. Another of his favourite setters is MASS, though he admits that he hasn't looked much at other compilers' work for some time. He dislikes long 'mechanical' clues which do not read well, and though he tries to adhere to 'Ximenean' principles, he is occasionally prepared to break the rules for the sake of brevity and coherence. He uses Crossword Compiler software, which takes the donkeywork out of filling grids, thus allowing him more time for the fun part, i.e. thinking up the clues. He prefers to fill his grids word by word, writing the clues at the same time, or at least to choose words which look as though they will lend themselves to easy cluing later. He tries to keep clues short and, if possible, amusing.

Ray enjoyed a moment of inspiration recently while watching a documentary on Jackson Pollock. Thinking of how an aficionado of the artist's works might describe his collection, he had the idea of 'A load of pollocks?' for SHOAL, and this became the starting point for his next crossword. His favourite clues are those which he believes cannot be bettered. A good example is DEREK's 'Hold hands' for STEVEDORES.

Ray is a weekly setter for the *Daily Telegraph*, and he also does work for *Channel Four* from time to time.

Twudge
See DOC

Victor
See **BROWNE, RICHARD**

Virgilius

Brian Greer was born in 1944 in Strabane, Ireland. He has three grown-up children from his first marriage; he remarried in 1998, and moved to the United States in 2000. Now settled in Portland, Oregon (dubbed 'Little Beirut' by George Bush Senior after he had eggs thrown at him there), he continues his academic career, working closely with his wife Swapna, on the cultural and political aspects of mathematics education. He has competed in the American crossword puzzle tournament on three occasions, without distinction, and gave the plenary talk at the event in 1996, including the much-appreciated short poem by Roger McGough: 'Got up/Shaved/Did the Times crossword/Shaved again.'

Brian's serious involvement in crosswords started when he was studying mathematics at Selwyn College, Cambridge, and produced amateurish and quirky puzzles for the university newspaper *Varsity*. Back in Belfast, having changed disciplines to psychology, he contributed more amateurish and quirky puzzles to a two-weekly political magazine called *Fortnight*. In 1975 he joined the team at *The Times*, where he became crossword editor from 1995 to 2000, and wrote *How to Do the Times Crossword* (2000). During his formative years on the paper he benefited greatly from the punctilious editing of Edmund Akenhead, particularly as regards precision in language. Becoming a crossword editor himself exposed a latent streak of authoritarianism, leading to such epithets as 'the Mutilator' being applied to him.

In early 2005 Brian became crossword editor for *The Independent* (which, unlike *The Times*, was happy with someone doing this job from the west coast of the USA), but he relinquished this position early in 2006 in order to devote more time to writing books and other academic activity. He continues to contribute to *The Independent* (as Virgilius), *The Times*, and now also *The Guardian* (as Brendan), and the *Daily Telegraph*.

Brian's puzzles have also appeared in *The Listener* (under the pseudonym Virgilius), and he has recently started setting for the *New York Times*. The pseudonym is not based on the Roman poet, but on the name of an eighth-century Irish scribe who inserted acrostics in his work.

Brian is a sporadic, and occasionally successful, competitor in the AZED competitions. On one occasion he won the Victor Verborum cup; the following month he mailed it on to the next winner, Rear-Admiral Ridley, who, on receiving an unexpected parcel from Belfast, took it into his garden and immersed it in a bucket of water until he established its provenance. Brian's nomination for 'best clue not even to get a VHC (very highly commended)' is 'Record total produced by working round the clock' for SEVENTY-EIGHT. His all-time favourite, which won the cup, is Les May's 'Bust down reason?' for BRAINWASH. Another favourite is Michael Macdonald-Cooper's 'Not a square meal' for PIZZA (*see* CALMAC). He has a weakness for cryptic definitions, which enliven otherwise prosaic American puzzles, an example being 'Rake over the coals' for DON JUAN IN HELL.

See the puzzle section for an example of this setter's work.

Vixen
See CRISPA

Waterloo

David Gribble was born in 1932 and educated at Eton and Magdalene College, Cambridge, where he read modern languages. He was a teacher for all of his professional life, briefly at the highly traditional Repton School and then, for more than thirty years, at the highly untraditional Dartington Hall School. When the latter closed he was one of the founders of the even less traditional Sands School in Ashburton, Devon. He has written several books about the kind of education he favours, including *Considering Children*; *Real Education: Varieties of Freedom*; *Lifelines*; and *Worlds Apart*.

David set his first crossword at the age of ten as a birthday surprise for his grandfather. It included, as was fashionable at the time, a quotation clue: '"To ——, or not to ——" (Shakespeare) (2)'. The first cryptic crosswords he attempted to solve, at about the same age, were in *Country Life*. He was pleased if he managed four or five clues. He progressed to *The Times*, still hardly ever completing a puzzle and regarding Ximenes as totally incomprehensible. Several years later he saw a friend, who was not a regular crossword solver and was therefore unaware that Ximenes puzzles were impossible, glance at one and immediately solve a clue. He realized that the clues were similar in method to those he had been used to solving, and after buying a Chambers dictionary he found he could usually complete them.

David's first *Listener* puzzle was a joint effort produced with a friend. It was called 'Deasil and Widdershins', and the solution was just a ring of digits. All the numbers which could be formed by reading round the circle in either direction, starting from any point, shared some ridiculous number of common prime factors. His first verbal puzzle had across clues in English with entries in French, and down clues in French with answers in English. The confusion of English and French was the origin of his pseudonym.

David's puzzles are usually quirky, each of them based on an idea he has not seen used elsewhere (though sometimes others have). In 'My Cousin's Bangle', for example, his fictitious cousin had made up the diagram, carelessly not always holding it the same way up, so that Ms might become Ws, Ns might become Zs, and his unconventional lower-case ds might turn into ps. The puzzle was originally rejected, with comments showing that the vetter had not fully understood it. David re-submitted the puzzle with explanations, and it was accepted, with minor changes. David's own particular favourite is probably a 'carte blanche' called 'An Unusual Symmetry'. The symmetry was in the arrangement of the letters, not the bars, so, for example, the extreme left-hand column read DRYADS/E/N/DEWPOND and the extreme right-hand column read D/N/O/P/WEDNESDAY/R/D.

For David puzzles are a hobby rather than a career, so he does not use software to help him with his grids, as the creation of these is, for him, part of the fun. He was astounded when a solver wrote that he solved a Playfair code (*see* page 7) by using a computer program; it seemed analogous to winning the quarter-mile on a motorbike. He does not submit crosswords to any other publication.

Woodworm
See JAGO

Xestobium
See JAGO

Xmas

Noel Jones was born in 1943 in Peebles, and spent most of his formative years in Edinburgh and Dundee. Having been educated to A level by Jesuits in Leeds, he then studied English language and literature at Queen Mary College, London. He maintains that the two strands of his degree reflect his love of the true cryptic clue: the linguistic precision of the definition together with the imaginative creativity of the wordplay. After doing Voluntary Service Overseas in Guyana, he became an English teacher, teaching mainly sixth-form pupils. Now retired, he lives in rural Norfolk and spends his time gardening, playing the tamborim (a Brazilian type of tambourine which has no jingles and is struck with a stick) in the Norwich Samba Band, and acting, all over Norfolk but especially at the Maddermarket in Norwich.

Noel's love of increasingly demanding puzzles led him to cross over from solving to setting in the late 1970s. His pseudonym is itself a sort of cryptic clue: definition Noel and wordplay X (crossword symbol) with 'mas' (Latin for 'male'). He does not have ten MAs unfortunately, but for the one he does have he produced a dissertation on puzzles. Most of his work has appeared in *Crossword*, the Crossword Club magazine, but he has also circulated privately (sometimes as Pundit) many puzzles thematically linked to the plays he has been in. His fondness for awful puns was also apparent in a puzzle called 'Pundit' which was included in *The (Almost) Impossible Crossword Book* (1984), edited by Gyles Brandreth. He has also had one puzzle in *The Listener*, written an article on puzzles for *Mensa Magazine*, and appeared on television, both in cameo acting roles and on the crossword-based *Commuter Quiz*.

Noel has had many ideas for crosswords, resulting in dozens of half-finished puzzles; he needs, he says, to stop acting and start doing. His favourite setters include Ximenes, AZED, Apex

(Eric Chalkley), MASS, and ARAUCARIA. He also likes the misleading definition clues common in *The Times* jumbo puzzles, and regards *The Chambers Dictionary* as his bible. His pet aversions, however, are clues which make no sense to read and computer-generated grids in which, for example, across inversions are indicated by 'up'. His favourite clues (all, noticeably, short and of the '& lit.' type) include 'All-points bulletin' for NEWS, and 'Bust down reason?' (BRAINWASH). Among his own he is quite pleased with 'I'm not well-disposed' for TIMON and (possibly the ultimate in concise clues) '–?!' for NONPLUSSED. His most embarrassing moment was when he was sent the proofs of a puzzle he had submitted many years earlier, only to find that he didn't recognize it and was unable to solve it.

Yorick
See LAWS, MIKE

Puzzles

The crosswords in this section have
been selected to represent a wide range
of styles and levels of difficulty. Each is
by a different setter and the puzzles are
arranged alphabetically according to the
setter's name or pseudonym, with the
name of the newspaper or periodical in
which they first appeared. The date of
original publication, where known, is
also shown. This may be relevant to
solving. Puzzles are presented as they
originally appeared, with minimal
editorial changes, as are the solutions
(sometimes with explanatory notes)
in the section that follows.

Puzzle 1

Alaun
Sunday Telegraph

Across

7 Good service (4,5)
8 For days off, you require authorisation (5)
10 Sound that will disturb the calm (6)
11 Person we've all come to see jump and possibly run (4,4)
12 Take-home pay! (6)
14 For information, go to the social elite (6)
16 Had been providing, from the rain, a little shelter (4)
17 Grant it's not as nice as a private room (5)
18 Unhappy to be trailing in the game (4)
19 Seem likely to fall for the accountant (6)
21 Achieve a decisive victory for the party (6)
24 Is it not happy as a lark? (8)
26 Went off, as the revolver did (6)
27 What the nut consulted the chiropodist about? (5)
28 Go on and on extracting? (5,4)

Down

1 All drink? Almost all (5)
2 Only thing the hungry burglar was interested in? (4,4)
3 These ordered a Sunday paper (6)
4 Creatures having since hollowed out a nest in it (4)
5 Used up, as it happened (4,2)
6 Too popular an artist's model to be in the red? (9)
9 Waited on, though very tired (6)
13 Met outside 'The Headless Man', as planned (5)
15 Call back to pick up again (9)
17 Getting a father to help, one's sorry to say (6)
18 Give medical assistance to first, amid the misery (8)
20 Overtips, they hold. That's what they think! (6)
22 An earthquake by mid-March or sooner (6)
23 He's really bad if a doctor's brought into the home (5)
25 What you have to do to get a title? (4)

© Telegraph group

Puzzle 2

Antico

This crossword was first published in The Oldie, issue 205, April 2004

1 Across is to be deduced. The letters belonging to it appear in thirty-five other squares in the completed puzzle; these should be shaded in, to reveal an item associated with 1 Across.

Across

1 *See preamble* (6)
4 Strike part of sleeve (4)
9 Second person in relay outpaced (3)
10 Dumplings made by companion, in frantic cooking, not satisfactory (7)
11 Nothing from Italy taken into Holland (3)
12 Field in part used for fold (5)
13 Forgiving party involved in cheating (9)
14 Eccentric letter (9)
17 A lord disregarding bishop and priest (5)
19 Box that's French is at rear of church (5)
20 Scornful leader of syndicate, very cold, when arrested (9)
22 Firm corporal, say, appearing before court, starts to excoriate rebellion's planner (9)
25 Article unbelievable in any way? (2,3)
26 Look around, going about island, for fuel (3)
27 Work, modish one, concerning belief (7)
29 Pub again needing cases (3)
30 Just endless stone around lake (4)
31 Revised column, with mass cut out, good and clear (6)

Down

1 Bird up with rodent among first items in eager naturalist's endless list (9)
2 Discern insult, left out (5)
3 Entertainer's beginning with energy and self-importance (3)
4 Sausage – hot one, cut up – received by puss on middle of plate (9)
5 Mushrooms? Enjoyable, man declared (5)
6 Minutes I copy wrongly, being short-sighted (6)
7 Image number 101 upside-down (4)
8 Connect architect with enthralled learner (4,2)
13 Quotes from script, messy, with odd bits missing (5)
15 Soldier for instance on boat occupied by journal and collection of poems (9)
16 Artist referring to king as 'more remarkable' (5)
18 Going back over dreadful art, cringe (9)
19 Bird about in country? There's expression of surprise about that (6)
21 Demure, accepting most of extensive settlement (6)
23 Tower-like structure, not soft, topped by new material (5)
24 Spare container to hold hydrogen (4)
25 Reverse from channel, unnavigable, going north (5)
28 Nothing to split inside atom? (3)

© Oldie Publications 2004

Puzzle 3

Araucaria

This crossword was first published as Puzzle No. 21/1034 in 1 Across, November 2004

Across

1 Swindles brought to court (7)
5 Sporting day ends in drama (7)
9 Bluebottle reported to be thickening (9)
10 Mason's partner sees a fellow about the foregoing (5)
11 Caught return of the German solution (6)
12 Accommodate as a baby the French dancer unexpectedly leading (8)
15 *See 28*
18 How are we different than ale and than oil? (8,6)
20 League takes the lot with ice-breaking article (8)
21 Get in the way of the basket (6)
24 Shoe for opponent of the present form of 8? (5)
26 Simultaneous arrivals of the lower classes spelt wrong (9)
27 More in 550 was turning to the right (7)
28 '15' 25 'A sensible 7, asked to state a preference between being 8, 4, 11, or 19, would ———' (Tony Wright MP in *The Guardian*) (4,3,4,2,3,5,3)

Down

1 Roman nonconformist or Etruscan ditto? (8)
2 Request to appear short with South American in sum (7,4)
3 Use 4-letter word that's a girl's name (5)
4 Attempt at showing variety of colour (4)
5 Volunteers made haste to report on a dance (10)
6 Not too bad a blunder (bad English) (9)
7 Deceive 25 with change of starter (3)
8 Barbarian boy was in the pink (6)
13 Further related occurrence in the dark room (11)
14 In some theatre seats one can see a tube in a starfish (5,5)
16 Speaker keeping split personality of prehistoric beast (9)
17 Bible character playing harp, setter understands (8)
19 Talked a lot of little good to silly journalist (6)
22 Preserving jelly so pretty? (5)
23 Speed tied by registrar (4)
25 Hedge spar (3)

© 1 *Across* 2004

Puzzle 4

Ascot
The Observer 23 January 2005

Across

1 Dish, lightly cooked portion (7)
5 One likely to have a nap? (7)
9 Horseman, leader of cavalry, with very big rifle (7)
10 Row back to vessel to attend a service (7)
11 Carol having drop of lime in drink (5)
12 Set aside popular book (2,7)
13 Crowd with sports league meeting with journalists (5,10)
15 Tense meeting patrolman on street, one one's not met before (7,8)
19 Deploy laser beam, almost following lead of 'Cubby' Broccoli (9)
21 News involving learner driver and the public (5)
22 Study large hospital in Welsh town (7)
23 Appropriate language, English (7)
24 Girl, one leaving drunken sailor at New York, on the way back (7)
25 One who entertains those at sea on steamship (7)

Down

1 Goes mad, discarding clubs, and accumulates points (5,2)
2 Sappers deliberately hurt causing temporary delay (7)
3 Sweetheart gets upset about ending in feature film (4,5)
4 Accept defeat stoically, as a boxer might? (4,2,2,3,4)
5 Powerful tractor? One's extremely dependable when needed (5,2,8)
6 Community's endless capital (5)
7 Article supports working there in Iran (7)
8 Full? Salesman allowed inside at the end (7)
14 Street repairs, radical round roundabout by factory? (9)
15 Horseman in cap Dior designed (7)
16 Decisions in game, good for East in more than one series (7)
17 Rubbish boy initially put in lockup, perhaps (7)
18 Compensation concerning clothing (7)
20 Excellent fish (5)

© Allan Scott 2005

Puzzle 5

Auster
The Guardian 19 January 2004

Across clues are related and have no definition.

Across

7 Exposed to drink (8)

9 Me, on this occasion (6)

10 Peek surreptitiously (4)

11 Cross-breed? (7,3)

12 Edward briefly involved in polo ruck (6)

14 Australian upset after losing Rugby Union (8)

15 Second-rate resource (6)

17 Poet wants bible classes included (6)

20 Abroad, confused between left and right (8)

22 A small amount cheat returned (6)

23 Brit in Oz has time in an organization (10)

24 Chinese take-away? (4)

25 Line leaving coal mine (6)

26 A fellow with nothing to say (8)

Down

1 It's up to me and mine, and it's set to go off with a bang (4,4)

2 Entertain a lot, say (4)

3 Pound given before Mamie ordered sailor's warm jumper (6)

4 He accuses falsely, as the ship's officer said (8)

5 The way to get food, we hear, for a community celebration (6,4)

6 Reason to break with the missus in Barcelona? (6)

8 Due to the wind, oil drifts in each direction (6)

13 500 severely treated – about 500 – and rightly so! (10)

16 Finished outside, the listener drew closer (8)

18 Medic, before operation, takes out leader of Soho's non-conformists (8)

19 Truman is inside after discarding an axiomatic statement (6)

21 Silver and gold changed to coins in Israel (6)

22 A band of black-fish (6)

24 Search for company doctor (4)

© Shirl O'Brien 2004

Puzzle 6

'Corgis in Castle' by Azed
The Observer 2 June 2002

This puzzle was first published on 2 June 2002. All clues are normal. The initial letters of the across answers may be arranged to form the first four words of a familiar five-word phrase. Further hints may be found elsewhere in the puzzle. *The Chambers Dictionary* (1998) is recommended.

Across

1 Eccentric saves wings on old butterfly (7)
6 Law officer keeping order – not the first for drug peddler (5)
10 In result favourite appears top in struggle to win (10)
11 Zilch given away by secretive star making appearance (4)
12 Attacks (sudden) capturing British, in chains (7)
14 Bring from interment what's old to set before doctor (6)
16 Energy, atomic, held in check (5)
17 The rising love-romp that is fashionable (6)
19 Have another go at matter pet spread about (9)
21 This sugar has emanated around a container (9)
24 Having internal ailment, pike is gutted (6)
26 Excel in nothing, as of old, just the same (5)
29 Sample from Schlegel: I cited extract (6)
30 Electronic data that's true, though corrupted – trouble within (7)
31 Can it answer hard king? (4)
32 One in the money, led by drugs giant, accepting new beginning (10)
33 Noblemen putting a thousand into club sub? (5)
34 Dower deviously held in credit for fiddler (7)

Down

1 Roughly styled as 'guv'? The nerve! (5)
2 One formerly the foremost on water, shimmering? (10)
3 Yanqui woman? Tanner's mad with love for her (7)
4 Ancient ring for which Cornish tourists'll climb (6)
5 Little breadth in scandals disturbed bare patches in US landscape (9)
6 Grayling found in Yorkshire river, headless (5)
7 Odd pieces? (6)
8 Leather lining provides protection for this barb (4)
9 Dispatched inside Indian territory takes ill (7)
13 Exult in claptrap about dodgy audit (10)
15 Niggle about the 'ouse – it registers absorbency rate (9)
18 Junky drug, A1 (soft initially), makes one hermit-like (7)
20 United perhaps engaged in an even contest? (7)
22 Besmirched like daggers used by Macbeth, depressed about dead one (6)
23 It blows dust on the Spanish gannet's egg (6)
25 Line in epos elaborated on sturgeon (5)
27 English in Roth novel that's 'something else again' (5)
28 Eccentric American, Scouser's chum (4)

© Jonathan Crowther 2002

Puzzle 7

Richard Browne
The Times 3 March 2006

Across

1 Soldiers wearing superior field dressing (6)
4 From fish and seaweed, sulphur that's perfect for chemist (5,3)
9 Criticise meat as tough from the start (7)
11 Put on edge, getting soaked touring hospital (7)
12 Poet concerned with capturing type (5)
13 In bad fall, arm is not right – broken (9)
14 In monument a single layer gets damaged on the outside (10)
16 To secure bird is a problem (4)
19 Worthless pudding (4)
20 Starter that's often mocked (6,4)
22 Closing searches, one perhaps cast in debate (9)
23 Jones's partner extremely senile: look for the twitch (5)
25 Spring-activated shaft for lacing ribbons (7)
26 Motorist just for fun runs into lorry (7)
27 Paper and its source, including a rejected model (8)
28 Capital only 10 in republic accepted (6)

Down

1 Wrongly lipread, so like some light (9)
2 Indian lost a million? Not that much (5)
3 Singular bowlers – they have a high trajectory (8)
5 Drinking the way in gated community? (7,6)
6 One's put in new gate, knocking down the old (6)
7 Concentrate on being miserable in poor area – not hard (3,4,2)
8 Party's over: order city to be destroyed (5)
10 Backs these after torture, king intervening, to receive mercy (5-8)
15 Presents, in sound and in colour, king's defence (5,4)
17 Well-hidden service area turned up (3-6)
18 Wait for delivery of metal fixing-rod, about a metre (4,4)
21 Feeble evasion, inviting expression in support of business (3-3)
22 Resign as last of agreed period's up (5)
24 Housewives organised for each to get a cleaner (5)

© *The Times* 2006

Puzzle 8

Bunthorne
The Guardian 31 December 2005

Across

1 *See 8*

4 *See 8*

9 The father of Waterloo? (4)

10 Seed spilling, see, his need disturbed the Church (10)

11 (*See 8*) Two-man quarry (6)

12 Morse's ménage backing code with stratagems (8)

13 Stardust is seen in some scanner by Protestant (9)

15 *See 8*

16 Poet speaking of Psyche (4)

17 Ruthless order to setter on Korean diet? (3,3,3)

21 Carter's wit, hopeless case (8)

22 Wholly enthusiastic without books (2,4)

24 I.e. sloop hut constructed for steersman's comfort (5,5)

25 *See 8*

26 Amazon in retreat from the Old Man's island (6)

27 Abraham's tomb here in The Bronx (6)

Down

1 The Severn Bore's starting as rain falls around (7)

2 Record turn in the lunar cycle (5)

3 Potentially bad sign for the corporation (7)

5 Volatile girl one grabs in the market! (2,4)

6 Agent surviving without pre-Euro currency (9)

7 They admit mates to the masters' circle (7)

8,1,4,11,16,15,25 Posh, his vice was her misfortune. That b— song a mama's woe? C-could be! (3,3,4,3,3,3,6,6,2,1,4,4,4)

14 Liberal taken in by pointless bloody self-approbation (9)

16 *See 8*

18 No harm in looking through it? On the contrary! (4,3)

19 Seat raised bearing a device (7)

20 Remove Oxford United? No, he's reunited! (6)

23 Woods imitated at Harfleur? (5)

© *The Guardian* 2005

Puzzle 9

'Eoegoetrn' by Calmac

The Independent (Saturday Magazine)   2 October 2004

This puzzle was first published on 2 October 2004 (a significant date). Twenty-six clues contain a misprint in their definition parts. The correct letters, in clue order, provide a simple substitution code for the letters of the alphabet, though characters of the destination code (not being all different) do not necessarily have unique equivalents. The remaining eight clues have no definitions. Seven of their answers are of a kind, and the other provides a link between them. All eight of these answers are to be entered in code. The puzzle's title has been similarly encoded; solvers should deduce its original form and write this below the grid.

Across

1 Amateur general running round about in furious rage (12, two words)
9 Nuns obstruct ruler (7)
10 Inference of divine in the self personal attendant initially ignored (5)
13 Scops in Edinburgh outside public school (6)
17 Hard American secures a large covered wagon (6)
18 Kick up without meaning to, on account of eating large bird (8)
20 Prospers having been exiled hence, making it look almost normal at first (5)
21 European queen once captivated by old English fork (6)
22 Copy Chairman, crushing fly (6, two words)
23 Home of some fat eastern types, a number found in Hawaii (5)
26 Pipal territory, say, arboriculturist vacated with big cat about (8)
28 Trailed in motorcycle event, stifling a disgusted expression (6)
31 A soldier from America about to run through a native (6)
32 Mail was burned here – error initially covered in circular director put out (5)
33 Like certain planes, rose, for instance, flying on the banks of Derwentwater (7)
34 Wine account initially raised by Rector in church (12)

Down

2 Folder of Unitarian doctrine found in old car going up Roman road northwards (8)
3 Wrapped in cloth, right tool for working in garth (6)
4 Tenor by Italian church – he's less brown than the others (5)
5 Spain's parliament comprehends nothing in a foreign language (10)
6 Extremity of meter, a point showing fuel absorption (4)
7 Leaves put on maypole in the spring primarily (5)
8 Best stop cutting college (4)
11 Like wood pigeon topically, as put into pie? (8)
12 Done out of one's life? Get on in plays, securing opening on Broadway (8)
14 Arrangement for clarinet, one pitched in setting that's low (10, two words)
15 One letting home by road, possibly, relatively quaint, with old decoration inside (8)
16 Bishop, one surrounded by excited throng (8)
19 Went for swims round end of cape (8)
24 Church in small square associated with council condemning Asian heresy (6)
25 Sear tips of asparagus under grill until ready (5)
27 Parts of contract order one to take rolls (5)
29 Of pins and needles: silver or gold, originally (4)
30 Club – Heart – One No Trump (4)

Puzzle 10

Casina
The Times 19 September 2005

Across

1 Paris producer welcoming youngster into part of theatre (6)
4 Festival swineherd always observed (8)
10 Preserve and equip a youth feeding a setter (9)
11 Whip early king used to restrain love (5)
12 Broadly, Jean Rhys's source of floating algae? (8,3)
14 Leading cardinal was most successful in speech (3)
15 Lack of purpose, cutting off head's gas, for example (7)
17 Lively wit runs into European bank (6)
19 Fanciful as a French coin once used in Spain (6)
21 To merely exist, some feel, breaks one of its rules! (7)
23 Act like one of eight, say, seeing deer (3)
24 Pedantry of Chesterton's remote and ineffectual attacker? (11)
26 Precious stone presented to Mexican poet (5)
27 Honour a new church, holding one's act of homage (9)
29 Right woman in group to introduce a piece of music (8)
30 Transparent case leader of investigation dropped (6)

Down

1 Unsophisticated Foreign Secretary's play on words (8)
2 Responsible person's occupation out East (5)
3 Stole last of meat from galley, perhaps (3)
5 Supervise deliveries, taking escort (7)
6 Behave ostentatiously, having just left the board? (4,1,6)
7 Coinage in Limoges – and no mistake (9)
8 Rabbit on part of ferry at terminal (6)
9 Not solidly grounded, a month before retiring (6)
13 Very cheap aid organised by fellows snatching a nap (1,4,1,5)
16 Accommodating type shot outside tower (9)
18 Possible customer's outlook (8)
20 Row over unacceptable rugby formation (4-3)
21 One of a thousand in the fillies' race? (6)
22 Free deserter arrested by private soldiers (6)
25 Bondsman ultimately slain in overthrow of republic (5)
28 Old man associated with southern resort (3)

© *The Times* 2005

Puzzle 11

Peter Chamberlain
Scotland on Sunday Late 2003

Across

1 End of the act (9)
10 Apologist to lean over person studying fossils (15)
11 No end of good fortune concerning money (5)
12 Master of ceremonies' letters written out in full (5)
13 Father during the month shortly found some glossy black lacquer (5)
15 Succeeded with toil and difficulty although had worn badly (4-3)
16 Properly in accordance with the true facts (7)
17 Tree, which said shaky lime I left? (4-3)
19 Owl with not entirely nice plague! (7)
21 Belonging to the second person of old, say, before Sunday (5)
22 Canines, they can be false (5)
24 Was destined to have been entertained at a feast as reported (5)
25 Trivial insolence, quaint variety (15)
26 Frank runs before nine to lady on board (9)

Down

2 Note if vicar be around (5)
3 One who used to carry the torch might be seen between programmes (7)
4 Worst at relocating hotel (3-4)
5 Circular region of bracing air (5)
6 Excess wasted horrendously to start with (6)
7 Current obstacle? (8,5)
8 Remain and check number with beer-mug in the country (13)
9 Way with fish at end of day is unfeeling (6)
13 Cheerful Joyce will shortly enter (5)
14 Nudist did not stop disturbing nest (5)
17 Fashionable comic success (4-2)
18 Dramatist found swirling oil in lake (7)
19 Block nickname, not so (7)
20 All-round demonstration of affection (6)
23 Deer has one tongue (5)
24 Mushrooms give pleasure to soldier (5)

© Peter Chamberlain 2003

Puzzle 12

'Contract' by Charybdis
Sunday Telegraph 6 March 2001

Twelve participants begin by *filling in a formal paper* (11 Across, three words). The crucial thematic contract spelt out by squares a to g, plus all grid entries passing through these same seven squares (except for 38 Across) illustrate a thematic progression, the final stages of which have been run together, for convenience, forming a non-word. The progression, when reordered, matches the composite clue: *Union contract can aim to voice one point by wearing away big man, one seeking a good deal.* Upon completion, 11 Across may be reallocated (and the contract destroyed) by 38 Across (three words). Each clue contains a letter which must be eliminated. They spell out a task to be completed consistently with the final stage of the progression. (If stuck, a pub quiz team or internet search should help.)

Across

1 Taking in some upset, spews, trembling – there's a nervous link (7)
6 Hero errs and drinks (6)
12 Engaged in a bit of corruption (4, two words)
13 They row a little more than Steven (5)
14 Mountain town where many used to weed after repeated dead-heading (4)
15 Heading off to toil at queen's address? (4)
22 Locally common plant I applied to the skin right away (7)
23 Bart takes a turn as storyteller (4)
25 Silly lass ploughing a PhD in English (7)
26 Hopes to dry out here, like in part of the bible (4)
27 Give a right foul tie to Len (7)
28 Sort of nasty imp – it inflamed fear (10)
33 Best before? (4)
35 Rood in the nave is cut with Latin inscription (4)
36 Some stars in the sky? No. Black over in Paris (5)
37 Made enquiries on phone for a Manx tiger (4)
39 Very little support in outskirts of Surrey (6)
40 Set to take assemblies on reflection and values (7)

Down

1 Should we suspend merger initially floated? (4)
2 Old copper deposited in a mixture of briniest salts (8)
3 Tracey accepted Thomas (4)
4 Surrounded by Scottish gnats, I cut (4)
5 For example, G&S role (4)
8 Rodeo excited man of action (4)
10 Southern Spain, a rocky shore, heading for sunny Tangiers (9)
13 Inspectors cut up rough mainly (by no means entirely) to upset sir (11)
17 Managers may be found in this firm (6)
19 Sets popular song that's sung (6)
29 Almost entirely fuse five vertebrae at the bottom – it's a sacrum (5)
30 Slimy incline (4)
32 Ring to get served (starters only) (4)
33 Composer's trained ear? No (4)
34 Big heads, heads of real giants, exceptionally large (4)

© Telegraph group 2001

Puzzle 13

CJM
The Herald (Glasgow) 16 February 2006

Across

1 Firm lawyer reached finale (4)
4 Cold? Puts on lights and hugs (6)
9 Are you drunk? (6,8)
11 Divert with team song (9)
12 Fifty-six? Old? Answer played on a fiddle ... (5)
13 ... arms spread – am I OK? Bassoonist begins to writhe (6)
15 Almost semi–retired and in the money? It's a dream (8)
17 Saw maps or extremely Irish plan (8)
18 Had verbose discussion in the qualifier (6)
21 Nicks rusty tools (5)
22 Sick en route – bring in the big guns (9)
24 Reform: gift? He'd initially expected to scrap for it (7,7)
25 Edwardian canes fashioned at this meeting? (6)
26 Refurbished Tech was up to scratch (4)

Down

2 Done time, that's plain (5)
3 Living uninvited in Sinatra's quatrains (6)
4 Game assessors (8)
5 Initiated and trod the boards, accepting one duty (9)
6 Expressions, or other parts of speech, are set in stone (14)
7 Secretary includes alms distribution: that's clear, naturally (6)
8 Is it taught at catering college? (8,6)
10 Metallic fabric without substance (4)
14 American who composed notes, or took them (9)
16 Look into flight dish (8)
17 Friend doesn't see launch of gathering (4)
19 They're found on Glasgow road, we're told (6)
20 Flits irrationally to English block (6)
23 Diary of guiding principles (5)

© *The Herald* 2006

Puzzle 14

Codex
Oxford Times

Across

1 You'll need one if tripe's to be dished up! (8)
5 One will give you two (6)
10 Without hesitation he'll knock a jar back (5)
11 I've a skill that's plied with ear bad? Right (3-6)
12 Secluded place – none there, we hear (7)
13 Tax I'm able to pay here? Peter's pence, no doubt (7)
14 Cut to its shortest, skirt's semi naughty (8)
16 Flower in her dress (5)
19 'Where your treasure is, there will your heart be also' (5)
21 Henchard's missus (8)
24 Agreed to take part in recital (Lieder) (7)
26 Rope specialist – unemployed since 1965 (7)
27 You'll find me rail so about right/wrong (9)
28 What you'd have if you weren't here (5)
29 Naughtily it 'ud show in any one peeling (6)
30 Not an affliction for invertebrates (8)

Down

1 Feature of corybantic sportiveness (6)
2 Dear me! (9)
3 Begin, for example (7)
4 Is granted to a tenant – like Iona is (5)
6 He'll give you a leg up Abraham H-height (7)
7 'Concerning Hindu philosophy' (Entry in definitive dictionary) (5)
8 More rum required (8)
9 Top people get up to very shady dealings (8)
15 I'm unassuming? I'm not! (8)
17 Can I start to sleep? No, I'm tossing and turning (9)
18 Flying Caledonian (8)
20 Could be the third one of pop's litter (7)
22 Spread fire, perhaps? (7)
23 'Silly swine' makes a non-U description of such a person (6)
25 It crops up in Richard I – ruler of ghastly quality (5)
26 Initially heard upon record running achievement, perhaps (5)

© *Colin Dexter*

Puzzle 15

Crispa
The Guardian 6 December 2004

After more than fifty years compiling for the *Manchester Guardian* and *The Guardian*, this was Crispa's last puzzle.

Across

7 A lot rent accommodation, all for freedom (8)
9 The man with a dog to collect (4,2)
10 Speak irritably, or quietly answer back (4)
11 Fruit for an old miner's daughter (10)
12 From September, berries form the main food of a North African (6)
14 Drinking song sung at Christmas all round America (8)
15 Radiant bishop in support (6)
17 A gorge subject to pollution (6)
20 Dealer taking a certain measure about a chest (8)
22 Sort of old pottery the French mix together (6)
23 The gardener's joy makes for an easy life (3,2,5)
24 Against a transport system change (4)
25 Panic, being about a hundred short (6)
26 Ought with little hesitation to assume responsibility (8)

Down

1 Eminent lady writing tot a letter (8)
2 The wild pear harvest (4)
3 Dressing right as the cup holder (6)
4 Source of sandalwood? (8)
5 Public schoolboy getting shut in a car by mistake (10)
6 The chaperone expected a girl to rise (6)
8 Ditch such a coat (6)
13 A drab block specially built for teachers' use (10)
16 Some soldiers wheeled around and came back (8)
18 This is sure to have an inflationary effect! (8)
19 Forces relax in quarters (6)
21 Putting a note in the pool would be fine (6)
22 Many a Northerner exhibits charm (6)
24 A hollow farewell! (4)

© *Ruth Crisp* 2004

Puzzle 16

Dac
The Independent 10 February 2005

Across

1 Nuts for a bird (6)
4 Certainly not enjoying a night out (6)
9 Fellow discovered form of nuclear energy (8)
10 Foreign cheeses said to give you mild wind (6)
12 Be determined to reject all time-servers? (4,2,9)
13 Do away with military report (8)
14 Journalist of the Year, perhaps, was a heavy drinker (5)
16 Father, say, is engaged in risky activity? (5)
18 Old composer going round ten universities (8)
20 It's the end for this sort of clue! (11,4)
23 Stabbed gruesome fiend with tip of dirk (6)
24 Talk to new teacher, at first (6,2)
25 Foreign language buff (6)
26 Source of sherry endlessly offered to my lad (6)

Down

1 Reject fish, laughing quietly (9)
2 How anti-pollution campaigners aim to make big profit? (5,2)
3 Kind of therapy almost everyone needed after hostile take-over (12)
5 Look left and see transport terminal (7)
6 Woman featured in Cheshire newspaper (5)
7 Supposed visitor should be given a hearing (7)
8 Allotment scheme (4)
11 Ill-fated soldiers ordered to carry equipment after daybreak (5,7)
15 Appearing on high structure topless servant makes quite a display (9)
16 Be upset to finish school (5,2)
17 Ill-starred merchants (7)
19 Wretched soldier picked up old gold coin (7)
21 Hot food one leaves to cool (5)
22 Generous daughter supporting family (4)

Puzzle 17

Roy Dean (Diplodocus)
The Times 6 December 2004

Across

1 Mineral stored in hospital cabinet (4)
4 Slandered about one's being crooked (10)
9 He's surly about black slime in egg (10)
10 Ruler rejecting poet's work (4)
11 With 2000 in foreign currency, Kelvin brought back liqueur (6)
12 Attempt to imprison one chief in ruling three (8)
14 Area once occupied by Crusaders (4)
15 A theatrical change of heart? (10)
17 Not in office, being slightly crazy (3,2,5)
20 Married help? Possibly (4)
21 Itching to see Indian city with unlimited enchantment (8)
23 One wrong about Harry's immaturity (6)
24 Technical points genius may introduce (4)
25 Bridge: you can change trains on it (10)
26 Fairly well, after daily visit? (3,2,5)
27 Herb's daughter was remorseful (4)

Down

2 A copper's flat used for medical treatment (11)
3 MP tucked into pet food (9)
4 One close to tyre being finally changed in estuary area (7)
5 Nothing to be gained by president chasing nice girl (5,5,5)
6 Pulse beating silently when cut short (7)
7 Customary number of men in college to start with (5)
8 American bowler seen in China (5)
13 Passing passion is extremely close (4,2,5)
16 One putting on sheets turns over degenerate beast (9)
18 Settled down and became cheerful (7)
19 Make pen sharper to achieve candour (7)
21 Tall tower's reported as 'stack' (5)
22 Proper happiness doesn't need clairvoyant around (5)

© The Times 2004

Puzzle 18

'Generalist' by Didymus

This puzzle was first published in the March 2005 issue of Prospect magazine:
www.prospect-magazine.co.uk

Across

1 Milton's pamphlet on the freedom of the press, written in 1644 (12)

7 Extreme right-wing Italians in the 1930s (8)

12 Snorri Sturluson's sixteen sagas on the lives of the early kings of Norway (12)

13 Resorted to mending? (8)

15 The rootlike stalk of a hydrozoan colony (9)

16 Solid figures whose faces are six equilateral triangles (11)

17 A doctor in *Gil Blas* whose sole remedies are bleeding and drinking hot water (8)

18 An independent state in the Leeward Islands, capital Basseterre (2,5-5)

20 Australian captain who scored the most runs in Test cricket (5,6)

21 In India, a place of retreat for a religious community (6)

25 A fungus causing a disease affecting plants of the carnation and pink family (10)

26 A green or yellow liqueur made from herbs and flowers (10)

29 A ragout of game stewed in a rich brown sauce (6)

31 1925 treaties acknowledging European frontiers, subsequently violated by Germany in 1936 (7,4)

35 A *Python* member who went from *Pole to Pole* (7,5)

36 A steeply dipping seam of fossil fuel (4,4)

38 Having beautiful buttocks (11)

39 Ornamental plant with tubular flowers that are fragrant at night (9)

40 An Australian species of acacia (8)

41 To quarrel disgracefully or to wrangle (12)

42 Distinct varieties of a plant occupying a particular habitat (8)

43 Taciturn US actor who was the first to refuse an Oscar (6,1,5)

Down

1 A brief pithy saying (8)

2 Aldine versions of Greek and Latin classics, published in Venice in 1490 (8)

3 A dialogue between a knight and a shepherdess (11)

4 Cockney gossips created by Elsie and Doris Walters (4,3,5)

5 An icicle or edible *Laminaria* (6)

6 Embellished vocal passages, including trills and runs (10)

8 Sour bitterness (8)

9 'Do you believe in fairies? If you believe, ... your ....!' (J. M. Barrie) (4,5)

10 Family of violin-makers from Cremona (12)

11 St Martin's late spell of fine weather (6,6)

14 Handy communication from a port in Alabama? (6,5)

19 They're obsessed with cleanliness (11)

22 Symphonic poem by Saint-Saëns, based on a poem by Henri Cazalis (5,7)

23 Cuban-born novelist who won the Premio Feltrinelli award in 1973 (5,7)

24 A very thin silk fabric (5,2,5)

27 Micro-organisms found in lice causing typhus in humans, after biting (11)

28 BBC1 news magazine, broadcast for 3,131 2 Down from 1969 until 1983 (10)

30 Utopia, Erewhon, Narnia, and Wonderland are such (9)

32 A large two-edged broadsword of the Scottish Highlanders (8)

33 A Roman tip (8)

34 Ptolemy's astronomical treatise (8)

37 The upas-tree or its poisonous latex (6)

© *Tom Johnson / Prospect magazine* 2005

Puzzle 19

'Fish Restaurant' by Dumpynose
The Spectator 26 June 2004

Just as HALFPENNY combines with CRONE to suggest MAGWITCH, so unclued across lights combine with down ones to suggest five names from another Dickens novel. Unclued lights include six varieties of fish. Twelve clues contain a definition (one or two words) and a concealed letter mixture of the answer; remaining clues are normal. Ignore one accent.

Across

12 Choice crappie eaten with peppers (10)
14 Fist to clasp and twist object in (7)
15 Violet and Earl sat sadly through Edmund's funeral (10)
16 Emptying certain pottery's also a priority (7)
22 Endless abuse with fashionable hormone (7)
23 Greenling catching gourmet's eagle eye (4)
24 Rex rumpled denims in jogs (7)
26 Aquarian vaults other bass die for (7)
30 Mega-meal nearly beginning to test plates (4)
31 Sing about Tosca at neglected theatre (7, two words)
34 Network with British LSE founder (4)
36 Bilge in dock (7)
38 For potential taxidermic gade, licensees like formalin (10)
39 Metal drum thrice I play (7)
41 Fresh cero sent from peninsula (10)
42 Island festival, Chinese introduced (6)
43 Roast doree, Beeton defended (8)

Down

2 Card game quite fuddled eminent scientists (8, hyphenated)
3 Stripped impious criminal betrays narcotic (5)
4 Pricey lant, praised abundantly (7)
5 Cultist at no time holds joker (7, two words)
6 Epicures swallow sea-born tai meunière (6)
7 Prisoner, unescorted, heartlessly breaks free (6)
8 Opinion of karate teacher I ignored (5)
9 Urbanest beluga as chef hits Herculean target (13, two words)
10 Multi-faith buff chewing at Holostei painlessly (13)
11 Detachment of Sloanes go to town (9)
19 Supernal dab any mega-star would eat (9)
21 Dad tamed a cross antelope (5)
25 Saw-edged spades, Queen esteemed (8)
29 Wonder about fortune? Singular poet's is amazing (7)
32 Ambrosian dace mesmerises London borough (6)
33 Algarroba in place close to chestnut (6)
37 College expelled fight gang member (5)

© *Christopher Brougham 2004*

Puzzle 20

'Crying Havoc' by Enigmatist
www.enigmatist.com 2001

Clues are numbered in alphabetical order of their solutions. This order includes the six *entries* to 2 23, 6, 9, 17, 18, and 19 (not their normally-clued *answers*, because their covers have been blown). Of the remaining (cryptic indication only) thematic answers, 12 and 14 5 lie (as they ended up) horizontally in the grid, completing the set of 25's 20 4. The shaded squares indicate the predictable position in the grid (also appearing cryptically in one of the normal clues) where 10 is stuck with 28. Remaining clues are normal. All solutions are to be entered in the grid jigsaw-wise, wherever they will go.

2 23 Live outside the Capital? Two thirds fail (she will, shortly!) in Harlow (6,9)

6 DT feature writer described by great footballer with acidity: 'a soldier' (4,8)

9 #a) fried potato; #b) worn out (4,5)

17 Gold coin (old) bearing 'p' is covering for something juicy (6,4)

18 Trace may have given young person this untidy (reputable) bed back, say (4,5,5)

19 *I've got my oats in a sausage skin:* Successful record awfully dud in flight (5,7)

12 Pre-1150 taxi obtained during Whit (3,5)

14 5 At Riviera location, ridiculed example of Cubism? (4,3,5)

25 Social worker in love with a sailor (9)

20 See again in Paris, Hampshire, and Kent? Runs on board (9)

4 Perform *The Mikado*? (4)

10 *Feste & Co*, setter, ... (4,1,2)

28 ...solvers (4,3) jesters...

1 Soon we might know who wrote this? (4)

3 Caught trapped, lady's broken foot (6)

7 Language kept by herself (4)

8 Ascetic's nature out of clubs (6)

11 She, two women in one, was asked to give 5 hope (6)

13 Dance with *Cambridge Platonists, PLC*? (7)

15 Witchdoctor batting for both sides in the Sultanate (3-3)

16 Possibly radial, but not true of the Rustler's Ring (6)

21 Finally take in clapped-out horse for this? (2-4)

22 Exercises dropping in to look for swimmer (3,5)

24 Works over the standard reproduction? Only a little here (7)

26 Paradoxically, he can't die without love: he believes evil must exist (10)

27 All that is in use is useless: churchman backed into it (8)

© *John Henderson* 2001

Puzzle 21

'Going for Gold' by Fawley
Sunday Telegraph

Twelve of the better-established representatives in a long-running series of events are 'Going for Gold'. Each could combine with one of the unclued lights as the first element in a two-word unit of vocabulary, phrase, or saying. Omitted clue-numbers should be entered in their appropriate positions. The latest editions of *Chambers* and *Brewer's* are recommended, except for a singer of rhyming slang.

Across

4 Take a look around, right away! (4)
9 Adequate support for writing work on medication (8)
16 A few feathers flying when lecturer enters hall? (5)
19 Be inclined to kick back (4)
23 Yearn for old poet's work in Latin and English (4)
24 The woman personally sent back uncooked meat without hesitation (7)
26 They're big wheels in the plant (9)
28 Gold and black ensemble for the ball (3)
29 Australian runner's rival late getting away (3)
31 Interact suspiciously with European heretic (9)
34 Severely criticize expert about universal cure (7)
36 King of Norway backed golfer Germany rejected (4)
37 Being cunning, become bent! (4)
41 Love risqué type of expression (5)
42 Hard cop they retrained for security in Scottish court? (8)
43 Too dark to see old toy daughter's dropped (4)

Down

6 A recipe involved in remedy for poison (6)
8 Sexologist from island in New York ... (5)
9 ... traced odd characters in Edinburgh, as well (3)
11 Element of literacy – cliché? Not occurring regularly! (7)
13 Barred old character – he'd got drunk! (3)
14 Quietly coming upon exotic arboreal creature (9, two words)
17 Yob's first urge – to become a burglar (4)
18 Restaged Theban play at last, in biblical location (7)
21 Dash to collar Dickens character – a dip of sorts (9, hyphenated)
22 Study Ian's broadcast about monster's habitat (7)
27 VIP from Spain in terrible danger (7)
32 Engineer in pain, shivering in a freezing block (6, two words)
33 Sea-bird depicted in crochet-work (4)
35 First-rate vehicle contained minor bugs (5)
38 Band rejects piano for old-fashioned rowdy sound (3)
39 It's supposed to lift an elephant – blimey! It's going up! (3)

© Telegraph group

Puzzle 22

'Bare Bones' by Chris Feetenby (Corylus)
Mail on Sunday 22 January 2006

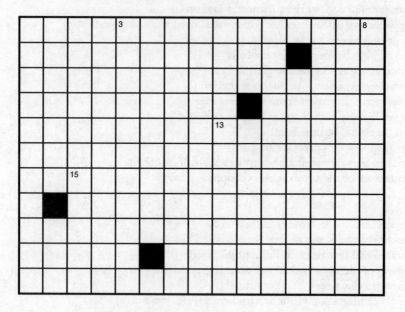

Across

1 Petrol suppliers getting people into Paddington etc. (two words)
9 Coming from home, is sensible to get some fine China
10 We hear man's to fight where letters go
11 Sentimental language is not quite advantageous
12 Senior woman performed to secure Japanese money
13 Lightly browned having gone off due East
14 Taking a chance, not good, in description of gait?
16 A name could be given to one cold with blood disorder
19 And not rejecting this man
20 Left one with company in colonnade
21 One attempting to take a millimetre off with this?
22 Study office worker misusing a Roneo with us at the same time

Down

1 Having cultivated land not right to be well-known
2 Make bet about it being non-clerical body
3 Drunken inn visit, see, could show one's not considerate
4 It seeks to enliven red set (two words)
5 A most unusual hat Ern sported? Could be (two words)
6 Affliction or a toil possibly borne by a tribune for the most part
7 Old card game bachelor in Rome played
8 Found gender from chromosome in offspring
14 Like endless choice of jelly
15 Poet next to 19 Across
17 Latin American dance giving mother body odour
18 Old king having no power in Mediterranean island

© *Mail on Sunday* 2006

Puzzle 23

Brian Greer (Virgilius)
The Times

Across

1 Reserve with claim to get on in the second half? (10)
6 Old piano accompanying you and me for musical piece (4)
9 Standard procedures getting girl confused about zero in complicated maths (10)
10 Just one part of me wanted extra (4)
12 Act of opposition – avenge it with veto, possibly (8,4)
15 Some Asians prepare them to go (6,9)
19 Security precaution involving a certain treatment for animals? (8,7)
24 Person who adds to spice of holiday time (6,6)
28 Asset – one of four seen in this puzzle ... (4)
29 ... and negative indications central to it (5,5)
30 Reduced in sales, sometimes (4)
31 Doctor X settles up for delivery in bulk at hospital? (10)

Down

1 Among Irish, a writer (4)
2 Mischievous spirit could be good in youth (4)
3 Boy cutting girl's herbaceous plant (7)
4 US president heading the wrong way – time to withdraw (7)
5 Irishman's identifying himself with grand contrivance (7)
7 Current in river, or is it still? (5)
8 Part of act viewed in audition (5)
11 Cheese with strong Greek character (4)
13 Move with difficulty, though not stiff (4)
14 Woodworking tool, say, for what joiner does (4)
16 Top honour for wartime hero (3)
17 One is associated with x (4)
18 To decline drug is prudent (4)
20 Low digits, normally five and five (4)
21 What's left of harvest I get inside (7)
22 Bridge ace in six diamonds usually cashes trumps initially (7)
23 Gets equipped, also, with a sort of 28 (5,2)
24 Animal swallows soft part of flower (5)
25 Assaults in shopping areas reported (5)
26 Feverish complaint from a guest? No way! (4)
27 Islands in part of Thames (4)

© The Times

Puzzle 24

Barbara Hall
Sunday Times

Across

1 Forcibly restrain two thousand disrupting traffic (8)
5 Out at elbow (6)
9 Kind of key that might be hidden in the cupboard (8)
10 Put on by one in a bustle? (6)
12 Flowery name for beef sauce? (5)
13 Europeans filter back into health resorts (9)
14 Irate lunatic oddly incoherent (12)
18 No end to it – blame inner turmoil! (12)
21 Seen to crumple and smell, when growing old (9)
23 Fury coming to a head in Scotland (5)
24 Hedges woman's planted around a dam (6)
25 Sinks full of coal? (8)
26 Use curtains in attempt to be fashionable (6)
27 Set off, have a row – then separate (8)

Down

1 Star seen in beaver fur (6)
2 Mule is chomping our dish (6)
3 One lifting the lid will have a big surprise! (3,6)
4 Stubborn, but has to get over reading difficulty (5-7)
6 Knife skill demonstrated by the chef, say? (5)
7 Many too wary to travel by fast route (8)
8 Does Bess panic, with bee in her bonnet? (8)
11 I can collapse after first payment – a levy reportedly prompting these reactions (5,7)
15 In this lake, bobbing around, the French trawl with us (9)
16 Hide from girl – having put letters in wrong order (8)
17 With this, sexton smashed oriental object buried inside? (5,3)
19 Clay duck turned up on tree, up north (6)
20 Hits out at live character thought dead by Pyramus (6)
22 The going rate for an amphetamine (5)

© *Sunday Times*

Puzzle 25

'Beelzebub' by Paul Henderson (Phi)
Independent on Sunday 22 January 2006

Across

1 Cheered charioteer, highly-regarded, upon comeback (7)
6 Mumbai drink one's given to girl (5)
10 Blasts eliminating silence? Shells (6)
12 One tucking into grandma's bread (4)
13 Ancient temple fragment, wide, afflicted, weak entirely (11, two words)
14 Burn found to include trace of mercury (7)
15 Forester in Minnesota, when wild, might be found amongst them (12)
16 Tailors' skill with men displayed on board (7)
20 Constituent of element I excavate – nothing in that (7)
21 Disgusting item criers never broadcast before end of harangue (12)
23 Child, small object, falling over, with lazy person neglecting one (7)
25 Mere leading astray? (11)
26 Fine Romans will include *me*? (4)
27 Catches – and where one catches it in seconds, repeatedly (6)
28 Army regulations covering criminal behaviour (5)
29 US city almost superfluous, a thing without life (7)

Down

1 Question over fellows in Scots pub (5)
2 Uranium row elevated sodium deposit (4)
3 Becomes less severe with reserve shown about period of fasting (7)
4 Vaguely rational set includes English philosopher (12)
5 US soldier turning up in uniform to make excursion (7)
6 Notes we run part of London in deal (12, two words)
7 Mineral: a mineral primarily swallowed by fish, given by one account (11, two words)
8 Dye seller has to change (6)
9 Enrage thus (7)
11 Junior priests ensuring good behaviour amongst kids (11, two words)
16 Outdated verse form fools upheld in the main (7)
17 Split, bleeding, but well supplied with water (7)
18 Ship's pennant not initially ragged (7)
19 Nothing to be seen in more depraved fiddler (6)
22 Artist's rigorous in cyclic form (5)
24 One set of tools brought up for greenstone ornament (4)

Puzzle 26

'Theme and Variations' by Jago
The Listener 15 January 1987

'Theme and Variations' is an innocent enough title for a puzzle, where you have to enter the answers in the manner prescribed by the unclued theme-word. Seven of the remaining unclued entries form *one* complete variation on the theme and the eighth defines the group of seven. (Incidentally, you should bear in mind how to fill space most appropriately.) Ignore punctuation.

Horizontals

12 Second-hand, nameless fish (4)
13 Old singer's occupation (6)
14 Delay going back to a festive gathering (4)
15 Trip up SRN, rather clumsily (5)
16 10^{12}, to such a degree, is *some* growth! (8)
17 Get news of second English Duke, taken off to a funeral, as it were (7)
18 Bore, for example, with hesitant interjection (4)
19 In real emergencies, first of all, there comes keen resentment (3)
20 Small monkey appearing in fez at intervals (4)
22 Himalayan beast Henry put into the zoo – being heartless (3)
23 Senior Gentleman: egghead? (4)
24 A bodyguard in Rome, getting a porter in a muddle (10)
26 Brushwood to be cut down – by this old woman? (3)
27 Elaborate flowerbed, often seen in wood (4)
28 Take one's time to score (3)
29 Swallow, dead on course (5)
32 Sounds like a sort of prepared fish, for example; cold (5)
33 Spiritual stronghold (5)
34 Old saying gives colour to English (4)
35 Observed a brood of pheasants, deserted (4)
37 A short time in that place where dramatic events happen (7)
38 Battered old casks for poor spirits (8)

Verticals

1 Part of a dagger, or heavy knife (2)
2 One of the team making progress; he should be in charge at HQ (10)
3 An enemy, clearly audible, voicing contempt (3)
4 Find us by the river, taking a great interest (5)
5 An incomplete doctrine, for one's pains (4)
6 Tut! For ties, you should arrange for these haberdashers (10)
7 That woman comes in every other day (3)
8 Make a speech of zero value (5)
9 Father's note, giving a statement of the time (4)
10 Look after such a flighty old girl with love, young man! (6)
11 First of all, give everyone legal maturity (3)
21 One of the three boatmen gets changed, head to toe, in the field of stubble (6)
23 Draw out newspaperman with a point or two (6)
25 The chief apartments of patriarchs (5)
30 Either hinder or help to rise (4)
31 Scottish herald seen in French city, taken short (4)
36 Gambling game which may be Old English, in hindsight (2)

© *Jim Coulson/The Listener 1987*

Puzzle 27

'Playfour' by Kea
Tough Crosswords February 2002

All clues are normal. From each entry in the central two rows and columns a letter must be removed wherever it occurs, and solvers must work out where the entry goes. Answers in rows and columns 5–6 and 9–10 are entered in Playfair code, with each pair of adjacent rows or columns using a different one of four connected key phrases. Another such phrase should be completed in the grid.

P	L	A	Y	F
O	U	R	B	C
D	E	G	H	I
K	M	N	Q	S
T	V	W	X	Z

In a Playfair code, a key word or phrase in which no letter recurs is written in a 5x5 square, followed by the rest of the alphabet in order, with I standing for I and J. To encode a word, e.g. REQUOTED, split it into pairs of letters and encode each pair as follows. If a pair forms the corners of a rectangle in the code square, take the opposite corners, in the same row order; thus RE codes to UG and QU to MB. If the pair are in the same row or column, take the neighbours to the right/below, cycling around to the start of the row/column if necessary; thus OT codes to DP and ED to GE. Reassembling the encoded pairs gives UGMBDPGE.

Central

Acme's reverse gives tense time during prosperity (6)

Bids show up whole battle (7)

Concerned with rumpled sheet that's left one in a rage (7)

Dishonest about one's dubious ends (5)

Elevation of plan overlooking central heating escapes (6)

Flipping tub containing margarine makes you jump (7)

Greatly opposed to old pounds (4)

Hard liquor reserves – they contribute to vision (6)

Ireland's sages once found over among the marsh-mallows (7)

Just the cases for parliamentary agent, a flier from Prestwick (4)

Across

1 Tunnel occupied with caution (6)

6 Rad's misguided crusade (7)

12 Tool for lifting meat left in iron, thus keeping hands unhurt (9)

13 Unpopular person won trick (4)

14 Neck pieces, specifically frills (7)

15 Cup-holder plays in Italy almost a year (7)

18 Teletubby relaxed, knocking out a verse (5)

20 Mental cases set on floors (6)

21 Solicitor-General carries drink back and forth, pulling with a line (8)

22 I'll turn in current Kea-ish puzzling (6)

23 Newspaper report gives away nothing indeed (6)

27 Losing partner upset legitimate composer (6)

29 Antelope lair hides almost nothing (6)

31 Starter from Oriental recipe with American caper dressing: I had sea slug (8)

32 Provincial fighters help us out of Germany (6)

33 Finally seeing heart of Talisker, a Scottish sight (5)

36 Annoyed after deductions were advanced (7)

37 Dab hand's first in prize-money with quick fix (7)

38 Old body marking that shows prestige when aboard ship (4)

39 Monarch swallows new fruit, mostly taking small bites (9)

40 Least aware of reduced size in portion (7)

41 Windy month with temperature dropping is marked by vessels (6)

Down

2 Mayor of Madrid one called corrupt (7)

3 Called up some abbreviated word of action (4)

4 No boarder beat up anybody without reason, ultimately (6)

5 Shakespeare's twisted and trod, bringing English almost to the fore (6)

7 Egyptian party has a following in Dominica (4)

8 Football manoeuvre was successful, as well you can hear (6)

9 Cap extensions arising from Scottish drinks (8)

10 Keep up most of the rising beer (7)

11 Animal shelter hero seizes monkey for branding (11)

16 We live together a little in county Hampshire (11)

17 Have to become a worker, possibly leading a dull life (8)

19 Very large whisky I can't put down (8)

24 Knife landed up in fight (8)

25 Scottish farm grass inhaled by doddery dons (7)

26 Words that are versatile and crudely forced on us (7)

28 Flay oneself, suffering but suppressing cry of pain (6)

29 Obsequious, cold and without refinement (6)

30 Exercising crossword setter weighed heavily for Shakespeare (6)

34 African tribesman's cutter going north, avoiding navy (4)

35 State of health is off-colour at the outset (4)

© *Estate of Michael Rich* 2002

Puzzle 28

Logodaedalus
The Guardian 7 March 2005

Across

7 Very large woman's jacket of a kind (8)

9 'About a Boy' ought to be kept in mind (6)

10 Friend having married, sure sign of a winner (4)

11 Loaf getting flatter, not for formal dinner (6,4)

12 Like Harlequin, pray when in the sea (6)

14 Plant expert born near station curiously (8)

15 Play with pots and kettles to repair (6)

17 I'm wearing nothing, having an affair (2,4)

20 Left to keep rent when let out of the nick (8)

22 A poet's dream increased by half a tick (6)

23 Downhearted little brother kept away (7-3)

24 To chat about a Forsyte novel, say (4)

25 They say the bird's a shade of blue (6)

26 Yet good man backed these points of view (8)

Down

1 Game bird is hot when swallowed by a hick (8)

2 Lifting short raincoats is a crafty trick (4)

3 Searched for 'The King and I' and then took flight (6)

4 This cow in marshy land preserves the right (8)

5 Moving round Spain with gusto, feeling faint (7,3)

6 Small horses take one sip without restraint (6)

8 Food's past, showing a wash is needed (6)

13 White-skinned, red-mottled, he at last succeeded (4,6)

16 Let years unhappy bring to mind a blow (8)

18 Extend the angle badly formed with toe (8)

19 Rose, half-cut, fills opening, being smart (6)

21 Nice little job for student who can't start (6)

22 I can't believe it when my bottom shows! (2,4)

24 Who helps make sausages? This person knows (4)

© D. G. Putnam 2005

Puzzle 29

'19 Across 54 Across' by Machiavelli
The Times Listener series 27 January 2001

Twenty-six entries are words formed by removing both the second and penultimate letters from a longer word. Each letter of the alphabet has been removed once from each position. Clues to these entries contain a one-word definition of the entry to be made at that number (to which the figure in brackets refers), but belong as a whole to the longer word used to form a thematic word elsewhere. Remaining clues and entries are normal. All words can be justified by *Chambers* (1998 edition).

Across

1 Day-scholar is wrong – enter 'X' (3,2)
7 Strong desires suppressed by Bahamas citizen (7)
12 Responsibility assigned to under-secretary (4)
13 Sort of IOU all right for some (3)
14 Show proof of French outing (6)
16 Band's commitment to a dance (4)
18 With no superior room left (4)
19 *Title* (12)
21 What lecturers do before leaving college (4)

24 Second one of five children having crossed eyes (4)
25 More Scots in West (3)
27 Marsh subject to savage criticism in speech (4)
28 An inamorata is ardent (4)
29 Cloak made of raw silk repelled water (4)
30 Runs away from sinister parcel (3)
32 Ornaments – knots, big – something added to letters (3)
33 Initial intelligence that can have you feeling uneasy (3)
36 Famous citizen – height six cubits (5)
37 Nigeria supports Zambian currency and South Africa Angolan currency (5)
39 In short, what company could be in Cincinnati (3)
40 Cover up accident (3)
41 Elfin child – well-informed about it being missing (3)
43 Omitting operation, let burn during cooking – a mistake (4)
44 Last guy to support (4)
47 Tapir has not advanced (4)
49 Parts of speech possibly to be featured in commercials (3)
50 Told stories about Clootie (4)
52 Light cut into creature with wings (4)
54 *Title* (12)
58 Housewife in van reversed (4)
59 Criticism New York PR man's voiced (4)
61 Simple sailors leave Farndale in disarray (6)
62 Medal in the form of a cross (3)
63 In the early days, you prosper (4)
64 Gnarled king unlucky, losing head after revolution (7)
65 I float around as lost property (5)

Down
1 Ragged tears do get mended (7)
2 Nails not correctly estimated – one third missing (6)
3 Frenchman consigned to gallows ends up dead (4)
4 Peg – that was a strong drink (3)
5 Adjutants put ideas into action (4)
6 African doctor has one of the cars covered by motoring organisation's 'No good' (5)

7 Plenty of support for exchanging yen invested for gemstone (3)
8 Ferry boat from Dover or Ostend (4)
9 Officer capturing OAP on the loose (12)
10 Part of crust is over a pound (4)
11 Henry absorbed in interminable TV series – he has a chair (5)
15 Suffering colic, Pooh-Bah is a man frightened by crowds (12)
17 Obsolete coin, one on which mint's given up (4)
20 Take part in animated game (3)
22 Marks card, by the sound of it (4)
23 To take effect unless something happens and I slip up (4)
25 Power? The French produce plenty (4)
26 Playful and variant animal I have to follow (3)
28 Insect's bristle shortened during disease (3)
31 Soda pyroxene – a measure I take round outside (4)
34 Cold force to serve in military attire (3)
35 One of the goats that have almost round heads (4)
36 Observes end of syllabary overwhelmed with honours (4)
38 Travelled for free (3)
42 Glance from Burns that's following homeless person (7)
45 About second of September, Rugby head abandoned first gathering of Old Boys (4)
46 Appearance and sound of one who's going to succeed (3)
48 Curse put on German car (6)
49 Upright creature, a knight (5)
51 Dame keeps pupil in as a punishment (5)
53 Troops run into giant ambuscade – $\frac{2}{3}$ escape (4)
55 Styles gown (4)
56 Realise about mum (4)
59 Predicts whose serf will go mad (3)
60 A month without a drop of water for plant (3)

© *The Times* 2001

Puzzle 30

'Button' by Mass
The Times Listener series 21 August 1999

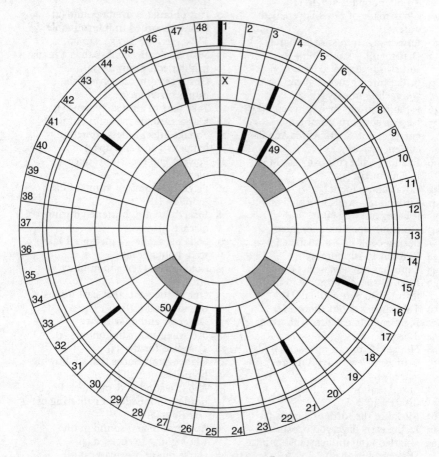

Radials: The definition in each clue gives a six-letter word from which one letter must be removed and entered in the appropriate numbered space in the outer circuit; the subsidiary wordplay leads to the answer's mutilated form. Thirty mutilations can be entered directly from the second circuit inwards. The others, deriving from the starred clues, are to be entered as jumbles.

Circuits: The outer circuit (comprising eleven words, one indefinite article and one abbreviation) refers to an expression relevant to the theme. The seven thematic entries in circuit X include two hyphenations, one a straightforward compound in the *Oxford English Dictionary*. 49 and 50, clockwise like the aforesaid circuits, are thematic variants (5,5; 5,5) in which one word is common to both.

Radials (6)

1 One's calling Mr Bond within?
2 Second layer, very small amount for Van Gogh
3 Such as spouts variable directions in Greek
4 Naval officer present for harbouring exercise
5 With onset of nosiness, peer in scrutinising way*
6 Teuton's head on sound old German coin*
7 Slow Yank's gotten into trouble*
8 Paper kite? Paper? Feasible*
9 Antique silver block, unusually long type of plate*
10 Field plan accommodating English ball game
11 Enclosure, with editor named*
12 Gifted, superlatively talented
13 Tidal flood engulfing eastern Irish lane
14 First hint of smoke, Indian signs of landslides
15 Racket? Not at all
16 Compared with second eleven?*
17 European coins, centimes, in e.g. alluvial deposits
18 Knight, against scoundrels, suffers*
19 Smears spoil manuscript*
20 Endless Welsh Sunday chimers
21 Tacks when sewing, while group spins
22 Cascading downpours: Japhet's last in ark, almost
23 Turning right, recognises northern migrating fawns
24 Spreads rare origin of radio in broadcasts
25 Daughter with oath rejected besotted lover
26 I struggle with leader in Derby, on the inside
27 Confused, sniffing cocaine, impregnated with pungency
28 Corroded lids of tin crates in swirling river
29 Mount tel's rough variegated surface*
30 Game, last of partridge among decaying elms*
31 Humble manners*
32 Hot wind, low during Sunday noon*
33 Tarot packs work like Wheel of Fortune?*
34 Clever commercial drivel
35 High spots in USA (except east and south)*
36 Most formal in attire as of old
37 Lightest drink imbibed by pint
38 Note flower bending over without odour
39 True hearts fit together
40 Dog lay before HM*
41 Is imbued with State standards of perfection
42 Old soldier? Thousands in France*
43 Obscure saga about Arthur's ultimate objects of quests*
44 Fijian toothache remedies – subject to anaesthetic
45 Eggs tinged with touch of neutral tones
46 Scouts leaving centre for new trails
47 Ancient book about southern summers
48 Eats courses audibly

© The Times 1999

Puzzle 31

'Wee Stinker' by John McKie (Myops)
The Herald (Glasgow) 3 April 2006

Across

1 Absurd caboc 9 live off (13)
8 Pitiless audio yarn (5)
9 Lady say cuts loaf (5)
10 Oz cat (5)
11 Bent upon thread (5)
12 Comestibles coup crans (5)
13 Tobacco snuffers (3)
15 Apple's raspberry source (5)
16 Tunis fixtures (5)
18 Marcel Marceau's tree (3)
21 Wick recorder (5)
23 A no longer pure prince (5)
24 Drives shivers away (5)
25 State Manx dialect (5)
26 Whiskey (5)
27 Mad Mungo? Nay! Mad Porter (5,5,3)

Down

1 To make safe resort – as Nice (2,4)
2 Dagger work? (13)
3 Stocking polyamide (5)
4 7 ton rides (6)
5 Rivals grasping bishop's feelings (5)
6 Dictatorship split celebrants (3,10)
7 What 23 Across may be in for a formal dress (6)
13 A heavy gas guitar (3)
14 Said to be sound of bbb or mmm (3)
17 Scourge of God (6)
19 Smoothly on to a switch (6)
20 Ashes holder's child – independent imp (6)
22 Queer game (5)
23 Continental as in hugs – advanced (5)

© *The Herald* 2006

Puzzle 32

'Royal Flush' by Merlin
The Times Listener series 26 January 2002

W3M2		G3	W2		R2	H1	Ja1		G5		S	W1
R3								H8				
	Jo		G2									
G4								Ed3				
H6				Ja2						Ed6		
	H2							Ed8	Ed2			
G1			El1		H3						Ed4	
G6						El2		H7				
R1							Ed7					Ed1
C2	A		H5			Ed5						
V							M1					
W4							C1					
			H4									

Some answers are clued normally and some using a definition and letter mixture: DLM clues contain a definition (in one or more words) of the answer and a consecutive mixture of its letters; the definition and the letter mixture do not overlap.

Each clue, read literally, alludes to a different king or queen of England from William I to Elizabeth II and their answers should be entered starting at the square thus indicated. Solvers must determine whether answers go across or down and insert the bars (which do not form a symmetrical pattern). One clue refers to no monarch, but is consistent with the theme; solvers must determine where its answer fits.

Normal clues

A little slip of a thing, I got put in Tower initially by father's brother (7)

A master on the box, head of the Commonwealth (13, two words)

A right source of gossip in me and Mrs Simpson (5)

Acquired crowns of nation only not by birth (10)

Aloof one's to evoke strong feelings when beheaded (6)

Arch enemy of Yorks cut down last of line Plantagenet (6)

Central figure with monarch and first of parliaments governing (7)

Done for by a hot object put up bottom (4)

'Hammer of the Scots' overturned mere Scots (5)

In flight used midst of greenwood in shelter (6)

Joint monarch with spouse first set up (6)

Joint monarch with spouse first set up in coup (10)

King long ago raised as German (7)

King, say, is what one associates with Bognor (5)

Last daring to get involved in battle (10)

Maybe melt gun to produce this monarch's special medal (10)

Monarch to go mad, one tormented at first, things screwed up (13)

Oh dear! Last of Stuarts obit – one's not the first person to know, that's very old (4)

One waiting to make the grade, a Catholic covertly (6)

One's come through being beset by explosive weapon (7)

Under me leader of rivals met fate in wine (6)

What's produced gloominess in me? – I lost a son at sea (13)

Would be rid o' an awkward priest (6)

DLM clues

An ingenu, me, restored briefly as another one possessed my throne (9)

As I ran nation I gave no pardon for peasants in revolt (4)

Called Rufus traditionally because of his red colouring (4)

Compiler of register of subjects who were taxed in return (7)

Favourite of East Enders when he came to see Luftwaffe's damage (4)

He made unique supplication for a horse (5)

Hearty leonine who fought in the Orient (6)

Her age struck fear into Protestants (3)

He's broken with the pope who made him England's defender of the faith (5)

His early death from disease exposed England to Catholicism (3)

His name is posted outside many a bar (5)

His passion for actresses can raise eyebrows in certain quarters (6)

I came through flood on Raleigh's cloak, I returned dry (6)

I was generally doing battle with Matilda (4)

My crest flew over Crécy where I'd great victory (5)

One forced to sign Magna Carta by barons' leaders he had fleeced (6)

One greatly admired after Agincourt (4)

Regent fed atrociously, put on too much weight (8)

Still she rules as the nation hails her jubilee (7)

Puzzle 33

'Mephisto' by Tim Moorey (Owzat)
Sunday Times 22 January 2006

Across

1 Forgive me when Mephisto puzzles jar (6)
7 Hard question: what was a creel called once? (4)
10 One mark for English, distinction coming soon (9)
11 Juveniles with yen for a little room in dwelling (4)
13 Marble appropriate on proscenium? Check carried out (6)
14 Tiring person, sort one repelled (6)
16 Work on street, east to west – picks needed (4)
18 Boycott housing close to mast and leave (6, two words)
20 Jack, a Conservative is for the high jump perhaps (9)
21 Soldier managed to distribute a number of mines linked together (9)
24 Muslim students overtaken by strain without lecturer (6)
25 Two daughters in very big dispute (4)
28 See fan fighting with fists as before (6)
30 A leader in Turkey, say tackling accepted heart of problem (6)
31 Tree seen when miles driven in remote parts of Africa? (4)
32 Endless civility shown by adjutant and one irregular fighter (9)
33 Rudimentary carriage from far back (4)
34 Always stick around for millet from India (6)

Down

1 Parasitic disease hits Posy sadly (8)
2 Press club (4)
3 Fish: tons turning up around loch (9)
4 Body folds with warning given to volunteers (6)
5 Odd people taking aim on English ornamental trees (10)
6 Critic is getting up on legs (6)
7 Damn the grating! (4)
8 Welshman losing his head in brawl, a sort of capital punishment! (8)
9 Bottom of back garden plot gets a layer of turf (4)
12 Writ said to be preposterous around Strand (10)
15 Person who is promising to protect cipher is a nut (9)
17 Nothing in new-fangled pattern? I would assess that (8)
19 Frank carries a lot for a cool walk (8)
22 Internal security permits small keys (6)
23 Malawians one's seen in two states (American) (6)
26 A vehicle overturned can become worthless (4)
27 Old boy indeed acting with charm as before (4)
29 Bush's schedule in Washington, Tony's first to be wheeled out (4)

© *Sunday Times* 2006

Puzzle 34

'Three Writers' by Mr Lemon
The Times Listener series 11 October 1997

One or more letters have to be omitted from the answer to each clue before it is entered in the grid. Definitions are to the full word, subsidiary indications to the grid entry. Numbers in brackets always refer to the grid entry. The single letter omitted from each of thirty-two answers in clue order describe the approach of the 'Three Writers', the remaining five clues drop a hint as to style. *Chambers* (1993) is recommended. Two of the 'Three Writers' are unclued; solvers should find and highlight the third.

Across

1 Routine clerks can be self assertive people (7)
7 Separate exercise in plain (5)
11 Sea-water's bad for birds (8)
12 Scotsman returns to take on Richard the Covenanter (6)
13 Song about king's skin colour (6)
15 Raps having no king among high cards (8)
16 Cable revised preview with report's introduction for Vatican (7)
17 Silver matrix absent in molten rocks (6)
18 Plaster of Paris ships in fashion (4)
21 Expects kisses (4)
24 The President once – a cutter of wood? (6)
26 Tension doesn't begin to relieve worry (7)
30 Old Tories excited harborer (8)
31 Estaminets keep a bit of Riesling inside flasks (6)
32 Warning sound as golf shot goes outside centre of belt (6)
33 Rapid eye movement timer worked by heart (8)
34 Councillor has pouch for a fox (5)
35 Torpedo goes around during (brief) constant measure of emission (7)

Down

2 Aphrodite's fluorescent salt (6)
3 Listen to inside of male's chest (5)
4 Old courtesy one finally gets to see in France (5)
5 Singer drew grebes swimming round lake (11)
6 Calls for woman's work basket (4)
7 Scraper is brought up round block to stop wheel (6)
8 Fort with exterior of round building stone (4)
9 Club price is cut at last (5)
10 German follows one big awkward girl – a truly monstrous bird! (5)
14 They keep the rain off school piano (4)
19 Heartless group of teachers forged paper (4)
20 Season in charge of the moon (6)
22 Yes! Forward's foot slipped back (5)
23 Leaders of profession mostly chosen to lecture (6)
25 Terribly drear worshipper (5)
27 Went for a swim – in the Tay – thereupon grandchild died (5)
28 As an example Prokofiev's sister exercised at first in judo costume (5)
29 Stifles restraints – figuratively speaking (4)
30 A swelling that is difficult to deal with (4)

Puzzle 35

'Site Map' by Mr Magoo
The Magpie June 2004

1	2	3	4	5	6	7	8	9	10	11	12
13						14					
15											
16											
17											
18						19					
20	21				22	23				24	
25											
26											
27											
28						29					
30											

Only **eight** bars in the symmetrical grid are shown, and therefore numbering may be inappropriate to the final grid.

    Eight of the listed clues are to three entries each, clued in any order. **Eight** other clues omit a certain six-letter word (and maybe punctuation), essential to the clue. Numbers in brackets refer to apparent grid lengths.

    Bars must be inserted and 1 Across (three words) completed. Finally, **eight** bars must be deleted again, and the resulting entries jumbled to form a two-word phrase beneath the grid.

    Three of the two-word entries are not in *Chambers* but are well-known phrases.

Across

13 One conducting arch in two pieces away from Greek taking overdose (6)

14 Kill, initially, after black slugs (6)

15 Almost exhausted after reversing craft built from 7, perhaps (12)

16 Stones track with crazy word for refusing bird broadcast – bird not dead! (12)

17 Some within Royal Box go on a trip to city platform and pour the tea, so to speak (12)

18 Oiled, jarred (not half) and smashed (6)

19 In trouble, deals crisply with disappearing monster (6)

20 Money for sex or drug (6)

23 Look back inside perhaps with God's country (6)

25 Struggle in snare: politician from non-independent republic grew old, having managed without servant (12)

26 Sucker not second in excellent programme: established law breaking for instrument with a point (12)

27 Fellowship of artist in place of gross debauchery (12)

28 What constructs briefly I see, having a specific purpose (6)

29 50% of Latin in respect of poetical land (6)

30 Gateman from the East roots for City (12, two words)

Down

1 Summons before breakfast? (12, two words)

2 Who has heard 'custard apple'? (6)

3 Streams coming from hill fissures (12)

4 Torero leaves content, hearing this surprised cry bull originally emits: animal's lair covered by rubbish (12)

5 Grass had hunch to change time when lifted note's taken from noon – in June 60 years ago? (12)

6 Acted like being adapted for paddling? (6)

7 Girders shown by glances, we hear (6)

8 Decay of hideous Toad is exposing affectation of superiority: a pass (and many other bids!) (12)

9 Pill Bill found in dusty larder, having elegance – amphibian, moreover (12)

10 I dropped a bombshell, and upset a single homosexual (12, two words)

11 Capital E in Ego (6)

12 Riding like a man is most excellent, getting redder! (12)

21 Perhaps concealing base in old harbour (6)

22 Love to mix drinks, following Southern Comfort (6)

23 Column that's incorrect breaking up paragraph (6)

24 Recently discovered Seychelles, full of gossip (6)

© Mark Goodliffe 2004

Puzzle 36

Mary O'Brien (Simplex)
Irish Times May 2006

Across

8 Hatred of women (8)

9 Root vegetable (6)

10 Aircraft supported only by air (6)

11 Put a name to (8)

12 Advancing slowly on the fringing? (6)

13 Catches in a trap (8)

15 Comfort; rest (4)

17 Running from (7)

19 By the time in question (7)

22 Find a cure, strangely, in the colour (4)

24 Distance north or south of the Equator (8)

27 'Tomorrow, and tomorrow, and tomorrow / ... in this petty place from day to day' (Macbeth) (6)

29 Money made or paid on money (8)

30 Have a mind to do (6)

31 In place (2,4)

32 Answer; reply (8)

Down

1 Sent down the wrong road (6)

2 Oddly enough, the edge of the thoroughfare is adored (8)

3 H (8)

4 They show the writers' names (7)

5 Emphasise the strain? (6)

6 Ex ...; optional (6)

7 Area rich in petroleum deposits (8)

14 Close in time or space (4)

16 Old (4)

18 Acquiring skill or knowledge (8)

20 Most blessed with good fortune (8)

21 Negatively-charged particle (8)

23 A hundred years (7)

25 Spain and Portugal (6)

26 Functional; handy (6)

28 Impose a penalty (6)

© *Mary O'Brien/Irish Times* 2006

Puzzle 37

Pasquale
The Guardian 22 February 2005

Across

9,10,21 Down Oh, excel, fervent Mr Toad – making this lot look silly! (3,6,3,2,6)

10 *See 9*

11 Start to rouse a man when one hardly ever reacts (4,3)

12 Rebelled with United Nations force being introduced (7)

13 Picture part of collection? (5)

14 Visitors' accommodation university established – old servant to guard them (5,4)

16 Real tale of war? Different manuscript from this fictional story (1,8,2,4)

19 With this ground condition, hope to get hoe (4,5)

21 Ape rushed into marsh, head disappearing (5)

22 Saint having a bit of a snack at home (7)

23 What nude's in with nothing on, the fool? (7)

24 Aggressive still on a physicist's scale? (5)

25 Like a nag man's got put off? (9)

Down

1 Birds mating rasp bizarrely (10)

2 Banks are going bust – in a state (8)

3 President frivolous in a tricky situation (6)

4 Folk singer participating in live sessions (4)

5 Nowadays, people of both sexes may put their foot in it (7,3)

6 A second beast turning up in romantic work of art (8)

7 A French company's taken over second international organisation (6)

8 Knock for six – trick Somerset's tail-ender unleashed! (4)

14 Incur anger wrecking poet's source of inspiration (7,3)

15 Miss toying around with a man who can't stand her? (10)

17 Ronay keeps good works up with something to help the eater (3,5)

18 Argued about a boy being given appropriate name (8)

20 Shy away from bird traversing lake (6)

21 *See 9*

22 Go through battle without army suffering reverse (4)

23 Home abandoned by a German astronomer (4)

© *Don Manley 2005*

Puzzle 38

Paul
The Guardian 7 September 2002

Across

5 Core, we hear, by going round fruit (6)
6 Wolves should be bats, such as 21 (6)
9 Exciting moment produced a hundred times capital investment (6)
10 Heading off for Egyptian town, one on endless river, with the wife (8)
11 13 between two of them at Towcester (4)
12 Wasp swallows unusual gem that's to be eaten crystallized (4,6)
13 Evidence of exciting race stolen from home is in pub (5,6)
18 Tell Hebrew about the leader of the flock (10)
21 5 Across thrice before ... (1,3)
22 ... 'There was this car, and two redheads got out' – that's the joke! (4,4)
23 Parade a personal design (6)
24 Choke from ... (6)
25 ... from choke (6)

Down

1 See some dynamism at Chelsea, when playing Rochdale Reserves, say? (8)
2 Persian king offering himself after fornication in lift (6)
3 Transport to horse's head pulled up (8)
4 African country accepting godhead is harmless (6)
5 Tolkien character embraces a Spanish city (6)
7 Drunk, so taken advantage of (6)
8 Working principle under King Tom? (4,2,5)
14 Leaves by 25, or in a different way (8)
15 Dress essential for capital gains? (5,3)
16 Singers producing notes for the audience (6)
17 Portuguese resort to be blasted beyond the horizon (3,3)
19 Little devil appears in top that's transparent (6)
20 Tripe consumed in turn (6)

© John Halpern 2002

Puzzle 39

'Gridlock' or 'Leaderless' by Plausus
ad familiares June 2006

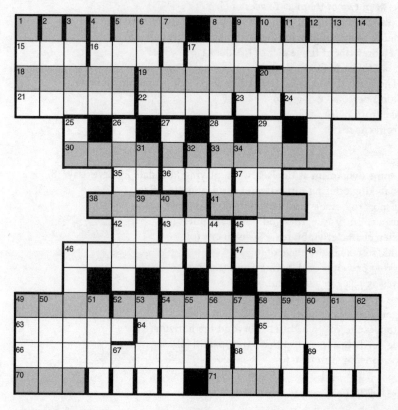

Solvers should deduce 71 from one of the titles and dog-Latin poetry in shaded squares and longer forms of 56, 57, and 58. All answers are in Latin except those indicated by a *.

Across

5 With (3)
12 I (3)
15 And not, neither, nor (3)
16 Salt or wit (3)
17* Put back in place (8)
18 By chance (5)
19 (See 33 Across) with reins (Abl.) (5)
20 I plough in (5)
21 Mythical hunter; constellation (5)
22* Did Cleo take them to heart? (4)
23 Out of (2)
24 Love (4)
30 Take away! (s.) from ancient Greek township district (4)
33 (See 19 Across) with reins (5)
35* Pater (joc.) (2)
36* Oculus (3)
37 By, from (2)
38 I take away in public protest (See 30 Across) (4)
41 Savage, grim, fierce (4)
42 You (Acc. s.) (2)
43 For a god-fearing man (Dat. m.) (3)
45 Goes (See 69 Across) (2)
46 'Et tu ———-!' Caesar (5)
47 Who? (4)
49 and 52* Plenus + Abl. (4,2)
54* Vaccae (4)
58* Oves (5)
63 Suitable, fitting (Acc. m. pl.) (5)
64* Vietnamese tunic's a zero to Welshman? (2,3)
65 Beautiful valley in Thessaly (5)
66 With city walls (Abl. pl.) (8)
68* Old Norse deus belli (3)
69 Went (See 45 Across) (3)
70* Et (3)
71 Unclued. See preamble (3)

Down

1* Gen on Fino? (4)
2 I think (Dep. vb) (4)
3 Hard (Nom. m. pl.) (4)
4 So be it! (4)
5* French urbs for cane-making (4)
6 Any (Nom. f. s.) (4)
7 ——— amicos My friends (Acc.) (4)
8 For the gods (Dat. pl.) (4)
9 To be (4)
10* Right (abbrev.) (2)
11 Gifts (4)
12 We were (Imp. 1. pl.) (6)
13 I wear or wage (4)
14 Smell (4)
17* Recommended Retail Price (abbrev.) (3)
20 Nine (2)
25 To, towards ... (not BC) (2)
26 Attack or force (7)
27 Buy! (s.) (See 60 Down) (3)
28 'Non ———' Vespasian of a public loo coin – 'It doesn't stink' (4)
29 Strawberry tree (7)
31 She or those things (2)
32 In purple I clothed by a novice (5)
34* Remus in a boat (3)
39* Came across at the Opera House (3)
40 O foot! What riches Goddesses of plenty (4)
44 '——- et amo' 'I hate and love.' Catullus (3)
45* Intelligence Quotient (abbrev.) (2)
46* ianuam obseravit or ran away and ate greedily (6)
48 If (2)
49 Repute or rumour (4)
50* Super + Abl. on top of, over (4)
51* No short yearn (4)
52 Bone (2)
53 Bean (4)
54* ——— d'etat (4)
55* Overdoses on Reichenbach's forces (3)
56* Bellum (3) guard hospital room
57 Sede! (3) in original position
58 Hara for Porci (3) underworld flower
59 Greek goddess = Juno (4)
60 Issue forth and buys (See 27 Down) (4)
61* E.g. Odyssey, Iliad, or Aeneid (4)
62 I seek mad poet (4)
67 It (2)

© David Dare-Plumpton 2006

Puzzle 40

'Sixes and Sevens' by Sabre
The Times Listener series 15 February 2003

Seven-letter answers are entered normally, but only the locations of two in each quadrant are given; clues for the remaining four in the quadrant appear in random order. Each across (down) five-letter diagram entry can be jumbled with one letter extracted from the seven-letter word in the same row (column) to form the six-letter answer to the respective clue. These extracted letters (taken in numerical order of the seven-letter entries, across, then down) spell out a message for the solver. One word in the south-east quadrant is not in *Chambers*, but is in the *Oxford English Dictionary*.

© *The Times* 2003

North-west

4 String back on sports shoe (7)
15 Cherishing sloth marks crazy Hebrew literalism (7)
   Left janitor's second floor store-room (7)
   Offensive person swears at first fiddle (7)
   GI's blacking out is too boring (7, two words)
   Every other car boasts it, one's means of defence (7)

South-west

22 Second mark in crustacean's claws (7)
37 Blocked passage is cut: gas ultimately lessens (7)
   Television only half of day backs up one's small bill (7)
   Strife as payee's middle payment for a year's right (7)
   It displays collies rampant for one armiger's term? (7)
   Representation (still life) of vegetable (aubergine) (7)

South-east

26 Dropping acceleration, dislike turning (7)
40 Fare well grasping Idaho's dance moves (7)
   A College in Oxford gets cut: universal spirit shows (7)
   Pre-dinner drink – O, John! Ros is drunk (7)
   Donut's left in sneaker (7)
   A silk dress: right away, tuck up tangle (7)

North-east

10 Osmanli official unloads bananas (7)
18 Weed with dead leaves ripped off (7)
   In mask, one travelling home gets in late (7)
   A tipsy Moor as lover (7)
   Are these fishermen poking fun? (7)
   His work showed little independence (7)

Across

8 Restrained contralto gets to speed up (6)
13 A slight convexity caught by orange light (6)
16 Washington's universal pest finished off woollens (6)
17 Draw symmetrical parts of necktie in a knot (6)
20 Relinquishes diamonds – utter strangeness (6)
21 Mismade Fiesta clutches, former discards (6)
29 A national accounting of Society in central America (6)
30 Maintenance: old American car in Paris lacks it (6)
38 Close of day – Countess changes out of cobalt (6)
39 LP ends up, most oddly, in Labrador's brush? (6)
42 Thailand boyfriend recalled rising (6)
43 Barmy stuff is penned by poet (6)

Down

1 A bicep's contraction, you hear, in spots (6)
3 Temptresses remove us from noisy entertainments (6)
5 St Andrews' puss – bad catty! (6)
7 Middle quarter missing from crude wall (6)
9 Scarlet at end of nose: re-use carbon for a time? (6)
11 Masseuse, maybe, kneading us with this oil (6)
31 Alto guy is free from anxiety (6, two words)
32 Fourth grades slated for reform (6)
33 A range of intromitted electrodes (6)
34 Adder-like Prince, energy lacking, is poisonous (6)
35 Fed coke, perhaps – Simon Templar approved (6)
36 Erysipelas follows with the result of swelling (6)

Puzzle 41

'Darts Final' by Salamanca
Sunday Telegraph

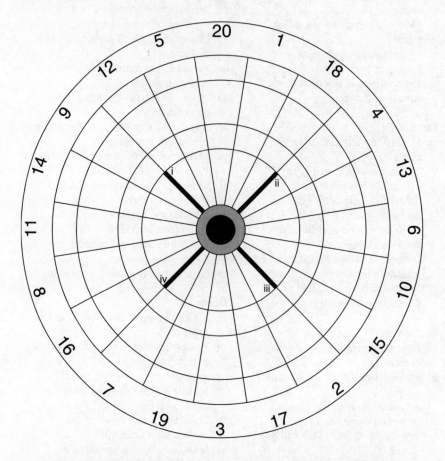

On the dart board, in this 'Darts Final', seven-letter radial answers must be arranged logically for entry (the outer ring containing doubles, the third trebles, the other two separate singles). In the outermost singles ring an observation appears reading clockwise from the sector nominated 20, and i–iv are normal clockwise words. Doubles and trebles have been reduced to a two-letter format (rearranged where necessary) for a help list of definitions in a not necessarily helpful order. *Chambers* (1998) is recommended.

Radials

1 Observe present and past society's ups-and-downs
2 Thin layer of plate shown by 'hit' girl (one of Spice group being hugged by Teletubby?)
3 Skin diseases (offensive in The 'Nam), requiring rest for curing
4 Early Syrian's success, pulling young girl with energy
5 Fatuous to include centre of plant – medicinal one
6 Drop, s-see, involved in fumble (two words)
7 What cowboy could wear a pop-group's stories?
8 How to provide a second helping of ice?
9 Opt to use épée after struggle – shoe cut off at end (hyphenated)
10 They looked for pop-chart success – and got it!
11 Queen-killer like one active, charming (but loose) woman
12 This group's played etc. in potter's outside shed
13 Muddled detective leaves Channel Islands in sentry-vessel
14 These plants have no name in collections
15 Bennett's girl takes 'Card' to radio-receiver
16 Witnesses to crucial cricket matches
17 Fermented liquid found in upper half of foreign butter tree
18 Such a short opera may touch one
19 Morning marks seen in partner with milk-glands
20 Old Bill arranged roses in borders of rhododendrons

Clockwise

i One responsible for some frenetic, low nonsense?
ii Awaken for sure in the night?
iii In middle of Leeds bishop went astray
iv One European left so I've amended former notification

Two-letter forms

See letter (and French note) to one live silver alien. Tree flourished on street early in the day. No Scots Spaniard, say, extended record while before Engineers' Club.

© *Telegraph group*

Puzzle 42

'Code Sequence' by Schadenfreude
The Times Listener series 5 July 2003

Two different letters must be omitted from the answer to each clue and the residue entered at the appropriately numbered location. The first letter to be omitted is always the first occurrence of that letter in the defined word. Where the second letter appears more than once after the first, solvers must deduce which to omit. Thus, if NI is the digraph to be omitted from UNIONIST the grid entry could be UONIST or UIONST, not UNIOST. Each clue has an extra word which contains the two letters to be omitted, each appearing once only and in the correct order. In most cases the redundant word leads unambiguously to the digraph. For example, if ALLOCATION is the extra word in a clue to ORDINAL then the digraph must be IN. Clues are presented in alphabetical order of their answers.

© *The Times* 2003

Clues

A thrash includes very vain chap drinking a liqueur (8)

Fine American mosque almost destroyed (6)

Amateur evening had tragicomedies approved (6)

Active queen meets retired heavyweight film stars (6)

Munro boy joins north European naval force (8, two words)

Reflecting instrument (electronic) failed inside coronograph cover (9)

Officer with nothing to stop Royal Navy's artillery (7)

Pluto, Felix, and Flush demolished the contents of more than one plate (8)

Fish (monstrously large ganoids) in Spain are unknown (8)

Helpline to induce a different culture (9)

They instruct nurse to go in with the Queen's conjuror (9)

Member of mystical Hindu sect takes cut hemp (6)

Is the denazified American zone somehow least well defined? (7)

This holds memos and letters belonging to three envoys (6)

Such as drape women from Thailand seeking exotic looks (8)

Lord's subject about to shred Government acquisition certificate (9)

I learn downland flying like some seabirds (6)

A stiff ointment in luminous noon sun undergoes softening (9)

Male wards meaning to get in order for possibly curative plants (8)

Stone wall crunched fresh tropical plants (7)

Girl with luxury flat wasted womanhood (8)

Second daughter and unruly youth keeping an important date kept designs within bounds (9)

Follower of fashion married modern poet (6)

Bill warmly embraces weak grandchild, a first-former perhaps (6, two words)

Guilty denial unclear about hospital department (6)

Five-eighths of about 13 acres, like the Oval? (7)

Doorkeepers sit relaxing in front of your old house (9)

China is about to finish a zigzag fence (8)

They receive money partly to smear retired judge (6)

Writers sharpen me randomly, never in the middle (6)

Infantry regiments ultimately overcome by God's butchery (7)

A trap rattling on unfinished road makes a ceaseless drumming sound (8)

This church official needs the ultimate in patience to convert hardy sectarians (9)

Old rocket perhaps crushed backward American city (6)

Nudist club recognised keenness to install new Director (9, two words)

Exclusive party accepting the count in Paris (6)

Fishwives about to stop working – unknowingly they show keen practical judgement (9)

One president attaining perfection has reshuffled, keeping the same Department (6)

It features in revised leasing without a levy on orthodox ground-rent (9, two words)

Expensive antique without marks mirrored in cubes of decorative glass (6)

Seven chaps after piece-work (including new ranchers) – they're paid danger money (8)

Midwives celebrate about state of conflict and see Jock's passing out (8)

A hospital in Cannock makes use of rails (7)

Etna erupted unfavourably close to trenchers strengthening fieldwork (9)

Twists in hybrid roots untangled by us? (8)

Caseworkers consult various kids about Oasis's first source of sound and vision (9)

Passion with Martha reduced wayward promiscuity (6)

To prevent iceboxes overheating engineer a lower temperature (about zero inside) (9)

Feeble lawyer, exchanging rook for knight, meekly crumbled ... (6)

... you and I justify swapping a bishop perhaps (6)

Puzzle 43

Roger Squires (Rufus)
The Times 12 January 1995

Across

1 Audience standing up, well-pleased with one's address (5-5)
6 Not a great deal of notice (4)
9 Uttered in a death rattle (10)
10 Vessel with a professional second mate (4)
12 Marine detachment (4)
13 and 16 Roman marbles missing (3,6,6)
15 Said sale was fiddled and became aggressive (8)
16 See 13 Across (6)
18 It's all right to return a large amount of money (6)
20 A pound of sultanas (8)
23 About time to adjust the height indicator (9)
24 Where barristers get refreshers? (4)
26 A fall gives work to the doctor (4)
27 Fast-service ammunition (6-4)
28 Scrape up and sweep back (4)
29 Soldiers in irregular wars need someone to provide intelligence (10)

Down

1 Stretcher-bearers? (4)
2 Reveals United Nations demand in writing (7)
3 Means being out of employment? (6,6)
4 Advanced in a rush, but thought better of it (8)
5 Such heroes are not celebrated (6)
7 Primate filling role as a source of protection (7)
8 Soldering irons start making an electronic device (10)
11 Fail to win a single game and get annoyed (4,8)
14 A gift for dishonesty? (10)
17 Directions for making machine parts (8)
19 Used for hanging pirate captain holding up vessel (7)
21 Neckline that may bring out a whistle (7)
22 New fears about opening the attack (6)
25 A slight incoherence in speech (4)

© The Times 1995

Solutions

Solution 1

Solution 2

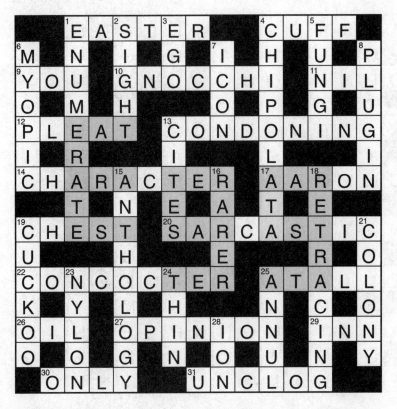

Thirty-five squares occupied by the letters of EASTER formed Egg.

Solution 3

Solution 4

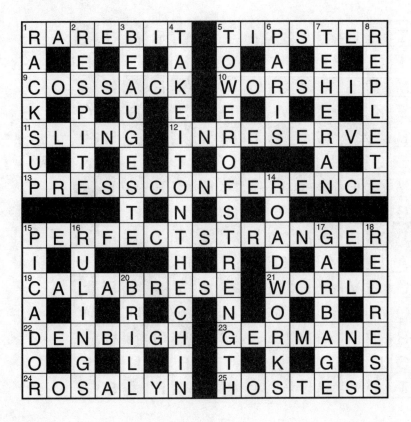

Solution 5

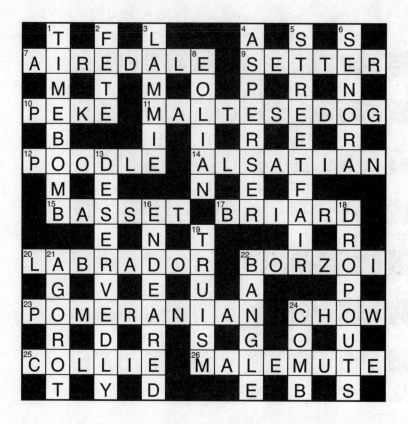

Solution 6

V	A	N	E	S	S	A	U	S	H	E	R
A	V	O	U	T	C	O	M	P	E	T	E
G	A	R	B	E	A	L	B	E	R	T	S
U	N	T	O	M	B	P	E	C	L	R	E
S	T	E	A	M	L	O	R	I	G	I	N
P	U	N	R	E	A	T	T	E	M	P	T
A	R	A	B	I	N	O	S	E	A	U	S
G	I	L	L	E	D	M	O	U	T	D	O
U	N	W	U	L	S	E	L	I	C	I	T
R	E	A	D	O	U	T	A	S	H	A	H
I	N	C	I	P	I	E	N	C	E	T	E
D	U	K	E	S	C	R	O	W	D	E	R

Anagram of initial letters of acrosses: 'God save our gracious (Queen)'; initial letters of clues (across, then down): ELIZABETH THE SECOND, ROYAL GOLDEN JUBILEE; title of puzzle: anagram of SINGLE ACROSTIC.

Across

1   an² in anag.
6   (p)usher
11   (Greta) Garb(o)
14   unto + MB
17   o rig in
26   o ut do (ditto)
30   ado in anag.
31   sh! + a h
32   n in ICI + I in pence

Down

2   a vant urine
4   emmets (rev.); sv stemma
6   (H)umber
7   anag. & lit.
9   sent in res
13   anag. in tripe
18   p + anag.
23   solan o

Solution 7

Solution 8

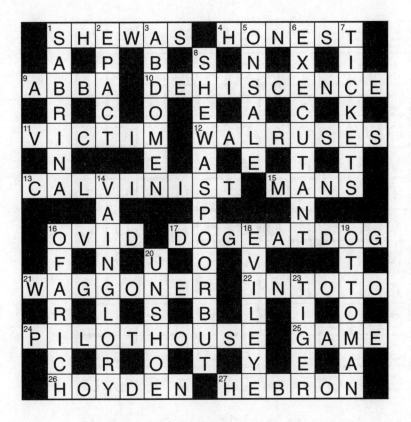

Solution 9

1 E	2 R	3 T	R	4 T	5 H	6 E	R	7 O	O	8 E	O
9 B	A	R	K	I	N	G	10 A	11 T	M	A	12 N
13 S	C	O	U	14 T	H	R	P	O	I	S	O
15 C	O	16 W	H	C	G	17 R	T	R	T	E	T
18 O	V	E	R	H	E	A	R	Q	S	19 W	B
20 M	I	L	A	N	G	O	21 E	U	V	R	E
22 M	A	K	E	D	O	E	23 H	A	24 N	O	I
U	N	25 A	R	26 L	E	G	27 A	T	I	O	N
28 T	29 A	U	G	30 H	T	O	C	E	C	G	G
E	G	G	G	I	R	31 Y	T	A	E	G	E
32 R	O	U	E	33 N	T	H	O	R	N	E	D
34 L	G	R	G	T	G	L	R	A	E	E	O

The code was: *The Power and the Glory*, G. Greene. The author is encoded at 1 Across, and other coded entries are places in his works: Havana (*Our Man in Havana*), Saigon (*The Quiet American*), Port-au-Prince (*The Comedians*), Corrientes (*The Honorary Consul*), Monte Carlo (*Loser Takes All*), Brighton (*Brighton Rock*), and Freetown (*The Heart of the Matter*). Graham Greene was born on 2 October 1904 and the title encodes CENTENARY.

Thematic answers are italicized. Correct forms of misprinted letters in definitions (printed in bold) spell out: *The Power and the Glory* – G. Greene.

Solution 9 *continued*

Across

1 *GRAHAM GREENE*   ham + re in Gen, within anag.
9 BARKING   Nuns/Nuts; bar, king
10 ATMAN   Inference/Inherence; (b)atman
13 SCOUTH   Scops/Scope; out within Sch
17 *HAVANA*   a van within H, A
18 OVERHEAR   Kick/Pick; rhea within over
20 MILAN   Prospers/Prospero; first letters
21 OEUVRE   fork/work; Eu, VR within O, E
22 MAKE DO   Copy/Cope; ked within Mao
23 HANOI   fat/far; a no. within HI
26 LEGATION   Pipal/Papal; e.g. a(rboriculturis)t within lion
28 TAUGHT   Trailed/Trained; a, ugh within TT
31 *SAIGON*   A, GI (rev.), within son
32 ROUEN   Mail/Maid; e within roun(d)
33 THORNED   planes/plants; anag. of on, the, D(erwentwate)r
34 *PORT-AU-PRINCE*   port, a-, up, R, in, CE

Down

2 RACOVIAN   Folder/Holder; O, car (rev.), via, N
3 TROWEL   garth/earth; R in towel
4 TITCH   brown/grown; t, It, Ch
5 *CORRIENTES*   *rien* within Cortes
6 RAPT   fuel/full; -r, a, pt
7 OMITS   put/out; first letters
8 EASE   Best/Rest; (C)ease
11 TORQUATE   topically/typically; qua within torte
12 NOT-BEING   Done/Gone; B- in anag. of get on in
14 *MONTE CARLO*   anag. of clarinet less I, within moo
15 COMMUTER   letting/getting; O, MM within cuter
16 *BRIGHTON*   B + I in anag. of throng
19 *FREETOWN*   -e in anag. of went for
24 NICENE   Asian/Arian; CE in nine (3x3)
25 AUGUR   Sear/Seer; first letters
27 ACTOR   rolls/roles; hidden
29 AGOG   Of/On; Ag, o-, g-
30 HINT   Club/Clue; H, I, NT

Solution 10

Solution 11

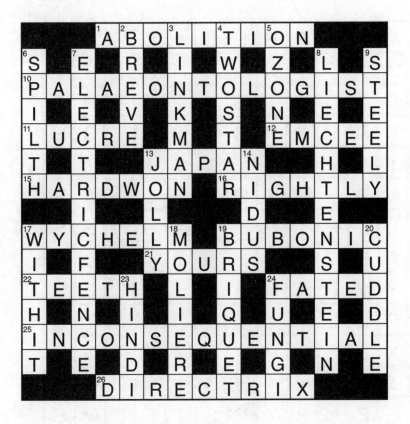

Solution 12

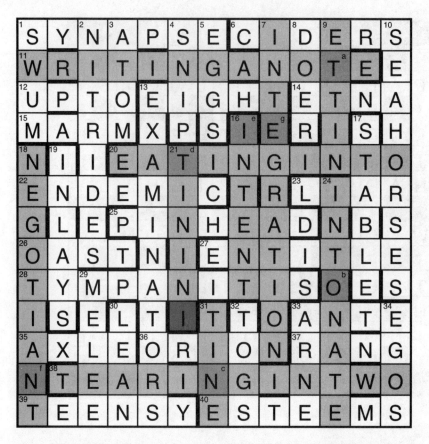

S	Y	N	A	P	S	E	C	I	D	E	R	S
W	R	I	T	I	N	G	A	N	O	T	E	E
U	P	T	O	E	I	G	H	T	E	T	N	A
M	A	R	M	X	P	S	I	E	R	I	S	H
N	I	I	E	A	T	I	N	G	I	N	T	O
E	N	D	E	M	I	C	T	R	L	I	A	R
G	L	E	P	I	N	H	E	A	D	N	B	S
O	A	S	T	N	I	E	N	T	I	T	L	E
T	Y	M	P	A	N	I	T	I	S	O	E	S
I	S	E	L	T	I	T	T	O	A	N	T	E
A	X	L	E	O	R	I	O	N	R	A	N	G
N	T	E	A	R	I	N	G	I	N	T	W	O
T	E	E	N	S	Y	E	S	T	E	E	M	S

Theme: TONTINE. Unclued lights were anagrams with one letter removed each time – ending with TIN, IN, I. (TEARING IN TWO = WRITING A NOTE redistributed.) Extra letters spelt WRITE TITLE OF SONG – IT'S BY GLORIA GAYNOR. This indicates I WILL SURVIVE.

A tontine runs its course by gradual elimination and final redistribution of the original to the survivor. The puzzle is constructed on the same principle. In this case, 'I' WILL SURVIVE.

Notes on clues
Composite clue: union = INTEGRATION, contract = TONTINE, can = TIN, aim = INTENT, to voice = INTONATE, one = I, point = TINE, by = IN, wearing away = EATING INTO, big man = ETTIN, one seeking a good deal = NEGOTIANT.

Solution 12 *continued*

Across

1	ANY (rev.) in SPE(w)S anag.	speWs
6	CID+ER(r)S	erRs
12	hidden	corruptIon
13	2 mngs	sTeven
14	(g)(r)ETNA	weEd
15	(s)MARM	Toil
22	ENDE(r)MIC	I
23	RAIL (rev.)	barT
25	anag: a PhD in E	Lass
26	AS in O.T.	hopEs
27	TIE T(o) LEN anag.	tO
28	anag.	Fear
33	2 mngs	beSt
35	L in AXE (see NAVE)	roOd
36	O+ NOIR rev.	No
37	RANG(e)	tiGer
39	TEE+N+S(urre)Y	In
40	MEETS in SE(t) (all rev.).	seT

Down

1	initial letters	Suspend
2	D in anag. of RINIEST	Briniest
3	A+TOM	traceY
4	I in SNP	Gnats
5	EG+G&S	roLe
8	anag. of RODE(o)	rodeO
10	S+E+A+SHORE (anag.) +S	tangieRs
13	AXE rev. +MAIN(ly) anag.+TO+S(i)R rev.	sIr
17	2 mngs	manAgers
19	IN+LAY+S (for sun)	sunG
29	MEL(t) + (fiv)E + (vertebra)E	sAcrum
30	2 mngs	slimY
32	TO+G(et) + S(erved)	riNg
33	anag. EAR N(o)	nO
34	E(al) + G(iants) +OS	Real

Solution 13

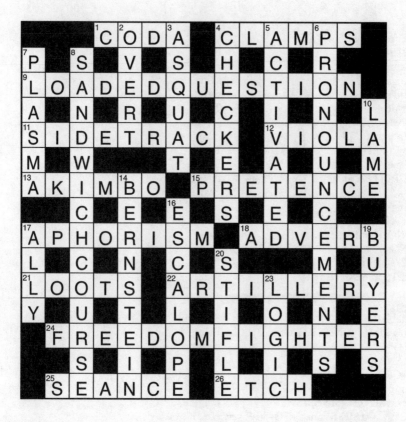

Solution 14

Solution 15

Solution 16

Solution 17

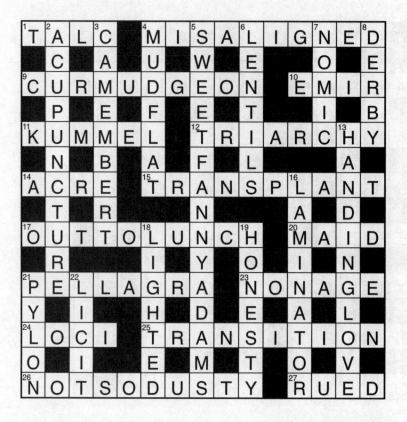

Solution 18

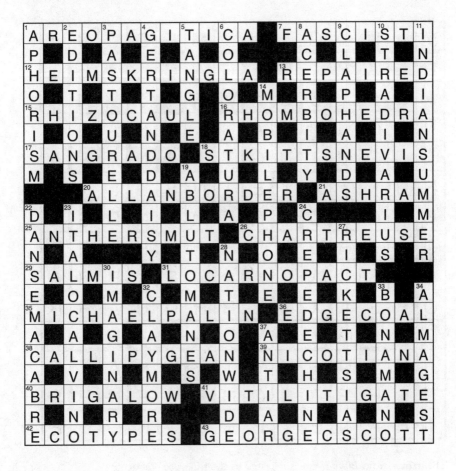

Solution 19

¹M	²A	³H	O	⁴G	⁵A	N	⁶Y	M	E	D	⁷U	S	⁸A	⁹A

M	A	H	O	G	A	N	Y	M	E	D	U	S	A
P	L	A	P	I	P	E	R	A	C	E	A	E	U
A	L	L	I	S	L	W	W	R	I	T	I	N	G
N	F	O	U	H	E	A	R	T	S	E	A	S	E
T	O	O	M	I	N	G	T	I	A	N	A	E	A
H	U	F	I	A	T	E	I	N	S	U	L	I	N
E	R	N	E	D	Y	R	E	M	I	N	D	S	S
O	S	E	R	D	A	B	S	A	D	F	E	E	T
L	A	S	C	A	L	A	A	W	E	B	B	R	A
O	P	S	A	X	O	R	R	H	U	B	A	R	B
G	E	R	M	I	C	I	D	A	L	I	R	A	L
I	R	I	D	I	U	M	I	P	S	K	A	T	E
S	C	H	E	R	S	O	N	E	S	E	N	E	S
T	H	A	N	E	T	B	E	S	T	R	O	D	E

The names, from *Bleak House* (suggested by the title), are Woodcourt (MAHOGANY/BAR: 1/27), Jellyby (MEDUSA/ASIDE: 6A/18), Chadband (ALLIS/TIE: 13/17), Carstone (FIAT/SARDINE: 20/28), and Skimpole (SKATE/PERCH: 40/35). BAR, MEDUSA, ALLIS, SARDINE, SKATE, and PERCH are types of fish. The twelve letter mixture clues each include a type of fish, the letters of which are either all included in the mixture, or, in one case (ERNE: 23A), include the whole mixture.

Solution 20

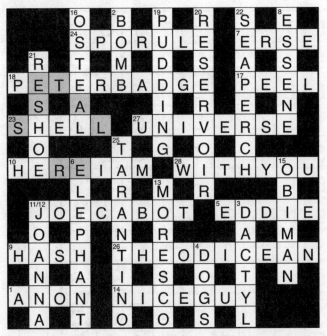

The theme is characters from Tarantino's *Reservoir Dogs*; nearly all of the characters shoot each other in the final scene if they haven't already come to grief. Messrs BLONDE, PINK, BROWN, ORANGE, BLUE, and WHITE have had their names removed from clue answers; Joe Cabot and Nice Guy Eddie also ended up horizontal. The shaded squares appropriately represent the word STEALERS (the film revolves around a failed bank robbery) in the shape of a wheel: Stealers Wheel were the group who had a hit with 'Clowns to the left of me, jokers to the right...(HERE I AM (setter)) Stuck in the Middle WITH YOU (solver)', part of the film's soundtrack and centrally located in the grid.

Tarantino's Reservoir Dogs:

2 23 B/LOND(on)/E/BOMB/SHE'LL ref. Jean H
6 P/INK/ELE//Ph/ANT
9 HASH B/ROWN anag.
17 OR/ANGE/PEE/L
18 BLUE PETER BAD/GE anag., rev; ref. Christopher Trace
19 W/HIT EP/UDD/ING
12 J/O.E. CAB/OT
14 5 NICE/GUYED/DIE
25 TAR/ANT IN O
20 RE-/S.E.,R/VOIR
4 DO G&S
10 (*Feste* & Co = Clowns, to the left of me) HERE I AM...stuck in...

28 ...the middle WITH YOU (Jesters = jokers, to the right)
1 ANON 2 mngs
3 DA/CT/YL anag.
7 ERSE hidden
8 ESSEN(c)E
11 JO/ANNA ref. Eddie Grant, 'Give me hope J'
13 MORES (&) CO
15 O/BI/MAN
16 O/STEAL i.e. radius
21 R/E/SHOE anag.
22 SEA/PE/RCH
24 SPO/RULE rev.
26 THEODICEAN anag.
27 UNI/VER/SE anag.

Solution 21

Theme: (wedding) anniversaries. Omitted clue-numbers associated with unclued words:

1   paper TIGER
2   cotton CANDY
3   leatherNECK
5   wooden HORSE
7   woollen-DRAPER
10 tin-OPENER
12 silk PURSE
15 crystal BALL
20 china CLAY
25 silverFISH
30 pearl BARLEY
40 Ruby MURRAY – 1950s singer and
    rhyming slang for curry

Solution 22

Solution 23

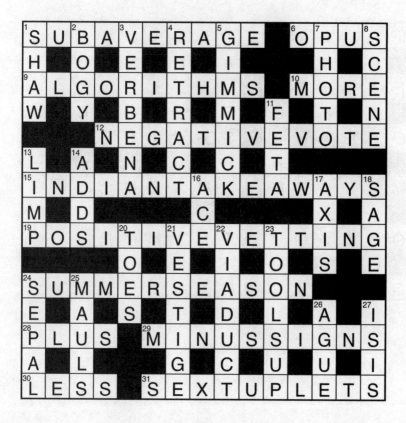

Solution 24

Solution 25

H	U	R	R	A	E	D	L	A	S	S	I
O	R	M	E	R	S	I	O	N	A	A	N
W	A	I	L	I	N	G	W	A	L	L	C
F	O	N	E	S	C	R	E	M	A	T	E
F	R	O	N	T	I	E	R	S	M	E	N
S	A	R	T	O	R	S	M	S	M	R	S
E	V	O	S	T	I	S	O	T	O	P	E
S	I	R	R	E	V	E	R	E	N	C	E
T	O	D	D	L	E	R	D	A	I	T	R
I	L	E	G	E	R	D	E	M	A	I	N
N	E	R	O	A	E	S	N	E	C	K	S
A	R	S	O	N	D	E	T	R	O	I	T

Across

1 Hur + dear (rev.)
6 lass I
10 (st)ormers
12 a in nan
13 w ailing w all
14 m in create
15 anag. inc. MN
16 art OR in SS
20 o in I stope
21 anag. + e
23 dot (rev.) + (I)dler
25 anag. & lit.
26 hidden & lit.
27 neck in s,s
28 ARs on
29 de tro(p) it

Down

1 how FF
2 U + oar (rev.)
3 Lent in res
4 E in anag.
5 GI (rev.) in dress
6 we r Morden in lot
7 a m in salmon I a/c
8 's alter
9 2 mngs
11 order in minors
16 nits (rev.) in sea
17 rive red
18 st(r)eamer
19 o in viler
22 cf. stern
24 I kit (rev.)

Solution 26

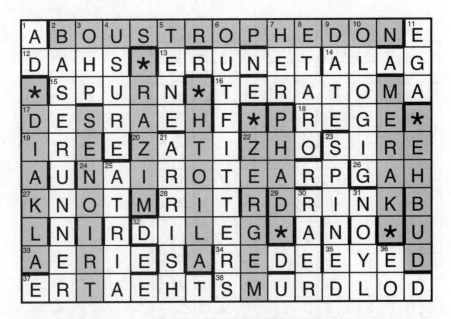

A	B	O	U	S	T	R	O	P	H	E	D	O	N	E
D	A	H	S	★	E	R	U	N	E	T	A	L	A	G
★	S	P	U	R	N	★	T	E	R	A	T	O	M	A
D	E	S	R	A	E	H	F	★	P	R	E	G	E	★
I	R	E	E	Z	A	T	I	Z	H	O	S	I	R	E
A	U	N	A	I	R	O	T	E	A	R	P	G	A	H
K	N	O	T	M	R	I	T	R	D	R	I	N	K	B
L	N	I	R	D	I	L	E	G	★	A	N	O	★	U
A	E	R	I	E	S	A	R	E	D	E	E	Y	E	D
E	R	T	A	E	H	T	S	M	U	R	D	L	O	D

The theme-word 'Boustrophedon' means 'plough-wise' – an ancient style of writing – which indicates that alternate lines must be written in opposite directions.

The variation 'Triones' defines the group of the seven stars of THE PLOUGH; whilst the remaining seven variations are their names: ALKAID, MIZAR, ALIOTH, MEGREZ, PHAD, MERAK, and DUBHE.

The 'space' to be filled at the end of each star name is most appropriately occupied by an asterisk: and when this is done, the resulting pattern is (of course) the constellation Ursa Major itself.

Solution 27

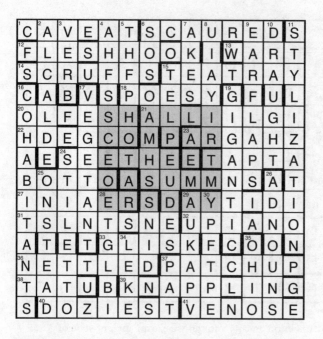

¹C	²A	³V	⁴E	⁵A	⁶T	S	⁷C	⁸A	⁹U	¹⁰R	¹¹E	D	¹¹S

The thematic phrases are all from Shakespeare's Sonnet 18: 'Shall I
Compare Thee to a Summer's Day?' in the grid; the Playfair key phrases
'Rough winds', 'do shake', 'the darling', and 'buds of May'; and 'more
lovely' from the omitted letters in clue order. Words with letters
omitted, in grid order, are: Across: seether, tapeta, bottom, summons;
Down: sovs, toe-loop, ollamhs, eludes, snide, pyat.

Explanations (* = anagram, << = reversed)

Central
bottom = acme's reverse; t(ense) t(ime) in boom (=prosperity)
summons = bids show up; sum (=whole) Mons (=battle)
seether = one in a rage; {re (=concerned with) sheet*}<<
snide = dishonest; ends* around I (=one)
eludes = escapes; {schedule (=plan) minus ch (=central heating)}<<
toe-loop = jump; {pot (=tub) around oleo (=margarine)}<<
sovs = old pounds; so (=greatly) v(ersu)s (=opposed to)
tapeta: they contribute to vision; tape (=hard liquor) TA (=reserves)
ollamhs = Ireland's sages once; (mar)sh-mallo(ws)<<
pyat = a flier from Prestwick; p(arliamentar)y a(gen)t

Across
1 caveat = caution; cave (=tunnel) + at (=occupied with)
6 scaured = rad (i.e. afraid, Scottish); crusade*
12 flesh-hook = tool for lifting meat; l(eft) in Fe (=iron) + so (=thus)
 around hh (=hands) + OK (=unhurt)

Solution 27 *continued*

13 wart = unpopular person; w(on) + art (=trick)
14 scruffs = neck pieces; sc(ilicet = specifically) + ruffs (=frills)
15 tea-tray = cup-holder; teatr(o = plays in Italy) + a + y(ear)
18 poesy = verse; Po (=Teletubby) + e(a)sy (=relaxed)
20 sickos = mental cases; sic (=set on) + KOs (=floors)
21 snigging = pulling with a line; S(olicitor-)G(eneral) around {gin (=drink)<< + gin (=drink)}
22 sakieh: I'll turn in current; Kea-ish*
23 Sunday = newspaper; sound (=report) minus o (=nothing) + ay (=indeed)
27 Ligeti = composer; {legitimate minus mate (=partner)}*
29 dzeren = antelope; den (=lair) around zer(o = nothing)
31 doridoid = sea slug; {O(riental) + r(ecipe)} in dido (=American caper) + I'd (= I had)
32 sogers = provincial fighters; SOS (=help us) around Ger(many)
33 glisk = a Scottish sight; (seein)g + (Ta)lisk(er)
36 nettled = annoyed; nett (= after deductions) + led (=were advanced)
37 patch-up = quick fix; pat (=dab) + h(and) in cup (=prize-money)
38 tatu = old body marking; when in SS (=ship) gives status (=prestige)
39 knappling = taking small bites; king (=monarch) around {n(ew) + appl(e = fruit)}
40 doziest = least aware; size* (reduced = adapted, disintegrated etc.) in dot (=portion)
41 venose = marked by vessels; Ventôse (=windy month) minus t(emperature)

Down

2 alcalde = mayor of Madrid; a (=one) + called*
3 verb = word of action; (ab)brev(iated)<<
4 day-boy = no boarder; anybody* minus (reaso)n
5 wealk'd = Shakespeare's twisted; walked (=trod) with E(nglish) moved almost to the beginning
7 Wafd = Egyptian party; {a + f(ollowing)} in WD (=Dominica)
8 one-two = football manoeuvre; homonym of {won (=was successful) + too (=as well)}
9 earflaps = cap extensions; frae (=from Scottish)<< + laps (=drinks)
10 draught = beer; guard (=keep)<< + th(e)<<
11 stylization = (commercial) branding; sty (=animal shelter) + lion (=hero) around zati (=monkey)
16 cohabitants: we live together; a bit (=a little) in {co(unty) + Hants (=Hampshire)}
17 vegetant = leading a dull life; (ha)ve + get (=to become) + ant (a worker, possibly)
19 gigantic = very large; gig (=whisky) {I can't}*
24 stiletto = knife; lit (=landed)<< in set-to (=fight)
25 onstead = Scottish farm; tea (=grass) in dons*
26 adnouns = words that are versatile; and* + {on us}*
28 flense = flay; oneself* minus O (=cry of pain)
29 crawly = obsequious; c(old) + rawly (=without refinement)
30 peazed = weighed heavily for Shakespeare; PE (=exercising) + Azed (=crossword setter)
34 Efik = African tribesman; knife (=cutter)<< minus n(avy)
35 Ohio = state; o(f) h(ealth) i(s) o(ff-colour)

Solution 28

Solution 29

```
R U N I N S B B U R G E S S
O N U S O U I R S O R T I E
A G M O G I G A P R O D A L
S U B C U T A N E O U S L L
T E C H T N E I N E P M A E
E S V L E I A M I E C A P A
D A K O E S W I T K A N E H
P R O P S I N C H A P A U F
B I S H S T A Y A N T A B R
A D S O D E I L R A A L A E
P E A B S T R A C T I O N S
E T U I I E F L A K N C G H
A E F A L D A D S O T H E E
K N U C K L Y Y H A V E R S
```

The longer words (with the related lights and their one-word definitions) were:

Across

1 E(X)TE(R)N	(53D giant)
14 E(V)IN(C)E	(24A eyes)
24 S(Q)UI(N)T	(5D action)
28 A(F)LA(M)E	(52A wings)
29 B(U)R(Q)A	(7D support)
32 K(N)OS(P)S	(31D measure)
33 I(T)C(H)Y	(34D Cold)
37 K(W)AN(Z)A	(36D syllabary)
49 A(D)VER(B)S	(65A property)
52 F(L)A(X)Y	(59D mad)
65 W(A)I(F)T	(33A intelligence)

Down

5 A(I)D(E)S	(49A commercials)
6 M(G)AN(G)A	(25D Power)
7 P(Y)ROP(U)S	(37A supports)
11 K(H)O(J)A	(60D plant)
25 A(M)P(L)E	(26D animal)
26 S(P)ORTI(V)E	(14A outing)
28 T(S)ET(S)E	(45D head)
31 A(C)MI(T)E	(28A inamorata)
34 C(Z)AP(K)A	(29A cloak)
36 O(B)E(Y)S	(32A letters)
42 S(K)ELL(I)E	(11D chair)
45 R(E)UNI(O)N	(1A enter)
53 B(R)IGA(D)E	(6D cars)
59 F(O)RESHE(W)S	(42D Burns)
60 A(J)W(A)N	(28D bristle)

Solution 30

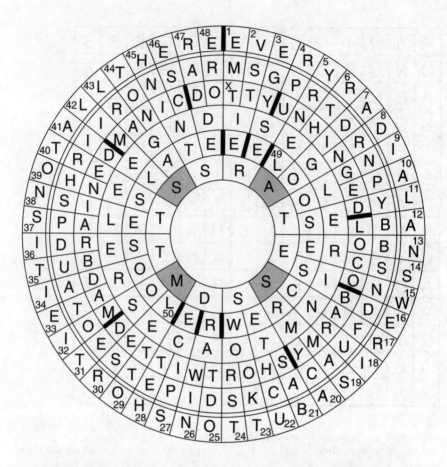

The expression 1–48 was suggested by the idiom 'Have all one's buttons (on)', in *Chambers* (1998 edition); and the adjectives in circuit X conveyed various kinds and degrees of craziness or derangement. The loose SCREW and SLATE (49 and 50) belong to related idioms.

1 M(E)TIER: M-tie-r
2 STI(V)ER: s+tier
3 G(E)YSER: G-y,S,E-r
4 PU(R)SER: p-use-r
5 NEARL(Y): n+earl
6 THALE(R): T+hale
7 AD(A)GIO: ad-GI-o
8 (D)RAGON: rag+on
9 L(I)NGOT: anag.+T
10 PELOT(A): p-E-lot
11 STY(L)ED: sty+ed
12 (A)BLEST: subsid. def.
13 BOREE(N): bor-E-e
14 SCREE(S): s+Cree
15 NO(W)ISE: subsid. def.
16 B(E)SIDE: B side
17 F(R)ANCS: fan-c-s
18 (I)NCURS: N+curs
19 (S)MARMS: mar MS
20 CYM(A)RS: Cymr(y)+S
21 (B)ASTES: as+set, rev.
22 CH(U)TES: ch-t-es(t)
23 KO(T)OWS: OK, rev.+ow(n)s
24 S(T)ROWS: s-r-ows

25 D(O)TARD: d+drat, rev.
26 I(N)WARD: I+war+D
27 (S)PICED: pi-c-ed
28 ETC(H)ED: t,c in Dee, rev.
29 M(O)TTLE: Mt+anag.
30 ME(R)ELS: e in anag.
31 MODES(T): subsid. def.
32 S(I)MOOM: S-moo-m
33 ROTAT(E): anag.
34 ADRO(I)T: ad+rot
35 BUT(T)ES: but E S
36 DR(I)EST: subsid. def.
37 PALE(S)T: p-ale-t
38 SILE(N)T: te, lis, rev.
39 H(O)NEST: H+nest, vb
40 SET(T)ER: set+ER
41 IDE(A)LS: i-Del.-s
42 MIL(L)ES: subsid. def.
43 GRAA(L)S: r in anag.
44 (T)ONGAS: on+gas
45 NINT(H)S: ni-n-ts
46 SC(E)NTS: n for ou in scouts
47 ADDE(R)S: Edda, rev.+S
48 (E)RODES: 'roads', hom.

Solution 31

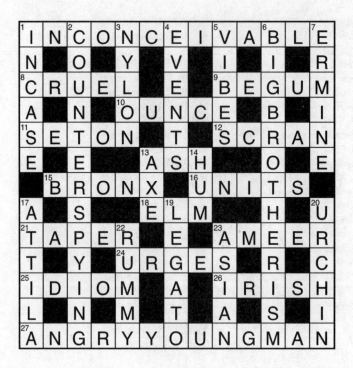

Across

24 grues

27 Jimmy Porter

Down

2 Cloak & dagger: are there two kinds of spies?

6 Is TV programme for 'celeb' rants?

7 AMEER + IN not A

14 bees

20 ur-ch.-I.-n

Solution 32

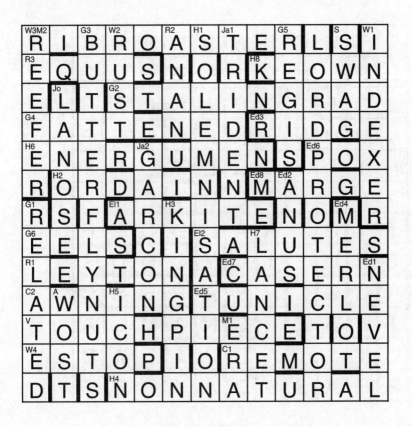

R	I	B	R	O	A	S	T	E	R	L	S	I
E	Q	U	U	S	N	O	R	K	E	O	W	N
E	L	T	S	T	A	L	I	N	G	R	A	D
F	A	T	T	E	N	E	D	R	I	D	G	E
E	N	E	R	G	U	M	E	N	S	P	O	X
R	O	R	D	A	I	N	N	M	A	R	G	E
R	S	F	A	R	K	I	T	E	N	O	M	R
E	E	L	S	C	I	S	A	L	U	T	E	S
L	E	Y	T	O	N	A	C	A	S	E	R	N
A	W	N	I	N	G	T	U	N	I	C	L	E
T	O	U	C	H	P	I	E	C	E	T	O	V
E	S	T	O	P	I	O	R	E	M	O	T	E
D	T	S	N	O	N	N	A	T	U	R	A	L

Solution 33

P	I	T	H	O	S	G	S	H	A	S	K
H	R	R	I	M	M	I	N	E	N	C	E
Y	O	O	F	E	D	N	I	C	K	A	R
T	N	U	D	N	I	K	P	K	C	F	F
O	P	T	S	T	S	G	E	T	O	F	F
S	A	L	T	A	T	O	R	Y	C	O	R
I	T	I	G	I	R	A	N	D	O	L	E
S	E	N	U	S	I	L	Y	O	D	D	S
R	N	G	O	L	N	E	A	F	E	S	C
A	T	A	B	E	G	S	N	A	M	L	A
C	O	M	I	T	A	D	J	I	E	A	D
A	R	B	A	S	S	B	A	J	R	E	E

Across

1 anag. less me
7 h + ask
10 I + eminence with m = mark for E = English
11 Y + oof
13 nick = appropriate + ar(ch)
14 rev.
16 op + St rev.
18 close to mast = t in Geoff B
20 salt + a Tory
21 GI ran dole
24 NUS in sei(l)
25 d d in os
28 anag.
30 a = accepted + (pro)b(lem) in A + T = Turkey eg
31 ml in A(fric)a
32 comit(y) + adj + I
33 hidden
34 rev. eer jab
320

Down

1 anag.
2 2 definitions
3 t + l in routing
4 omen TA
5 goal E in ginks
6 rev.
7 2 definitions
8 (t)aff in scold
9 k erf
12 string in said rev.
15 code in comer
17 o in anag. pattern
19 scad in free
22 is lets
23 a in NY NJ + A
26 rev.
27 OB I a
29 sla(t)e

Solution 34

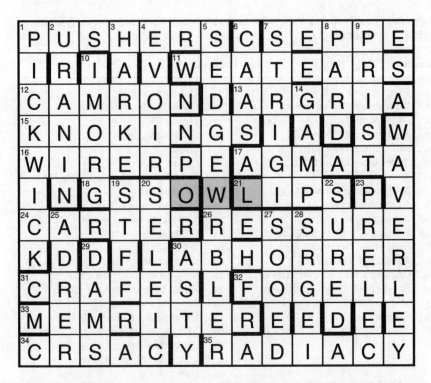

P	U	S	H	E	R	S	C	S	E	P	P	E
I	R	I	A	V	W	E	A	T	E	A	R	S
C	A	M	R	O	N	D	A	R	G	R	I	A
K	N	O	K	I	N	G	S	I	A	D	S	W
W	I	R	E	R	P	E	A	G	M	A	T	A
I	N	G	S	S	O	W	L	I	P	S	P	V
C	A	R	T	E	R	R	E	S	S	U	R	E
K	D	D	F	L	A	B	H	O	R	R	E	R
C	R	A	F	E	S	L	F	O	G	E	L	L
M	E	M	R	I	T	E	R	E	E	D	E	E
C	R	S	A	C	Y	R	A	D	I	A	C	Y

Letters omitted from the Across clues spelt – THEY COME AS A BOON, and from the Down clues – AND A BLESSING TO MEN. In addition five clues each dropped the letters PEN, they were: 1A (PEN)-PUSHERS, 21A LIP(PEN)S, 24A CAR(PEN)TER, 8D PAR(PEN)D, and 29D DAM(PEN)S. The full quotation in the *Oxford Dictionary of Quotations* (4th edition), being an advertisement for PENS:

They come as a boon and a blessing to men,
The Pickwick, the Owl, and the Waverley pen

PICKWICK and WAVERLEY were unclued. Solvers should have highlighted the third 'writer' OWL in the central squares.

Extract from *ODQ* 4th edition
They come as a boon and a blessing to men,
The Pickwick, the Owl, and the Waverley pen

Advertisement by MacNiven and H. Cameron Ltd (c.1920); almost certainly inspired by J. C. Prince 'The Pen and the Press' in E. W. Cole (ed.) *The Thousand Best Poems in the World* (1891):

It came as a boon and a blessing to men,
The peaceful, the pure, the victorious PEN!

Solution 34 *continued*

# denotes clues dropping PEN, other notes show full word with dropped letter **THUS**. * denotes anagram.

Across

1# 2 mngs
7 STeppe; Sep + PE
11 WHeatears; Sea-water*
12 CamEron; Mac (rev.) + R + on
13 ArgYria; Aria around GR
15 KnoCkings; No + K in Kings
16 Wire rOpe; R(eport) for V in preview*
17 Magmata; Ag + mat + a
18 GEsso; SS in go
21# 2 mngs
24# 2 mngs. Ref. President Carter
26 ReAssure; (P)ressure
30 AbhorrerS; Harborer*
31 CArafes; Cafes around R(iesling)
32 Fog-Bell; Golf* around (b)el(t)
33 MemOriter; REM + timer*
34 COrsac; Cr + sac
35 RadiaNcy; Ray around dia + c

Down

1 PICKWICK unclued
2 UraniAn; 2 mngs
3 HarkeN; He around ark
4 Devoir; (On)e + voir
5 Sedge-wArbler; drew grebes* around L
6 CaBas; 2 mngs
7 StrigiL; Is (rev.) around trig
8# Pa +r(oun)d
9 PriEst; Pr + is + (cu)t
10 Simorg; G after 1 + mor
14 GampS; Gam + p
19 StIff; St(a)ff
20 SeleNic; Sele + i/c
22 SurGed; Sure + (forwar)d
23 PrelecT; Pr(ofession) + elec(t)
25 AdOrer; Drear*
27 SooMed; So + oe + d
28 SErgei; Sr + e(xercised) in gi; ref. Prokofiev
29# 2 mngs, both 'figurative'
30 Nasty; A + sty

Solution 35

W	O	R	L	D	W	I	D	E	W	E	B
E	A	N	O	D	E	B	O	F	F	S	E
D	N	T	R	A	B	E	A	T	E	E	S
D	O	O	R	Y	B	A	T	S	N	O	T
I	N	R	O	B	E	M	A	T	O	U	R
N	A	R	D	E	D	S	C	Y	L	L	A
G	R	E	E	N	S	P	O	L	A	N	D
B	E	N	N	T	O	I	L	A	G	E	D
E	S	T	T	E	L	L	A	R	A	W	L
L	E	S	O	D	A	L	I	T	Y	S	I
L	T	E	L	I	C	A	R	A	B	Y	N
S	T	P	E	T	E	R	S	B	U	R	G

FUNNEL-WEB SPIDERS

The word 'spider' had been omitted after the following words in eight clues: 13 Greek 14 Kill 19 disappearing 23 inside 28 What 29 Latin 6 like 21 Perhaps; two of these (14 and 19) used the letters of 'spider'; two (23 and 21) used 'other' meanings of 'spider'; two (28 and 6) referred to webs; and two (13 and 29) used the Classical words for 'spider'.

   1 Across was a different sort of 'web', and the anagram below the grid – formed from the two-letter 'entries' left in the web-design grid – utilized both theme words, as an aid to solving it.

Solution 36

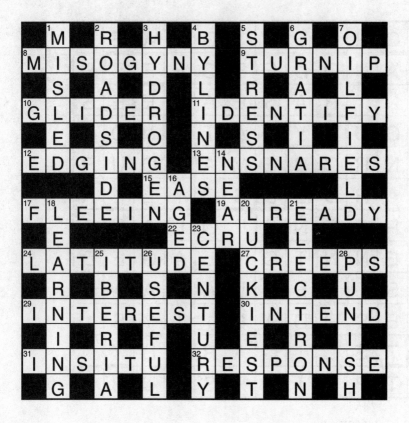

Solution 37

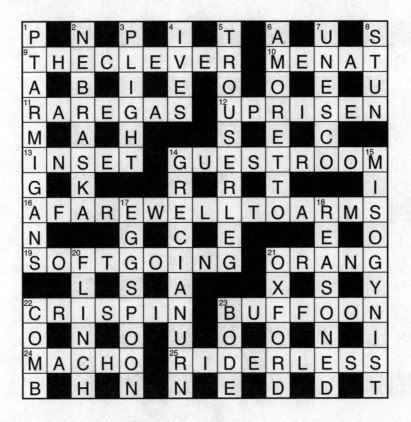

Solution 38

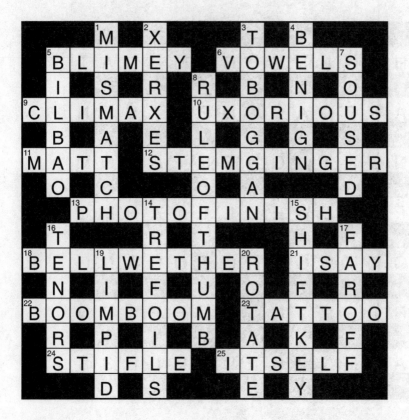

Solution 39

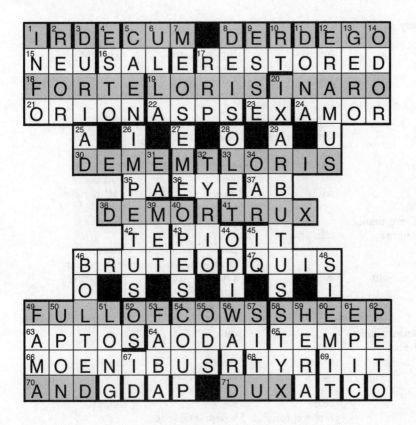

Glossary

ab	by, from	**meus, -a, -um**	my, mine
ad	to, towards	**moenia, -ium** (n. pl.)	city walls
amo	I love		
amor	love	**neu** *or* **neve**	neither, nor
amicus	friend		
aptus, -a, -um	suitable, fitting	**obsero, -serare**	lock, close up
arbutus	strawberry tree	**oculus**	eye
		odi	I hate
bellum	war	**odor**	smell
		olet	it stinks
cum	with	**opes**	wealth, riches
		os	bone
demo, -ere, demi,		**ovis**	sheep
demptus	take away		
deus	god	**pater**	father
donum (n)	gift	**peto, -ere, -ivi**	seek, ask for
durus, -a, -um	hard	**pius, -a, -um**	god-fearing
		porcus	pig
ea	she	**plenus, -a, -um**	full
ego	I		
emo, emere, emi,		**quis**	who
emptus	buy		
esse	to be	**remus**	oar
ex	out of	**reor, reri, ratus**	think
faba	bean	**sal**	salt, wit
fama	renown, rumour	**sedeo, -ere, sedi,**	
forte	by chance	**sessus**	sit
		si	if
gero, -ere, gessi,		**situs**	situated, site
gestus	wear, wage		
		te (tu)	you
hara	sty	**trux, trucis**	savage, fierce
		Tyrius, -a, -um	Tyrian purple
ianua	door		
id	it	**ullus, -a, -um**	any
impetus	force, attack	**urbs**	city
inaro, -arare, -aravi	plough in		
it (eo, ire, i(v)i)	goes	**vacca**	cow
lora (n. pl.)	reins		

Solution 40

L	A	S	T	A	G	E	C	A	S	E	H
C	B	E	R	M	A	M	O	R	O	S	O
K	A	R	A	I	S	M	D	E	U	A	W
E	T	C	I	N	W	I	D	D	L	E	D
S	T	I	N	K	E	R	E	T	D	M	I
F	I	S	E	D	L	A	R	V	A	T	E
E	S	C	R	O	L	L	S	E	N	U	S
U	E	R	A	V	O	L	O	R	O	S	O
D	E	A	D	E	N	S	U	S	E	S	T
U	S	M	E	L	D	O	S	I	D	O	S
T	A	B	L	E	A	U	V	O	T	R	E
Y	A	S	S	T	S	L	I	N	K	E	R

The extracted letters (indicated in parentheses in the six-letter answers) spell 'TAKE SECOND LETTERS OF CLUES' which in turn gives 'THE FIVE LETTER ACROSS ENTRIES ARE IN ALPHABETICAL ORDER', thus allowing unique completion of the diagram.

Solution 40 *continued*

Across

1 l.-(j)a(nitor)-stage
8 CHAS(T)E: c-haste
13 C(A)MBER: c.-amber
14 A-Moor (anag.)-so
15 'ai' in marks (anag.)
16 WAU(K)ED: Wa-U-ked, 's = has
17 ENTIC(E): nec(k)tie (anag.)
18 w.-(d.)iddled, weed = past tense
19 s(wears)-tinker
20 DEMIT(S): d.-emit-s.
21 DEFI(E)S: hidden
24 l-a R.V.-ate
28 collies (anag.): for I, (armige)r
29 (C)ENSUS: cen.-S.-U.S.
30 AV(O)URE: A(merican)-vo(it)ure
33 O lo-ROS-o
37 deaden(d)-(ga)s
38 SU(N)SET: (co)untess (anag.)
39 LE(D)UMS: odd letters
40 do s-ID-o's
41 hidden
42 REVO(L)T: T-lover (rev.)
43 Y(E)ASTS: Yea-'s-ts
44 s-l.-inker, 's = has

Down

1 (F)LECKS: cf. flex
2 (c)a(r)b(o)a(s)t(s)-'t-I's
3 CIR(C)ES: circ(us)es
4 train-re (rev.)
5 MA(L)KIN: mal-kin
6 G(Is)-as well
7 IMM(U)RE: imm(at)ure
8 2 mngs
9 REDAT(E): red-at-(nos)e
10 anag.
11 SE(S)AME: masse(us)e (anag.)
12 showed-I. (anag.), His = plural hi,
work = vb
21 feud-ut-(pa)y(ee)
22 s. cra-m.-bs
23 telev(ision)-o'd. (rev.), one's = one
has
25 All Soul(s)
26 (a.)version
27 t(r.)uss-ore
31 A(T) EASE: a tease
32 DEL(T)AS: anag.
33 ANOD(E)S: An-o'-des
34 VI(R)OUS: vi(P.e)rous
35 (S)TOKED: ST-OKed
36 TOR(O)SE: to-rose

Solution 41

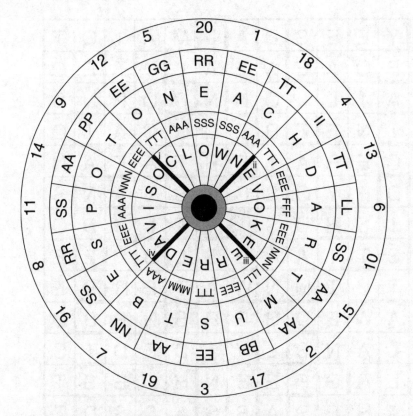

The seven-letter radial clues all lead to words with one double-letter and one triple-letter entered in the appropriate 'bed'. The message in the outermost singles ring is EACH DART MUST BE SPOT ON.

Radials
1. seesaws; see saw S
2. lam Ella & Mel in Lala
3. tetters; Tet + *
4. Hittite; hit tit + e
5. galanga; lan in gaga
6. fall off; l-lo in faff
7. bandana; band + ana
8. reserve; re-serve
9. peep-toe; *
10. Seekers; mngs
11. Aspasia; asp (cf. Cleopatra) + Asia
12. octette; * in (p)otte(r)

13. vedette; * less CI
14. Annonas; no n in anas
15. antenna; ten in Anna (ref. A. Bennett)
16. attests; at tests
17. bebeeru; beer in beu(rre)
18. cantata; can tat a
19. mammate; am M in mate
20. rossers; * in r(hododendron)s

Clockwise

i	hidden	iii	RR in (L)eed(s)
ii	OK in eve	iv	a + * less E

Two-letter forms

la	an	fl	Sr
es	be	re	EP
et	Ag	St	as
te	ET	am	an
at	ti	na	SE

Solution 42

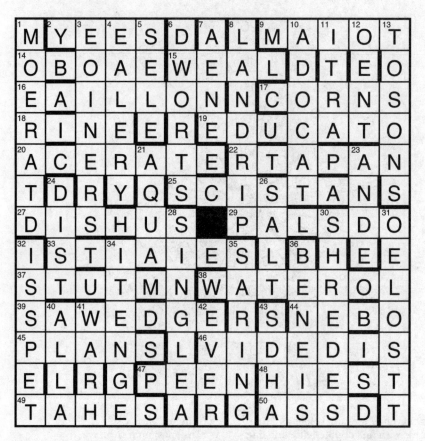

	¹M	²Y	³E	⁴E	⁵S	⁶D	⁷A	⁸L	⁹M	¹⁰A	¹¹I	¹²O	¹³T
¹⁴O	B	O	A	E	¹⁵W	E	A	L	D	T	E	O
¹⁶E	A	I	L	L	O	N	N	¹⁷C	O	R	N	S
¹⁸R	I	N	E	E	¹⁹R	E	D	U	C	A	T	O
²⁰A	C	E	R	²¹A	T	E	²²R	T	A	P	²³A	N
T	²⁴D	R	Y	²⁵Q	S	²⁶C	I	S	T	A	N	S
²⁷D	I	S	H	U	S		²⁹P	A	L	³⁰S	D	³¹O
³²I	³³S	T	³⁴I	A	I	³⁵E	S	L	³⁶B	H	E	E
³⁷S	T	U	T	M	N	³⁸W	A	T	E	R	O	L
³⁹S	⁴⁰A	⁴¹W	E	D	G	⁴²E	R	S	⁴³N	E	B	O
⁴⁵P	L	A	N	S	L	⁴⁶V	I	D	E	D	I	S
E	L	R	G	⁴⁷P	E	E	N	⁴⁸H	I	E	S	T
⁴⁹T	A	H	E	S	A	R	G	⁵⁰A	S	S	D	T

The omitted digraphs were the fifty USA ZIP codes, with the treated answers entered at the numbers corresponding to the order in which the states joined the Union; see *Brewer's Dictionary of Phrase and Fable*. The clue answers, with number and state were: 10(VA) advocaat, 23(ME) amende, 7(MD) amened, 21(IL) Aquila, 36(NV) Ben Nevis, 31(CA) coelostat, 17(OH) cohorns, 27(FL) dishfuls, 4(GA) eagle-ray, 19(IN) education, 3(NJ) enjoiners, 50(HI) Hassid, 48(AZ) haziest, 11(NY) in-tray, 34(KS) kitenges, 8(SC) land-scrip, 18(LA) larine, 20(MS) macerates, 6(MA) madworts, 9(NH) Manihot, 32(MN) misspent, 1(DE) moderated, 24(MO) modist, 44(WY) new boy, 12(NC) nocent, 14(VT) obovate, 33(OR) ostiaries, 29(IA) palisado, 2(PA) payees, 47(NM) penmen, 45(UT) pultans, 22(AL) rataplan, 25(AR) sacristan, 40(SD) sallad, 39(ND) sand wedge, 5(CT) select, 30(WI) shrewdies, 43(ID) siddha, 28(TX) single tax, 26(MI) smalti, 37(NE) stuntmen, 35(WV) swarving, 49(AK) takahes, 16(TN) tenaillon, 13(RI) torsions, 46(OK) videodisk, 41(MT) warmth, 38(CO) water-cool, 15(KY) weakly, 42(WA) weaver.

Solution 43

¹H	O	²U	S	³E	P	⁴R	O	⁵U	D		⁶S	P	⁷O	⁸T
O		N		A		E		N				A		R
⁹D	E	M	O	R	A	L	I	S	E		¹⁰P	R	O	A
S		A		N		E		U		¹¹L		A		N
	¹²I	S	L	E		¹³N	O	N	C	O	M	P	O	S
¹⁴B		K		D		T		G		S		E		I
¹⁵A	S	S	A	I	L	E	D		¹⁶M	E	N	T	I	S
C		N		D		¹⁷B		P						T
¹⁸K	O	P	E	C	K		²⁰S	E	R	A	G	L	I	O
H		O		O		²²S	A		T		A		R
²³A	L	T	I	M	E	T	E	R		²⁴I	N	N	S	
N		H		E		R		I		E		Y		²⁵S
²⁶D	R	O	P		²⁷C	A	N	N	O	N	B	A	L	L
E		O			F		G		C		R			U
²⁸R	A	K	E		²⁹N	E	W	S	R	E	A	D	E	R

Index

This index presents an alphabetical list of the main newspapers, magazines, etc. mentioned in the biographical section, followed in each case by the setters whose work has appeared therein. Where appropriate, the relevant name or pseudonym of a setter is given in round brackets.

Moodim, Mr Lemon, MynoT, Owzat, Phi, Piccadilly,
Quark (EB), Rufus (Bower, Hodge, Icarus),
Schadenfreude, Smokey, Virgilius

Independent on Sunday
Calmac (Beelzebub), Columba (Beelzebub), Duck
(Quixote), Mass, Mordred, Mr Magoo, Phi (Beelzebub)

Irish Times
Alaun, Simplex

Listener (including *Times Listener* series)
Adam, Apex, Aragon, Armonie, Ascot, Auctor, Azed
(Gong), BeRo, Bufo, Calmac, Caper, Columba, Corylus,
Derek, Dimitry, Doc ('Twudge), Duck, Dumpynose,
Enigmatist, Jago, Kea, Laws (Jude), Llig, Loda,
Logodaedalus (Dogop), Machiavelli, Mass, Merlin,
Mordred, Mr Lemon, Mr Magoo, Nibor, Obiter, Phi,
Piccadilly, Pieman, Plausus, Quark (Phiz), Rover, Sabre,
Salamanca, Schadenfreude, Smokey, Virgilius, Waterloo

Magpie
Adam, Charybdis, Dimitry, Mordred, Mr Magoo,
MynoT, Piccadilly, Pieman, Schadenfreude

MoneyWeek
Owzat

My Weekly
Axe

New Internationalist
Axe

New Scientist
Alaun

New Statesman
Salamanca

New York Times
Virgilius

Observer
Ascot, Azed, Rufus

Oldie
Columba (Antico)

Oxford Today
Calmac (Michael Macdonald-Cooper)

Physics World
Merlin (Richard Palmer)

Plain English
Diplodocus

Private Eye
Brummie

Prospect
Doc (Didymus)

Puzzler
Doc, Logodaedalus (Don Putnam)

Quest
Diplodocus

Radio Times
Crispa, Doc

Scotland on Sunday
Calmac, Derek

Scotsman
Calmac (Andrew Campbell)

Sketch
Alaun

Spectator
Columba, Doc, Dumpynose, Mass, Smokey

Sun
Rufus

Sunday Telegraph (Enigmatic Variations)
Alaun, Auctor, BeRo, Bufo, Caper, Columba, Dimitry, Duck (Giovanni), Hypnos, Jago, Kruger, Laws (Fawley), Loda, Mass, Mordred, Mr Lemon, MynoT, Owzat, Phi (Kcit), Piccadilly, Plausus, Quark (Quota), Salamanca, Schadenfreude (Oxymoron), Smokey

Sunday Times
Apex, Caper, Corylus (Mephisto), Crispa, Hall, Laws (Mephisto), Owzat (Mephisto)

Teacher
Rover

Times
Aragon, Ascot, Browne, Caper, Casina, Crispa, Dimitry, Diplodocus, Grant, Hall, Hesketh, Kea, Laws, Machiavelli, Mutch, MynoT, Paul, Phi, Rufus, Smokey, Virgilius

Times Educational Supplement
Rufus

Times Law
Dumpynose

Times Literary Supplement
Tantalus

Varsity
Azed (Gong), Virgilius

Verbatim
Hypnos

Week
  Owzat (Tim Moorey)

Woman's Weekly
  Derek

World Digest
  Hall

Yorkshire Post
  Derek, Hall, Mutch